Teach Yourself VISUAL

Microsoft 365

T0093381

by Paul McFedries

Visual

A Wiley Brand

About the Author

Paul McFedries is a full-time technical writer. Paul has been authoring computer books since 1991, and he has more than 100 books to his credit. Paul's books have sold more than four million copies worldwide. These books include the Wiley titles *Teach Yourself VISUALLY Windows 11*, *Teach Yourself VISUALLY Excel 2016*, *Excel Workbook For Dummies*, *Excel All-in-One For Dummies*, and *Excel Data Analysis For Dummies, Fifth Edition*. Paul invites you to drop by his personal website at www.paulmcfedries.com or follow him on Twitter @paulmcf.

Author's Acknowledgments

It goes without saying that writers focus on text, and I certainly enjoyed focusing on the text that you'll read in this book. However, this book is more than just the usual collection of words and phrases. A quick thumb-through of the pages will show you that this book is also chock-full of images, from sharp screenshots to fun and informative illustrations. Those colorful images sure make for a beautiful book, and that beauty comes from a lot of hard work by Wiley's immensely talented group of designers and layout artists. I thank them for creating another gem. Of course, what you read in this book must also be accurate, logically presented, and free of errors. Ensuring all of this was an excellent group of editors that included project editor Lynn Northrup, technical editor Doug Holland, copy editor Kim Wimpsett, and production editor Barath Kumar Rajasekaran. Thanks to all of you for your exceptional competence and hard work. Thanks, as well, to acquisitions editor Devon Lewis for asking me to write this book.

How to Use This Book

Who This Book Is For

This book is for the reader who has never used this particular technology or software application. It is also for readers who want to expand their knowledge.

The Conventions in This Book

① Steps

This book uses a step-by-step format to guide you easily through each task. **Numbered steps** are actions you must do; **bulleted steps** clarify a point, step, or optional feature; and **indented steps** give you the result.

② Notes

Notes give additional information — special conditions that may occur during an operation, a situation that you want to avoid, or a cross reference to a related area of the book.

③ Icons and Buttons

Icons and buttons show you exactly what you need to click to perform a step.

④ Tips

Tips offer additional information, including warnings and shortcuts.

⑤ Bold

Bold type shows command names, options, and text or numbers you must type.

⑥ Italics

Italic type introduces and defines a new term.

Table of Contents

Part I Microsoft 365 Features

Chapter 1 Microsoft 365 Basics

Start and Exit Microsoft 365 Apps 4
Explore the App Window 6
Work with Backstage View 7
Change the Color Scheme 8
Search for a Ribbon Command.................................. 10
Work with the Ribbon.. 12
Customize the Quick Access Toolbar......................... 14
Using a Microsoft 365 App with a Touch Screen.......... 16

Chapter 2 Working with Files

Create a New File 18
Save a File.. 20
Open a File 22
Print a File.. 24
Select Data 26

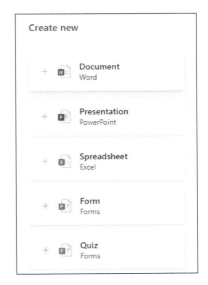

Chapter 3 — Microsoft 365 Graphics Tools

Insert a Picture from Your PC.................................... 28

Insert an Online Picture... 30

Resize and Move Graphic Objects............................ 32

Understanding Graphics Modification Techniques........ 34

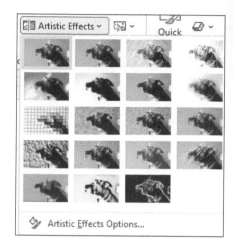

Chapter 4 — Working with Microsoft 365 Files Online

Microsoft 365 and the Cloud................................... 36

Sign In to Microsoft 365 38

Share a Document from Microsoft 365 40

Sign In to OneDrive... 42

Using an Online App in OneDrive............................. 44

Open a Document in a Desktop App from OneDrive...... 46

Upload a Document to OneDrive.............................. 48

Share a Document Using OneDrive........................... 50

Table of Contents

Part II   Word

Chapter 5   Adding Text

Change Word's Views 54

Type and Edit Text 56

Insert Quick Parts 58

Insert Symbols 60

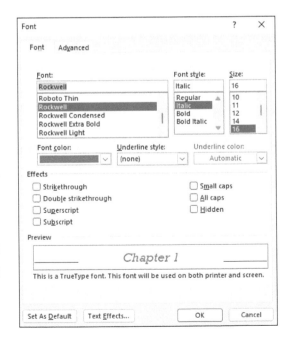

Chapter 6   Formatting Text

Change the Font, Size, and Color............................... 62

Align Text.. 66

Set Line Spacing.. 67

Indent Text... 68

Set Tabs 70

Set Margins... 72

Create Lists.. 74

Copy Formatting 76

Clear Formatting 77

Format with Styles 78

Using a Template.. 80

Chapter 7　Adding Extra Touches

Insert an Online Video.. 82

Assign a Theme 84

Add Borders.. 86

Create Columns... 88

Insert a Table.. 90

Apply Table Styles... 92

Insert Table Rows or Columns 93

Add Headers and Footers 94

Insert Footnotes and Endnotes 96

Table
Pictures

Shapes
Icons
3D Models

4x3 Table

Insert Table...
Draw Table
Convert Text to Table...
Excel Spreadsheet
Quick Tables

Chapter 8　Reviewing Documents

Work in Read Mode View 98

Find and Replace Text 102

Navigate Document Content 104

Check Spelling and Grammar..................................106

Customize AutoCorrect...108

Using Word's Thesaurus and Dictionary..................110

Translate Text 112

Track and Review Document Changes 114

Lock and Unlock Tracking.......................................116

Combine Reviewers' Changes..................................118

Work with Comments...120

Editor

Editor Score　**89**%

Formal writing

Corrections

Spelling　✓

Grammar　8

Refinements

Clarity　13

Conciseness　5

Table of Contents

Part III Excel

Chapter 9 Building Spreadsheets

Enter Cell Data 124

Select Cells 126

Using AutoFill for Faster Data Entry 128

Turn On Text Wrapping 130

Center Data Across Columns.................................. 131

Adjust Cell Alignment... 132

Change the Font and Size..................................... 134

Change Number Formats...................................... 136

Increase or Decrease Decimals 137

Add Cell Borders and Shading 138

Format Data with Styles...................................... 140

Apply Conditional Formatting 142

Insert Rows and Columns 144

Resize Columns and Rows..................................... 146

Freeze Column and Row Titles On-Screen 147

Name a Range 148

Clear or Delete Cells 150

Chapter 10 Worksheet Basics

Add a Worksheet..152

Rename a Worksheet 153

Change Page Setup Options 154

Move or Copy Worksheets 156

Delete a Worksheet 157

Find and Replace Data 158

Create a Table 160

Filter or Sort Table Information............................162

Analyze Data Quickly 164

Understanding Data Analysis Choices 165

Insert a Note 166

Chapter 11 Working with Formulas and Functions

Understanding Formulas 168

Create a Formula...170

Apply Absolute and Relative Cell References.............172

Understanding Functions 174

Insert a Function 176

Total Cells with AutoSum 178

Table of Contents

Chapter 12 — Working with Charts

Create a Chart 180

Move and Resize Charts..182

Change the Chart Type..184

Change the Chart Style 185

Change the Chart Layout.....................................186

Add Chart Elements...187

Format Chart Elements..188

Change the Chart Data..189

Using Sparklines to View Data Trends.....................190

Understanding PivotTables 192

Create a PivotTable 194

Create a PivotChart 196

Insert a PivotTable Slicer 198

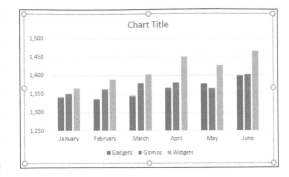

Part IV — PowerPoint

Chapter 13 — Creating a Presentation

Create a New Presentation....................................202

Create a Photo Album Presentation........................204

Change PowerPoint Views.....................................206

Insert Slides 208

Change the Slide Layout 210

Change the Slide Size 212

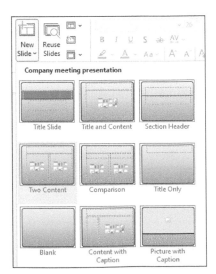

Chapter 14 — Populating Presentation Slides

Add and Edit Slide Text 214

Change the Font, Size, and Color..........................216

Apply a Theme..220

Set Line Spacing...221

Align Text...222

Add a Text Box to a Slide......................................223

Add a Table to a Slide 224

Add a Chart to a Slide 226

Add a Video Clip to a Slide 228

Move a Slide Object..230

Resize a Slide Object 231

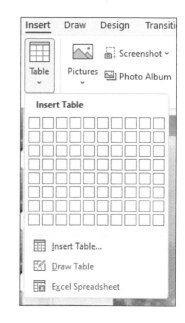

Chapter 15 — Assembling and Presenting a Slideshow

Reorganize Slides..232

Reuse a Slide 234

Organize Slides into Sections.................................236

Define Slide Transitions 238

Add Animation Effects...240

Create a Custom Animation 242

Record Narration...244

Insert a Background Song 245

Create Speaker Notes..246

Rehearse a Slideshow 248

Run a Slideshow 250

Table of Contents

Part V   Access

Chapter 16   Database Basics

Understanding Database Basics.............................256
Create a Database Based on a Template...................258
Create a Blank Database....................................260
Create a New Table...262
Change Table Views...264
Add a Field to a Table.....................................266
Delete a Field from a Table................................267
Hide a Field in a Table....................................268
Move a Field in a Table....................................269
Create a Form..270
Change Form Views..272
Move a Field in a Form.....................................273
Delete a Field in a Form...................................274
Format Form Fields...275

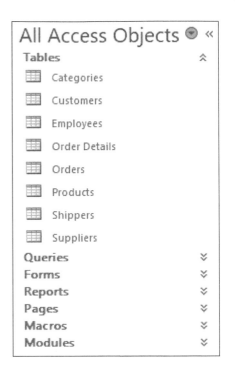

Chapter 17   Adding, Finding, and Querying Data

Add Records to a Table.....................................276
Add a Record Using a Form..................................278
Navigate Records Using a Form..............................280
Search for a Record Using a Form...........................281
Delete a Record from a Table...............................282
Delete a Record Using a Form...............................283
Sort Records...284
Filter Records...286
Perform a Simple Query.....................................288
Create a Report..292

Part VI Outlook

Chapter 18 Organizing with Outlook

Navigate in Outlook 298

Schedule an Appointment 300

Create a New Contact 302

Create a New Task 304

Add a Note 306

Customize the Navigation Bar 308

Peek at Appointments and Tasks 310

Chapter 19 E-mailing with Outlook

Compose and Send a Message 312

Send a File Attachment... 314

Read an Incoming Message 315

Reply to or Forward a Message 316

Add a Sender to Your Outlook Contacts 318

Delete a Message 319

Screen Junk E-Mail.. 320

Create a Message Rule 322

Index.. 324

PART I

Microsoft 365 Features

The Microsoft 365 applications share a common look and feel. You can find many of the same features in each program, such as the Ribbon, Quick Access Toolbar, program window controls, and the File tab. Many of the tasks you perform, such as creating and working with files, share the same processes and features throughout the Microsoft 365 suite. In this part, you learn how to navigate the common Microsoft 365 features and basic tasks.

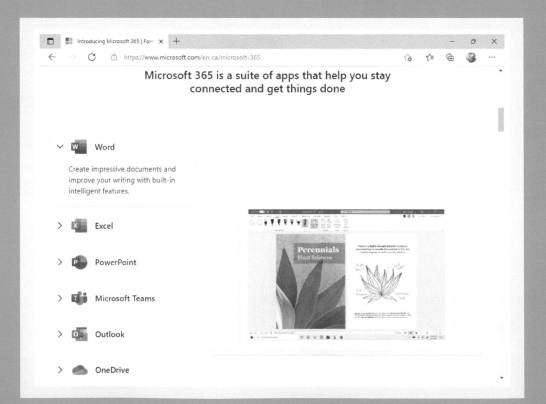

Chapter 1: Microsoft 365 Basics 4

Chapter 2: Working with Files 18

Chapter 3: Microsoft 365 Graphics Tools. 28

Chapter 4: Working with Microsoft 365 Files Online 36

Start and Exit Microsoft 365 Apps

A Microsoft 365 installation creates an icon for each Microsoft 365 app either on the Start menu or in the All Apps list. To work with an app, you need to know how to launch the app on your PC. When you are finished with an app, you also need to know how to exit the app.

This section uses Word to demonstrate how to open an app from Windows 11. Once a Microsoft 365 app opens, its Start screen appears, where you can find a recent document or start a new document. For other ways to open or create a document, see Chapter 2.

Start and Exit Microsoft 365 Apps

1 Click **Start** ().

The Start menu appears.

Ⓐ Alternatively, you can click **Search** ($\mathcal{O}$), type the name of the app, and then click the app in the search results.

2 Click the Microsoft 365 app you want to start.

Note: If you do not see the Microsoft 365 app you want, skip to step **3**.

3 Click **All apps**.

Windows displays the All Apps list.

4 Click the app you want to open.

4

The app launches and displays its Start screen.

Ⓑ You can use the Home panel to start a blank document or open a recent document.

Ⓒ You can use the New panel to start a new document.

Ⓓ You can use the Open panel to open an existing document.

Ⓔ This area indicates whether you have signed in to your Microsoft 365 subscription.

Note: See Chapter 4 for details about signing in to Microsoft 365.

⑤ To exit the app, click the **Close** button (✕).

Note: If you have multiple documents open, you must click **Close** (✕) for each file to exit the app.

Can I create a shortcut to open a Microsoft 365 application?

Yes, you can pin the app to the Windows Start menu or taskbar. Follow steps **1** to **4** in this section, and then right-click the app name in the All Apps list. From the menu that appears,

either click **Pin to Start** to add the app to the Pinned section of the Start menu or click **More** and then click **Pin to taskbar** to pin the app to the Windows taskbar. To open the app, click the app's tile in the Pinned section of the Start menu or the app's button on the taskbar.

Explore the App Window

All Microsoft 365 apps share a common appearance and many of the same features, and when you learn the features of one Microsoft 365 app window, you can use the same skills to navigate the windows of the other Microsoft 365 apps. These common features include the title bar, program window controls, zoom controls, and the Ribbon. The Ribbon is an important Microsoft 365 feature because it contains the app commands and features that you will use most often. You learn more about the Ribbon later in this chapter.

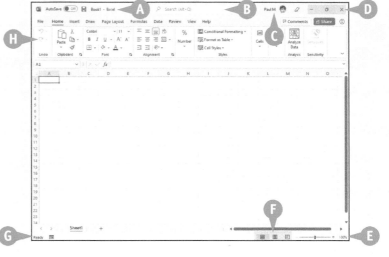

A Title Bar

Displays the name of the open file, the name of the Microsoft 365 app, and the AutoSave and Save buttons.

B Search

Enables you to search for items within the app.

C Microsoft 365 Indicator

Displays your Microsoft 365 sign-in status. If you see your name, you are signed in to your Microsoft 365 subscription. You can click your name to display a menu that enables you to manage your Microsoft account settings or switch to a different Microsoft account. If you are not signed in, this area shows a Sign In link.

D Program Window Controls

Enable you to control the appearance of the app window. You can minimize the Ribbon, and you can minimize, maximize, restore, or close the app window.

E Zoom Controls

Change the magnification of a document.

F View Shortcuts

Switch to a different view of your document.

G Status Bar

Displays information about the current Microsoft 365 document.

H Ribbon

Displays groups of related commands in tabs. Each tab offers buttons for performing common tasks.

Work with Backstage View

Y ou can click the File tab to display Backstage view. In Backstage view, you find a list of actions that you can use to open, save, print, remove sensitive information, and distribute documents as well as modify the app's settings. You can also use Backstage view to manage the places on your computer hard drive or in your network that you use to store documents and to manage your Microsoft 365 account.

Work with Backstage View

1 Click the **File** tab to display Backstage view.

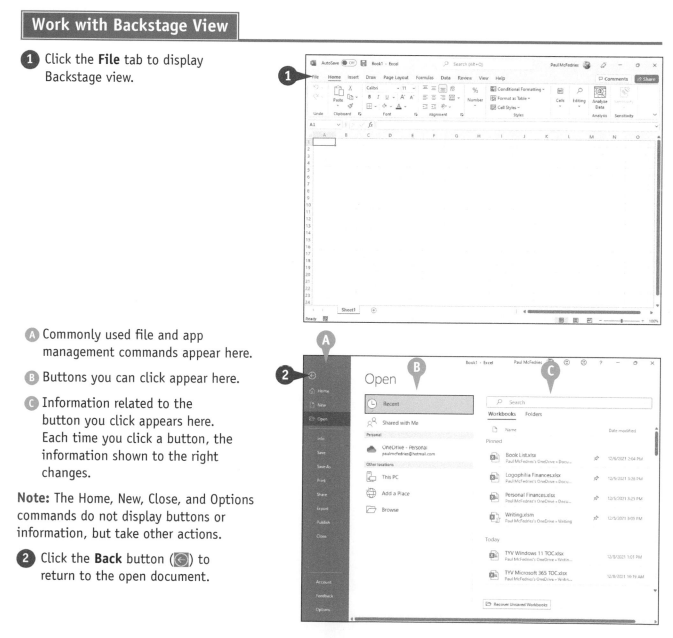

A Commonly used file and app management commands appear here.

B Buttons you can click appear here.

C Information related to the button you click appears here. Each time you click a button, the information shown to the right changes.

Note: The Home, New, Close, and Options commands do not display buttons or information, but take other actions.

2 Click the **Back** button (⬅) to return to the open document.

Change the Color Scheme

You can use Microsoft 365 themes and background patterns to change the appearance of the app screen. Themes control the color scheme the app uses, and background patterns can add interest to Backstage view. Color schemes can improve your ability to clearly see the screen, but be aware that some schemes might be distracting.

Microsoft 365 themes are available even if you are not signed in to Microsoft 365, but to use background patterns, you must sign in to Microsoft 365. For details on how to sign in and out of Microsoft 365, see Chapter 4.

Change the Color Scheme

Note: Make sure you are signed in to Microsoft 365. See Chapter 4 for details.

1 Click **File** to open Backstage view.

2 Click **Account**.

3 Click the **Office Theme** ▼.

4 Click a theme.

The colors of your app change.

Note: Some theme changes are more subtle than others.

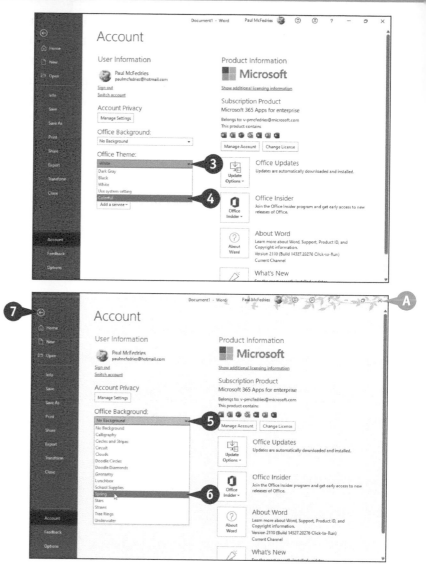

5 Click the **Office Background** ▼.

6 Click the pattern you want to use or click **No Background**.

A As you point the mouse (⯈) at a choice in the menu, a background pattern appears at the top of the window. The pattern appears only in Backstage view; it does not appear as you work on documents.

7 Click the **Back** button (⯇) to return to your document.

The Microsoft 365 theme you selected appears.

What happens if I select a background and then sign out of Microsoft 365?
The background no longer appears in the app but will reappear when you next sign in to Microsoft 365. Similarly, theme changes you make while signed in to Microsoft 365 might disappear when you sign out of Microsoft 365. With themes, however, you do not need to be signed in to Microsoft 365 to make a selection. Just complete steps **1** to **4** in this section.

Search for a Ribbon Command

All the Microsoft 365 apps enable you to search for Ribbon commands. Searching can be useful when you need to perform a task that you do not perform regularly and so are not sure where to find the command you need. Rather than wasting time looking through various Ribbon tabs and groups, the Search feature can help. By entering some or all of the command name, the Search features can take you directly to the command you want to run. You can still use the Ribbon directly, as described in the next section, "Work with the Ribbon."

Search for a Ribbon Command

1 Open a document in a Microsoft 365 app.

Note: See Chapter 2 for details on opening a Microsoft 365 document.

2 Select an object or some text in the document, if required by the Ribbon command you want to run.

3 Click inside the **Search** text box.

Note: You can also select the Search text box by pressing [Alt] + [Q].

A A list of your recent Ribbon commands appears in the Recently Used Actions section.

B A list of suggested Ribbon commands appears in the Suggested Actions section.

4 Type the name or a brief description of the command you want to run.

C The app lists possible commands you can use to complete your task.

5 Click a command to use it.

D Commands with arrows (⟩) display additional commands.

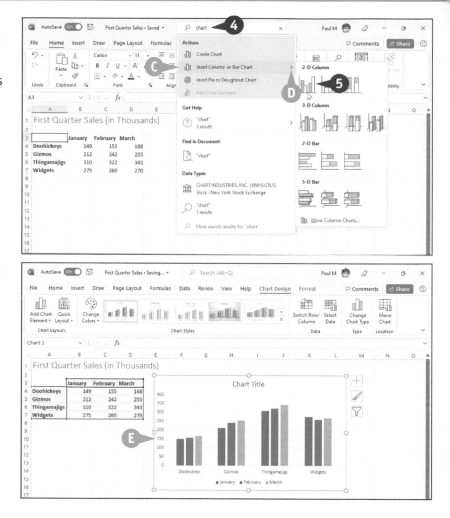

E The app performs the action you selected; in this example, Excel charts the worksheet data.

Will I need to type a description of the action I want to take if it is the same action I have previously taken?

No. The Search feature remembers your previous searches and displays them in the Recently Used Actions section of the menu that appears when you perform step **2**.

If I no longer want my previous searches to appear, can I clear them from the list?

No. The Search feature retains your searches in the Recently Used Actions section of the menu that appears when you click in the Search box.

Work with the Ribbon

You use the Ribbon to access an app's commands. The Ribbon is divided into tabs, the names of which vary depending on the app. Excel's Ribbon, for example, includes tabs named Home, Insert, Formulas, and Data. Each Ribbon tab is divided into groups of related commands. The Home tab includes the Clipboard group for copying and pasting data and the Font group for applying text formatting.

Each Ribbon command does one of four things: run a task, display a menu of commands, display a gallery, or launch a dialog box.

Work with the Ribbon

Run a Command

1 Click the tab containing the command you want to use.

2 Click the command.

The app runs the command.

Run a Command from a Menu

1 Click the tab containing the menu you want to use.

A Many Ribbon buttons have two parts: The top part runs the standard command, and the bottom part displays the menu.

2 Click the button's arrow (▼).

A menu of additional commands appears.

B Hover the mouse (⟡) over a command to see a tooltip that displays the command's name.

3 Click the command you want to run.

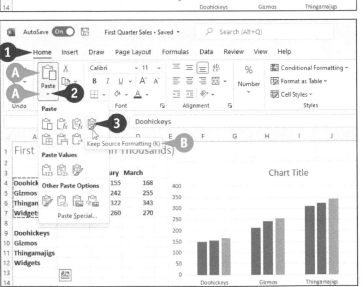

Choose an Item from a Gallery

1 Click the tab containing the gallery you want to display.

2 Click the gallery's **More** button (⤓).

3 Click the gallery item you want to apply.

C When you hover the mouse (⇖) over a gallery item, the app displays a preview of the effect.

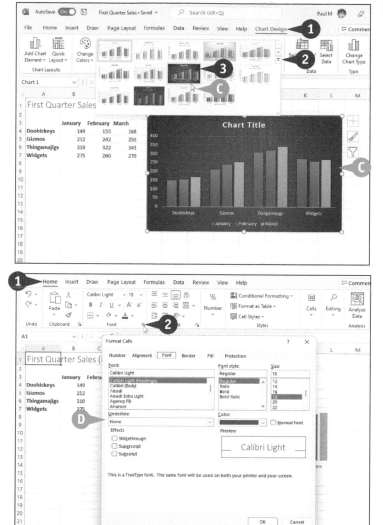

Launch a Dialog Box

1 Click the tab containing the group you want to work with.

2 Click the group's dialog box launcher (⌐⌐).

D The app displays a dialog box containing additional settings related to the group.

TIPS

Why do some Ribbon tabs appear and disappear?
Tabs that come and go on the Ribbon are known as *contextual tabs*. They are contextual in the sense that they appear only when you select an object in a document. For example, if you select a chart in Excel, the Chart Design and Format tabs appear. These contextual tabs contain commands related to working with charts. When you click outside the chart to deselect it, the contextual tabs disappear because you no longer need them.

Can I make the Ribbon take up less room?
Yes. Right-click any section of the Ribbon and then click **Collapse the Ribbon**. You now see just the Ribbon tabs. You can display the full Ribbon temporarily by clicking a tab.

Customize the Quick Access Toolbar

The Quick Access Toolbar offers one-click access to your frequently used commands. The Quick Access Toolbar is hidden by default, so to use it you must first display it. Its default position is below the Ribbon. Also by default, the Quick Access Toolbar either is empty or contains just one or two buttons, so you must customize this toolbar to add the commands you use often, such as the New, Open, Save, and Quick Print commands.

You can also reposition the Quick Access Toolbar so that it appears above the Ribbon, and you can configure it to show only the command icons.

Customize the Quick Access Toolbar

Display the Quick Access Toolbar

1 Right-click the Ribbon.

2 Click **Show Quick Access Toolbar**.

The app displays the Quick Access Toolbar below the Ribbon.

Add Commands to the Quick Access Toolbar

1 On the Quick Access Toolbar, click the **More** button (▽).

2 Click a command.

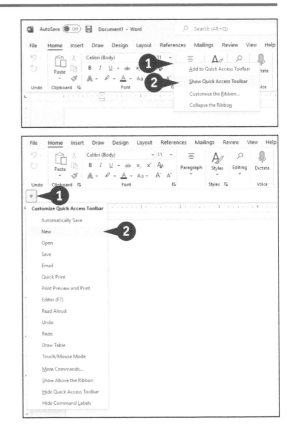

Ⓐ The app adds the command to the Quick Access Toolbar.

❸ Repeat steps **1** and **2** in this subsection for each command you want to add.

Customize the Quick Access Toolbar

❶ On the Quick Access Toolbar, click the **More** button (▼).

Ⓑ You can click **Show Above the Ribbon** if you want to display the Quick Access Toolbar above the Ribbon.

Ⓒ You can click **Hide Command Labels** to display just the command icons on the Quick Access Toolbar.

Ⓓ You can click **Hide Quick Access Toolbar** if you want to temporarily remove the toolbar from the app window.

TIPS

How do I remove a button from the Quick Access Toolbar?

To remove a command, click the Quick Access Toolbar's **More** button (▼). In the menu that appears, click the command you want to remove. The button no longer appears on the Quick Access Toolbar.

Can I add commands that do not appear in the Quick Access Toolbar's menu?

Yes. You can add commands to the Quick Access Toolbar directly from the Ribbon. Click the tab containing the command that you want to add, right-click the command, and then click **Add to Quick Access Toolbar**. The command now appears as a button on the Quick Access Toolbar.

Using a Microsoft 365 App with a Touch Screen

Ⅰf you use Microsoft 365 on a touch-screen device, you can take advantage of Touch mode to make using the apps easier and more efficient. You can configure the Quick Access Toolbar with a command that toggles between the default Mouse mode and the tablet-friendly Touch mode.

In Mouse mode, the Quick Access Toolbar and Ribbon button are closely spaced because it is relatively easy to select buttons accurately with a mouse. In Touch mode, the Quick Access Toolbar and Ribbon buttons are spaced farther apart to make it easier to select buttons accurately by tapping them with a finger.

Using a Microsoft 365 App with a Touch Screen

Add Touch/Mouse Mode to the Quick Access Toolbar

 On the Quick Access Toolbar, tap the **More** button (▾).

Note: If you do not see the Quick Access Toolbar, see the previous section, "Customize the Quick Access Toolbar," to learn how to display it.

2 Tap **Touch/Mouse Mode**.

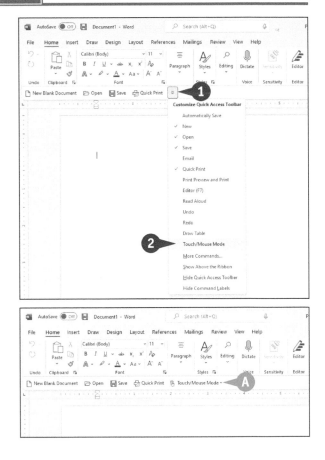

Ⓐ The Touch/Mouse Mode command appears on the Quick Access Toolbar.

Switch to Touch Mode

1 On the Quick Access Toolbar, tap **Touch/Mouse Mode**.

2 Tap **Touch**.

B The Microsoft 365 app increases the spacing between the buttons on the Quick Access Toolbar and the Ribbon, grouping Ribbon buttons as needed.

TIP

Are there any other features in Microsoft 365 apps that make the apps easier to use on touch devices?
Yes, Word's Read Mode contains buttons (and) on the left and right sides of the screen (A) that you can tap to change pages. See Chapter 8 for details on switching to Read Mode. For a more touch-friendly experience, consider using Microsoft 365 on an iPad or Android device.

in the same sentence (or else shooting's-too-good-for-'em puns such as "the abominable showman"). The nouveau riche dot-commers were mere **sneaker millionaires, MOPs** (millionaires on paper), and **optionaires** (people with millions of dollars in stock options). The older managers who were often brought in to help with the business side of things were called **gray matter**, as though they were the *real* brains behind these operations.

Create a New File

When you are ready to create new content, rather than adding to an existing document, you can create a new file. The Start screen that appears when you open a Microsoft 365 app (except Outlook, OneNote, and Teams) enables you to create a new file, as described in Chapter 1. If Word, Excel, PowerPoint, Access, or Publisher is already open and you want to create a new document, workbook, presentation, database, or publication, you create a new file using Backstage view. You have the option of creating a blank file or basing the file on a template.

Create a New File

Create a New Blank File

1 Click the **File** tab.

2 Click **New**.

The New screen appears.

3 Click the **Blank *Type*** thumbnail, where *Type* is the type of file, such as Document (Word), Workbook (Excel), or Presentation (PowerPoint).

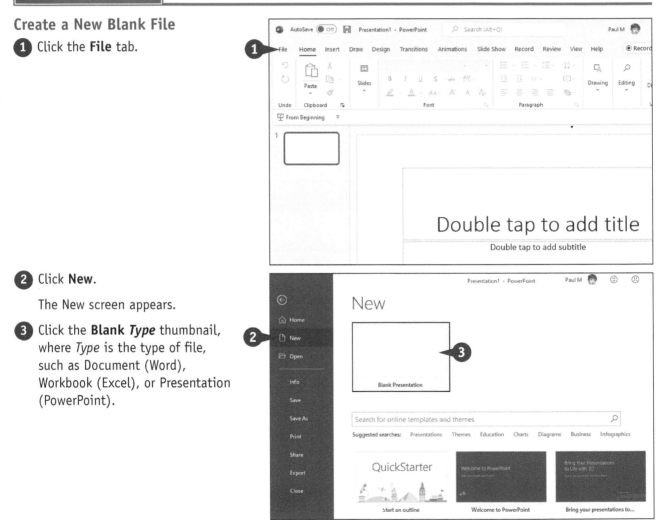

Create a New File from a Template

1 Click the **File** tab (not shown).

2 Click **New**.

The New screen appears.

3 Click the template that represents the type of file that you want to create.

A You can use this Search box to search for the template you want.

Note: A template contains predefined text and formatting that serve as the starting point for your document, saving you the effort of manually adding that text and formatting it.

A preview and description of the template appears.

4 Click **Create**.

The Microsoft 365 app creates and then opens a new file based on the template.

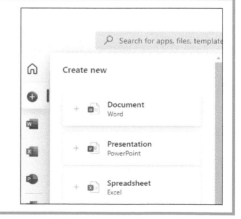

TIP

Is there another way I can create a new Microsoft 365 file?

Yes. Click the **Start** button (▦) and then click the **Office** app to launch it. Click **Create** (⊕) and then click a file type from the menu that appears. Windows opens or switches to the app and creates the new file.

Save a File

You save files you create in Microsoft 365 apps so that you can use them at another time. When you save a file, you can give it a unique filename and store it in the folder or drive of your choice.

After you save a file for the first time, you can click the **Save** button (🖫) in the app's title bar to save it again. The first time you save a file, the app prompts you for a filename. Subsequent times, when you use the Save button (🖫) in the title bar, the app saves the file using its original name without prompting you.

Save a File

Ⓐ Before you save a file, the app displays a generic name in the title bar (such as Document1 for a Word document, as shown here).

1 Click the **File** tab.

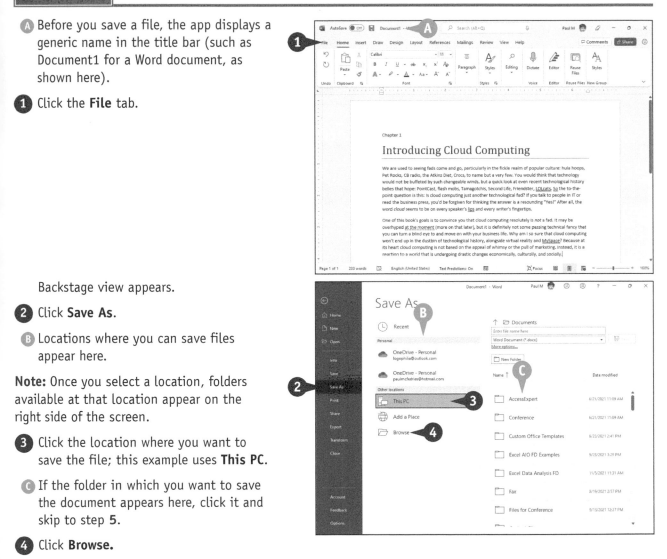

Backstage view appears.

2 Click **Save As**.

Ⓑ Locations where you can save files appear here.

Note: Once you select a location, folders available at that location appear on the right side of the screen.

3 Click the location where you want to save the file; this example uses **This PC**.

Ⓒ If the folder in which you want to save the document appears here, click it and skip to step **5**.

4 Click **Browse.**

The Save As dialog box appears.

5 Type a name for the document.

D You can click in the folder list to select a location on your computer in which to save the document.

E You can click **New folder** to create a new folder in which to store the document.

6 Click **Save**.

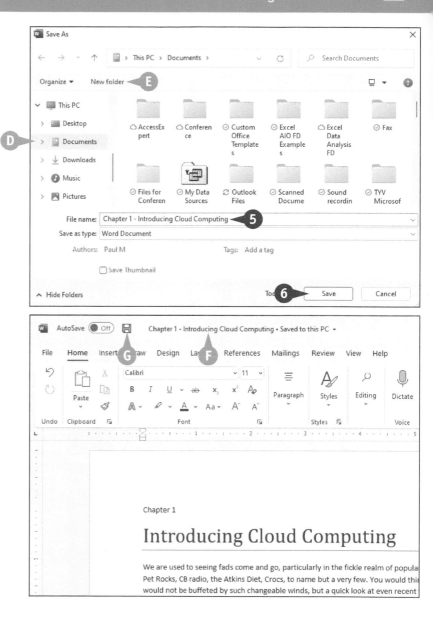

F Word saves the document and displays the name you supplied in the title bar.

G For subsequent saves, you can click the **Save** button (⊟) on the Quick Access Toolbar to quickly save the file.

Can I save a file using a different file type?

Yes. Each Microsoft 365 app saves to a default file type. For example, a Word document uses the DOCX file format, and Excel uses the XLSX file format. If you want to save the file in a format compatible with previous versions of the Microsoft 365 app, you must save it in the appropriate format, such as Word 97-2003 Document for previous versions of Word. To save a file in a different format, follow steps **1** to **4**, click the **Save as type** ⌄ in the Save As dialog box, and choose the desired format from the list that appears.

Open a File

Y ou can open documents that you have saved previously to continue adding data or to edit existing data. If you are not sure where you saved a file, you can use the Open dialog box's Search function to locate it.

In Word, you can open and edit PDF files. Because Word optimizes PDF files to enable you to edit text, editing a PDF file in Word works best if you used Word to create the original PDF file. If you used a different app to create the PDF file, the result might not look exactly like the original PDF.

Open a File

1 Click the **File** tab (not shown).

Backstage view appears.

2 Click **Open**.

A By default, the Microsoft 365 app displays recently opened documents. If you see the file you want to open, you can click it to open it and skip the rest of these steps.

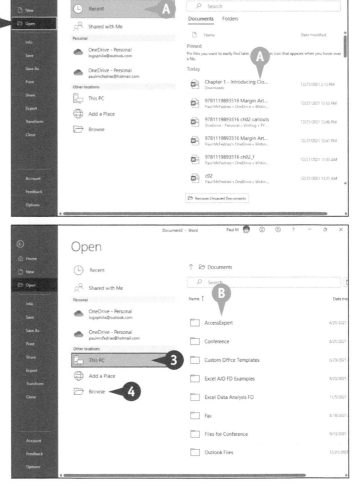

3 Click the place where you believe the document is stored. This example uses This PC.

B If the folder containing the document appears here, click it and skip to step **6**.

4 Click **Browse**.

The Open dialog box appears.

C If you chose the wrong place, you can search for the file by typing part of the filename or content here.

5 Click in the folder list to navigate to the folder containing the document you want to open.

6 Click the document you want to open.

7 Click **Open**.

The file opens in the app window.

D To close a file, click the **Close** button (✕) in the upper-right corner. If you have not saved the file, the app prompts you to save it.

Are there any tricks to searching for a file?

Yes. To search most effectively for a file, start by following steps **1** to **5** to locate and open the folder in which you believe the file was saved. Then, type all or part of the file's name in the Search box and press Enter. Files containing the search term in either the filename or as part of the file's content appear highlighted in the Open dialog box. Word also displays files containing a close match.

Print a File

If a printer is connected to your computer, you can print your Microsoft 365 files. For example, you might distribute printouts of a file as handouts in a meeting.

When you print a file, you have two options: You can send a file directly to the printer using the default settings, or you can open the Microsoft 365 app's Print screen to change these settings. For example, you might opt to print just a portion of the file, print using a different printer, print multiple copies of a file, collate the printouts, and so on. (Printer settings vary slightly among Microsoft 365 apps.)

Print a File

1 Click the **File** tab.

Backstage view appears.

2 Click **Print**.

A You can specify the number of copies to print by clicking the **Copies** ⬍.

B You can choose a printer from the **Printer** drop-down list.

C You can choose to print a selection from the file or specific pages using the available settings in the Settings list.

D You can select additional print options under Settings. For example, you can choose from various paper sizes and to print in landscape or portrait orientation.

E If you do not see the setting you want to change, click **Page Setup** to view additional settings.

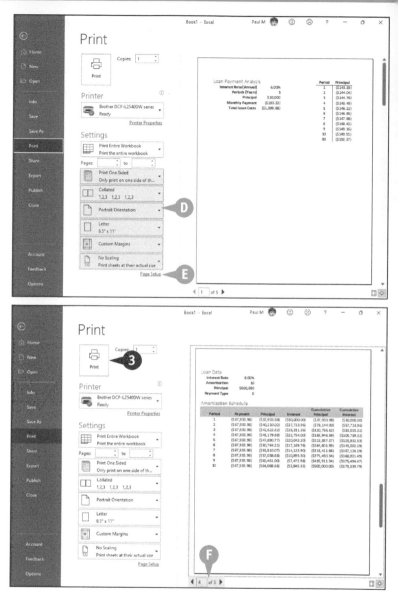

F You can page through a preview of your printed file by clicking the previous arrow (◀) and the next arrow (▶).

3 Click **Print**.

The Microsoft 365 app sends the file to the printer.

TIP

How do I print using default settings?

If you do not need to change any of your default print settings, you can simply click the **Quick Print** button on the Quick Access Toolbar (QAT). If you do not see the QAT, see Chapter 1 to learn how to display it.

If the Quick Print button does not appear on your QAT, you can add it. To do so, click the **More** button (▾) on the QAT and then click **Quick Print** in the list of commands that appears. You can also add a **Print Preview and Print** button to the QAT; clicking that button opens the Print screen from Backstage view.

Select Data

You can select data in your file to perform different tasks, such as deleting it, changing its font or alignment, applying a border around it, or copying and pasting it. Selected data appears highlighted.

Depending on the app you are using, Microsoft 365 offers several different techniques for selecting data. For example, in Word, PowerPoint, Outlook, and Publisher, you can select a single character, a word, a sentence, a paragraph, or all the data in the file. In Excel and Access tables, you typically select cells. In OneNote, use the technique appropriate to the type of data you want to select.

Select Data

Select Data in Word, PowerPoint, or Publisher

Note: You can use this technique to select characters, words, sentences, and paragraphs.

1 Click to one side of the word or character that you want to select.

2 Drag the mouse (⟨⟩) across the text that you want to select.

Ⓐ The app highlights the characters to indicate that they are selected.

Ⓑ To cancel a selection, click anywhere outside the text or press any arrow key on your keyboard.

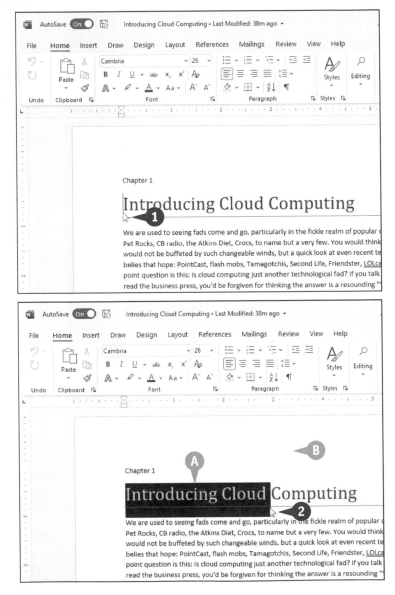

Select Cells in Excel or Access

1 Click the cell representing the upper-left corner of the cells you want to select.

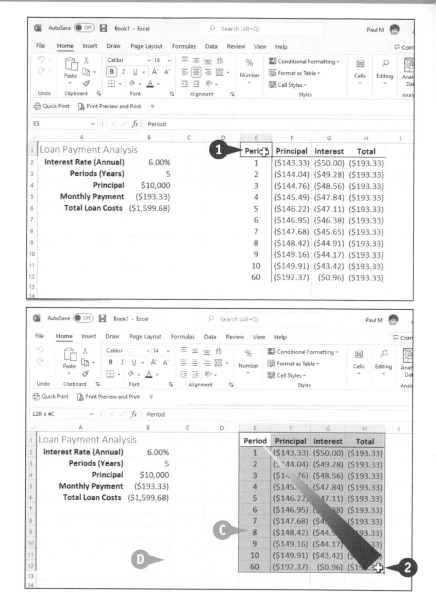

2 Drag the cell pointer across the cells you want to select.

C The app highlights the characters to indicate that they are selected.

D To cancel a selection, click anywhere outside the text or press any arrow key on your keyboard.

TIP

How can I use my keyboard to select text?

To select text or cells to the left or right of the insertion point or cell pointer, press Ctrl + Shift + ← or Ctrl + Shift + →. To select a paragraph or cells above or below the insertion point or cell pointer, press Ctrl + Shift + ↑ or Ctrl + Shift + ↓. To select all text or cells from the insertion point or cell pointer location onward, press Ctrl + Shift + End. To select all the text or cells above the insertion point or cell pointer location, press Ctrl + Shift + Home. To select all the text or cells containing data in the file, press Ctrl + A.

Insert a Picture from Your PC

You can illustrate your Microsoft 365 files with images that you store on your computer. For example, if you have a photo or graphic file that relates to the subject matter in your document, you can insert the picture into the document to help the reader understand your subject. After you insert a picture, you can resize and move the image as described in the section "Resize and Move Graphic Objects," later in this chapter. You can also modify the graphic in a variety of ways, as described in the section "Understanding Graphics Modification Techniques," later in this chapter.

Insert a Picture from Your PC

1 Click in your document where you want to add a picture.

Note: You can move the image to a different location after inserting it onto the page. See the section "Resize and Move Graphic Objects," later in this chapter.

2 Click the **Insert** tab.

3 Click **Pictures**.

4 Click **This Device**.

The Insert Picture dialog box appears.

A The folder you are viewing appears here.

Note: Image files come in a variety of formats, including GIF, JPEG, and PNG.

B To browse for a particular file type, you can click ∨ and choose a file format.

C You can click in the folder list to navigate to commonly used locations where pictures may be stored.

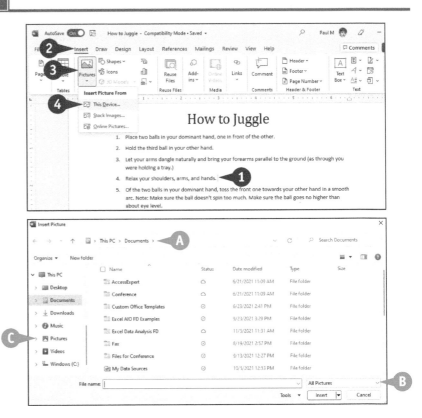

5 Navigate to the folder containing the picture you want to add to your document.

6 Click the picture you want to add.

7 Click **Insert**.

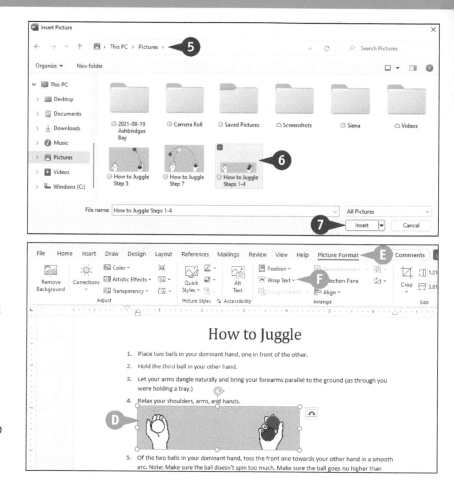

D The picture appears in your document.

E The Picture Format contextual tab appears on the Ribbon; you can use these tools to format the selected picture.

F In the **Picture Format** tab, you can click **Wrap Text** to control text flow around the picture.

To remove a picture that you no longer want, you can click the picture and press Delete.

TIPS

If I am sharing my file with others, can I compress the pictures to save space?
Yes. To compress an image, click the image, click the **Picture Format** tab, and then click the **Compress Pictures** button (🖼) in the Adjust group. In the Compress Pictures dialog box, fine-tune the settings as needed and then click **Compress**.

When I first insert a picture, I see a band labelled Alt Text along the button of the image. What is alt text, and how do I edit this text?
Alt (short for alternative) text is an accessibility feature that describes a picture for people with visual impairments. To edit the alt text, click the picture, click the **Picture Format** tab, and then click **Alt Text**.

Insert an Online Picture

If you want to illustrate a document but do not have an appropriate photo or other image stored on your computer's hard drive, you can still add interest to your Microsoft 365 files by inserting a picture or clip art image from an online source. You can insert online pictures into a Word, Excel, PowerPoint, Publisher, Outlook, or OneNote document. Be careful when choosing an online picture and make sure that it either falls into the public domain, meaning you can use the picture without requiring permission, or you have written permission to use the picture.

Insert an Online Picture

Note: If you are working in Word or Excel, switch to Print Layout view by clicking **View** and then **Page Layout**.

1 Click in your document where you want to add a picture.

Note: You can move the graphic to a different location after you insert it. See the section "Resize and Move Graphic Objects," later in this chapter.

2 Click the **Insert** tab.

3 Click **Pictures**.

4 Click **Online Pictures**.

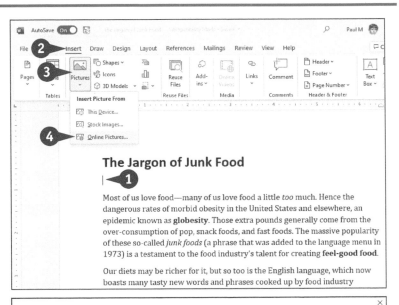

The Online Pictures dialog box appears.

5 Click in the Search box and type a description of the kind of image you want.

Ⓐ You can also click a category to display images related to that subject.

6 Press Enter.

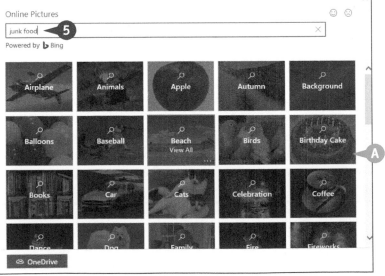

The results of your search appear.

Ⓑ You can click the up and down arrows (⋀ and ⋁) to navigate through the search results.

Ⓒ You can click **Back** (←) to return to the Online Pictures dialog box and search for a different image.

⑦ Click the picture you want to add to your document.

⑧ Click **Insert**.

Ⓓ The picture appears in your document.

Ⓔ The Shape Format and Picture Format contextual tabs appear on the Ribbon; you can use these tools to format the selected picture.

Ⓕ You can click the Picture Format tab's Wrap Text button or the Layout Options button (⬕) to control how text flows around the picture.

⑨ When you finish working with your online picture, click anywhere else in the work area.

Why must I make sure that the image I choose falls into the public domain?

Privately owned images are often available for use only if you agree to pay a fee and/or get the owner's permission to use the image. You can use a public domain image without paying a royalty and/or obtaining the owner's permission to use the image.

How does Creative Commons work?

At creativecommons.org, you find links to license or search for images at several places, such as Flickr or Google Images. Search results do not guarantee an image is licensed by Creative Commons. You need to click an image to examine its licensing information.

Resize and Move Graphic Objects

If a picture or other type of image — which is also called a *graphic object* — is not positioned where you want it, you can move it. Similarly, if a graphic object or is too large or too small, you can resize it. When you select a graphic object, handles appear on each side of the graphic object; you can use these handles to resize it. Alignment guides — green lines — appear as you move a graphic object to help you determine where to place it. Once you have picked the spot for the graphic, the alignment guides disappear.

Resize and Move Graphic Objects

Resize a Graphic

1 Click a graphic object.

A Handles (○) surround the graphic.

2 Position the mouse over one of the handles (the app's default mouse pointer changes to ⬉, ↕, ⬈, or ↔).

3 Drag the handle inward or outward until the graphic object is the size you want (⬉, ↕, ⬈, or ↔ changes to +).

4 Release the mouse button.

The graphic object appears in the new size.

5 Click outside the graphic object to cancel its selection.

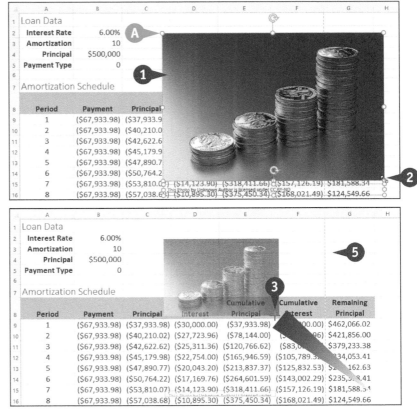

32

Move a Graphic

1 Click a graphic object.

B Handles (○) surround the graphic.

2 Position the mouse over a graphic object or the edge of a text box (the app's default mouse pointer changes to ✥).

3 Drag the graphic object to a new location.

4 Release the mouse button.

The graphic object appears in the new location.

5 Click outside the graphic object to cancel its selection.

	A	B	C	D	E	F	G	H
1	Loan Data							
2	Interest Rate	6.00%						
3	Amortization	10						
4	Principal	$500,000						
5	Payment Type	0						
6								
7	Amortization Schedule							
8	Period	Payment	Principal	Interest	Principal	Cumulative Interest	Remaining Principal	
9	1	($67,933.98)	($37,933.98)	($30,000.00)	($37,933.98)	($30,000.00)	$462,066.02	
10	2	($67,933.98)	($40,210.02)	($27,723.96)	($78,144.00)	($57,723.96)	$421,856.00	
11	3	($67,933.98)	($42,622.62)	($25,311.36)	($120,766.62)	($83,035.32)	$379,233.38	
12	4	($67,933.98)	($45,179.98)	($22,754.00)	($165,946.59)	($105,789.32)	$334,053.41	
13	5	($67,933.98)	($47,890.77)	($20,043.20)	($213,837.37)	($125,832.53)	$286,162.63	
14	6	($67,933.98)	($50,764.22)	($17,169.76)	($264,601.59)	($143,002.29)	$235,398.41	
15	7	($67,933.98)	($53,810.07)	($14,123.90)	($318,411.66)	($157,126.19)	$181,588.34	
16	8	($67,933.98)	($57,038.68)	($10,895.30)	($375,450.34)	($168,021.49)	$124,549.66	

	A	B	C	D	E	F	G	H
1	Loan Data							
2	Interest Rate	6.00%						
3	Amortization	10						
4	Principal	$500,000						
5	Payment Type	0						
6								
7	Amortization Schedule							
8	Period	Payment	Principal	Interest	Cumulative Principal	Cumulative Interest	Remaining Principal	
9	1	($67,933.98)	($37,933.98)	($30,000.00)	($37,933.98)	($30,000.00)	$462,066.02	
10	2	($67,933.98)	($40,210.02)	($27,723.96)	($78,144.00)	($57,723.96)	$421,856.00	
11	3	($67,933.98)	($42,622.62)	($25,311.36)	($120,766.62)	($83,035.32)	$379,233.38	
12	4	($67,933.98)	($45,179.98)	($22,754.00)	($165,946.59)	($105,789.32)	$334,053.41	
13	5	($67,933.98)	($47,890.77)	($20,043.20)	($213,837.37)	($125,832.53)	$286,162.63	
14	6	($67,933.98)	($50,764.22)	($17,169.76)	($264,601.59)	($143,002.29)	$235,398.41	
15	7	($67,933.98)	($53,810.07)	($14,123.90)	($318,411.66)	($157,126.19)	$181,588.34	
16	8	($67,933.98)	($57,038.68)	($10,895.30)	($375,450.34)	($168,021.49)	$124,549.66	

TIPS

Can I control how text wraps around an object?

Yes, if you insert the object into a Word or Publisher file. Click the object, click **Wrap Text** in the Picture Format tab, and then choose a wrap style.

Does it matter which handle I use to resize a graphic?

Yes. If you click and drag any of the corner handles, you maintain the proportion of the graphic as you resize it. The handles on the sides, top, or bottom of the graphic resize only the width or the height of the graphic, causing your graphic to look distorted.

Understanding Graphics Modification Techniques

Besides inserting, moving, and resizing pictures as described in this chapter, you can insert and modify other types of graphic objects — shapes, screenshots, SmartArt, WordArt, and charts — in all Microsoft 365 apps except Access. The available graphic objects vary from app to app; the specific types of available graphic objects appear on the Insert tab of the program. You insert these objects using basically the same techniques you use to insert pictures.

You can modify an object's appearance using a variety of Ribbon buttons that appear on a contextual tab specific to the type of graphic object you select.

Crop a Picture

You can use the Crop tool to create a better fit, to omit a portion of the image, or to focus the viewer on an important area of the image. You can crop a picture, screenshot, or clip art image. When you crop an object, you remove vertical and/or horizontal edges from the object. The Crop tool is located on the Picture Format tab on the Ribbon, which appears when you click the object you want to crop.

Rotate or Flip a Graphic

After you insert an object such as a piece of clip art or a photo from your hard drive into a Word document, you may find that the object appears upside down or inverted. Fortunately, Word makes it easy to flip or rotate an object. For example, you might flip a clip art image to face another direction, or rotate an arrow object to point elsewhere on the page. Or, for dramatic effect, you can rotate or flip pictures, clip art images, and some shapes. Keep in mind that you cannot rotate text boxes.

Correct Images

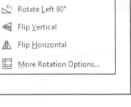

You can change the brightness and contrast of a picture, clip art, or a screenshot to improve its appearance, and you can sharpen or soften an image. Suppose, for example, the image object you have inserted in your Word, Excel, or PowerPoint file is slightly blurry, or lacks contrast. You find the image-correction tools on the Picture Tools Format tab on the Ribbon, which appears when you click to select the object to which you want to apply the effect.

Make Color Adjustments

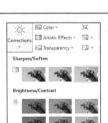

You can adjust the color of a picture, screenshot, or clip art image by increasing or decreasing color saturation or color tone. You can also recolor a picture, screenshot, or clip art image to create an interesting effect.

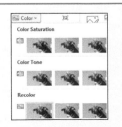

Color saturation controls the amount of red and green in a photo, whereas color tone controls the amount of blue and yellow.

Remove the Background of an Image

You can remove the background of a picture, screenshot, or clip art image. For example, suppose that you inserted a screenshot of an Excel chart in a Word document; the screenshot would, by default, include the Excel Ribbon. You can use the Remove Background tool in the Adjust group on the Picture Format tab to remove the Excel Ribbon and focus the reader's attention on the chart.

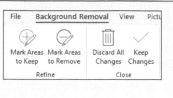

Add an Effect

You can use tools to assign unique and interesting special effects to objects. For example, you can apply a shadow effect, create a mirrored reflection, apply a glow effect, soften the object's edges, make a bevel effect, or generate a 3-D rotation effect. You can find these tools on the Picture Format tab of the Ribbon, which appears when you click to select the object to which you want to apply the effect. (Note that the Picture Effects tool is not available in Publisher.)

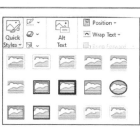

Apply a Style to a Graphic

You can apply a predefined style to a shape, text box, WordArt graphic, picture, or clip art image. Styles contain predefined colors and effects and help you quickly add interest to a graphic. Applying a style removes other effects that you may have applied, such as shadow or bevel effects. Sample styles appear on the Picture Format or Shape Format tab when you click the **More** button (⏷) in the Picture Styles or Shape Styles group.

Add a Picture Border or Drawing Outline

You can add a border to a picture, shape, text box, WordArt graphic, clip art image, or screenshot. Using the Picture Border or Shape Outline tool, which appears on the Picture Format or Shape Format tab, you can control the thickness of the border, set a style for the border — a solid or dashed line — and change the color of the border.

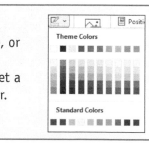

Apply Artistic Effects

You can apply artistic effects to pictures, screenshots, and clip art to liven them up. For example, you can make an image appear as though it was rendered in marker, pencil, chalk, or paint. Other artistic effects might remind you of mosaics, film grain, or glass. You find the Artistic Effects button on the Picture Format tab, which appears when you click to select the object to which you want to apply the effect.

Microsoft 365 and the Cloud

Today, people are on the go but often want to take work with them to do while sitting in the waiting room of their doctor's office, at the airport, or in a hotel room. Using Microsoft 365, you can work from anywhere using almost any device available because, among other reasons, it works with SharePoint and OneDrive, Microsoft's cloud space. From OneDrive, you can log in to cloud space and, using Microsoft 365 web apps — essentially, tools with which you are already familiar — get to work.

Sign In to the Cloud

Signing in to Office Online or to your Microsoft 365 subscription connects your Microsoft 365 apps to the world beyond your computer. Office Online offers free access to the online, limited-edition versions of the Microsoft 365 apps that you can use on any computer. Purchasing a Microsoft 365 subscription gives you access to full versions of the Microsoft 365 desktop programs and the online versions of the products. Signing in gives you access to online pictures and clip art stored at Office.com and enables Microsoft 365 to synchronize files between your computer, OneDrive, and SharePoint.

OneDrive and Microsoft 365

OneDrive is a cloud storage service from Microsoft that you can use with Microsoft 365; 15GB are free, and you can rent additional space. Microsoft 365 saves all documents by default to your OneDrive space so that your documents are always available to you.

Using Microsoft 365 Web Apps

You can create, open, and edit Word, Excel, OneNote, and PowerPoint documents from your OneDrive using Microsoft 365 web apps. These online apps are scaled-down editions of Microsoft 365 desktop apps that you can use to review documents and make minor changes.

Take Your Personal Settings with You Everywhere

Microsoft 365 keeps track of personal settings like your recently used files and color theme and makes them available from any computer just by signing in to Microsoft 365. Word and PowerPoint also remember the paragraph and slide you were viewing when you closed a document, and they display that location when you open the document on another machine, making it easy for you to get back to work.

Your Documents Are Always Up-to-Date

Microsoft 365 saves your documents by default in the OneDrive folder you find in File Explorer. As you work, Microsoft 365 synchronizes files with changes to your OneDrive in the background. This technology does not slow down your work environment because Microsoft 365 uploads only changes, not entire documents, saving bandwidth and battery life as you work from wireless devices.

Share Your Documents from Anywhere

You can share your documents both from within a Microsoft 365 app and from your OneDrive. From either location, you can email a document to recipients you choose, post a document to a social media site, or create a link to a document that you can provide to users so that they can view the document in a browser. You can also use Microsoft's free online presentation service to present Word and PowerPoint documents online.

Open Documents Online or Locally

When you select a Microsoft 365 document online, OneDrive gives you the option of opening the document using either the online version of the app or the desktop version of the app.

Online Document Tools

OneDrive offers several file management tools that you can use with the documents that you store online. These tools include Download, to download a copy to your computer; Delete, to remove the document from OneDrive; Move to, to move the document to another OneDrive folder; Copy to, to copy the document to another OneDrive folder; Rename, to change the document name; and Version history, to see previous versions of the document.

Sign In to Microsoft 365

You can use Microsoft 365 Online or your Microsoft 365 subscription to work from anywhere. While signed in from any device, you can use one of the free Microsoft 365 web apps. Microsoft 365 shares some of your personal settings — such as your Recent Documents list — across devices so that you always have access to them. Desktop product users sign in using a Microsoft 365 subscription, as described in this section and, for the most part, throughout the book.

When you work offline, Microsoft 365 creates, saves, and opens your files from the local OneDrive folder. Whenever you reconnect, Microsoft 365 automatically uploads your changes to the cloud.

Sign In to Microsoft 365

1 Open a Microsoft 365 app.

The program's Start screen appears.

2 Click **Sign In**.

Note: If you are viewing a document, click **Sign In** near the upper-right corner of the screen.

The Sign In window appears.

3 Type the Microsoft account email address associated with your Microsoft 365 subscription.

4 Click **Next**.

5 Type your password.

Ⓐ If you have trouble signing in, you can click this link to reset your password.

6 Click **Sign in**.

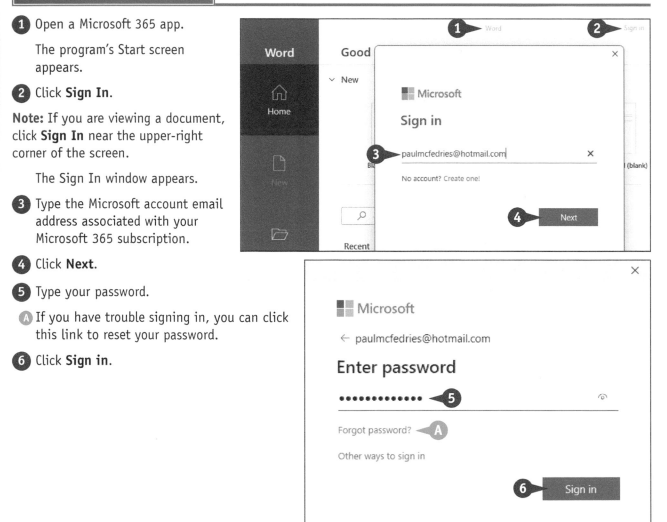

Ⓑ This area indicates that you have signed in to Microsoft 365.

Note: Microsoft 365 Online offers free access to the online, limited-edition versions of the Microsoft 365 programs that you can use on any computer. Microsoft 365 is a subscription you purchase to use full versions of the Microsoft 365 programs; Microsoft 365 includes both the desktop and the online versions of the products.

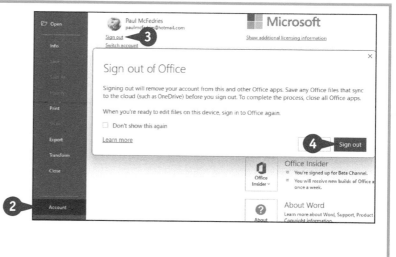

TIP

How do I sign out of Microsoft 365?
Sign in to Windows using a local account and follow these steps:

① Click the **File** tab (not shown).

② Click **Account**.

Note: In Outlook, click **Microsoft 365 Account**.

③ Click **Sign out**.

The Sign out of Office dialog box appears, warning you to save any files that sync to the cloud before continuing.

Note: In most cases, it is perfectly safe to click **Sign out**. If you are unsure, save all open Microsoft 365 files.

④ Click **Sign out**.

Share a Document from Microsoft 365

You can easily share documents using Microsoft 365. You can share a Microsoft 365 document by posting it to a social network or blog or sending a document as an email attachment. You can also take advantage of a free online presentation service Microsoft offers and share your document by presenting it online. Or, as shown in this section, you can send a link to your OneDrive — as part of Microsoft 365, you receive free cloud space at OneDrive — where the recipient can view and even work on only the shared document. When you finish, you can stop sharing the document.

Share a Document from Microsoft 365

Note: You must be signed in to Microsoft 365, and the document you want to share must be stored in the cloud.

1 With the document you want to share on-screen, click **Share**.

The Share Link dialog box appears.

2 In the **To** box, type the email address of the person with whom you want to share.

3 Click the person's name, if it appears; otherwise, press `Enter`.

4 Repeat steps **2** and **3** as needed.

5 Click ⌄ and specify how these people can interact with the shared document:

- **Can edit:** Click this permission to allow the people to view and make changes to the document.

- **Can view:** Click this permission to allow the people to view but not make changes to the document.

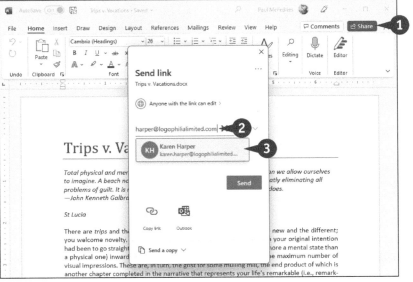

You can type a personal message to include with the invitation.

6 Click **Send**.

Microsoft 365 sends emails to the people you listed.

Send link

Trips v. Vacations.docx

Anyone with the link can edit ›

KH Karen Harper ✕

BS Becky Solnit ✕

Add another ✏ ⌄

A—Here's the essay ready for proofreading.

Send ─ **6**

Copy link   Outlook

Send a copy ⌄

TIP

How do I stop sharing a document?

Follow these steps:

1 Open the document you want to stop sharing and click the **Share** icon.

2 In the Share dialog box, click **More Options** (›).

3 Click **Manage access**.

4 Click ⌄ under the recipient with whom you no longer want to share.

5 Click **Stop Sharing**.

The app updates document permissions and removes the user from the sharing.

← **Manage access**

Trips v. Vacations.docx

https://1drv.ms/w/s!Ak23... ✕

Anyone with the link can edit

PM Paul McFedries
Owner

K karen.harper@logophilia...
Can edit ⌄ ─ **4**

PM Change to view only

Stop sharing ─ **5**

Sign In to OneDrive

You can use your OneDrive and Microsoft 365 apps to work from any location in the world on any trusted device. OneDrive offers you online storage from Microsoft. With Microsoft 365, you automatically receive a small amount of storage space for free, and you can rent additional storage space for a nominal fee.

You use a browser and a Microsoft account to sign in to OneDrive. Once you have signed in to OneDrive, you can use the Microsoft 365 web apps to open and edit documents. Microsoft 365 technology synchronizes documents stored in your OneDrive with documents stored on trusted devices.

Sign In to OneDrive

1 Open your browser.

2 In the address bar, type onedrive. com and press **Enter**.

You are redirected to the OneDrive Home page.

3 Click **Sign in**.

The Sign in dialog box appears.

④ Type your email address.

⑤ Click **Next**.

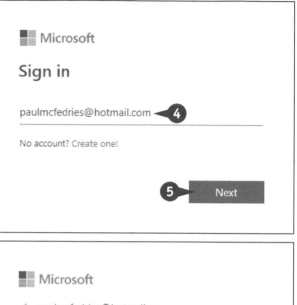

OneDrive prompts you to enter your password.

⑥ Type your Microsoft account password.

⑦ Click **Sign in**.

Your OneDrive space appears.

TIP

How do I sign out of OneDrive?
On the right side of the OneDrive toolbar, click your avatar (A) and then click **Sign out** (B). Microsoft signs you out of your OneDrive.

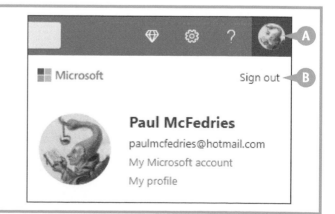

Using an Online App in OneDrive

From OneDrive, you can use the Microsoft 365 web apps to open documents and modify them using many of the same editing tools you use in the desktop apps.

Although the web apps do not include every desktop feature, you can use the online editing tools to perform basic functions in each app. For example, in the Word online app shown in this section, you can apply character and paragraph formatting, such as bold or italics, and you can align text. You can change margins, edit headers and footers, and insert a table or a picture from your computer.

Using an Online App in OneDrive

Open the Document

1 Sign in to OneDrive at https://onedrive.com.

2 Open the folder containing the document you want to view.

3 Click the document.

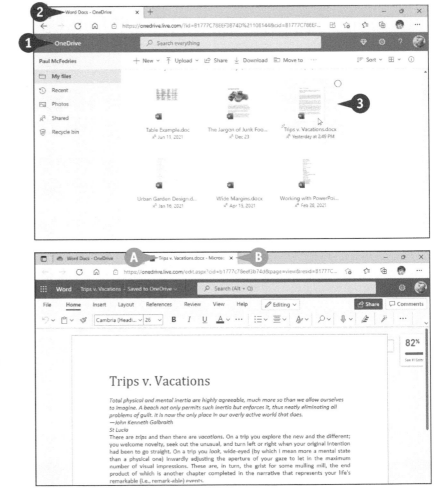

The document appears in the web app.

A The document opens in its own browser tab.

B To close the document, click the browser tab's **Close** button (✕).

Switch Modes

1 Perform steps **1** to **3** in the previous subsection, "Open the Document."

2 Click the **Mode Menu** button.

3 Click the mode you want to use.

Note: See the first tip in this section to learn what each mode means.

The web app switches to the new mode (Viewing mode, in this example).

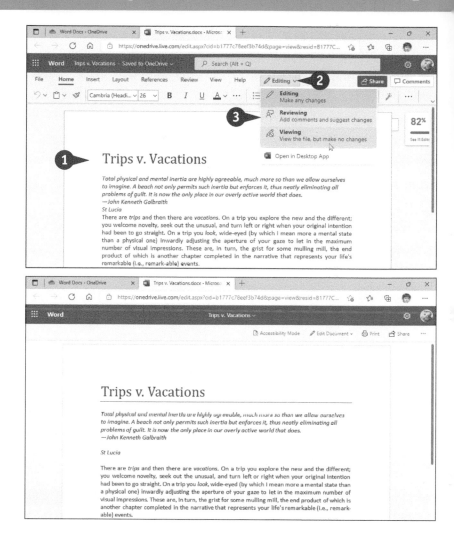

TIPS

What is the difference between the three document modes?

Editing mode means you can modify the document text and formatting. Reviewing mode means you can add comments, and you can make suggested changes that will later be accepted or rejected by the document owner. Viewing mode means you can read the document, but you cannot make any changes.

How do I save my work in an online app?

The answer depends on the online app. All the web apps automatically save changes as you work. In the Word, Excel, and PowerPoint web apps, you save your work as a new document by clicking the **File** tab and then clicking **Save as**.

Open a Document in a Desktop App from OneDrive

When you are using a Microsoft 365 online app to work on a document, you can open that document in the corresponding Microsoft 365 desktop app. For example, suppose that while you are working on a document stored in your OneDrive space, you discover that you need one or more tools that are not available in the online app. If Microsoft 365 is installed on the computer you are using, you can use OneDrive to open the file in the corresponding Microsoft 365 desktop app.

Open a Document in a Desktop App from OneDrive

From an Online App

1 Open a document using an online app.

Note: See the previous section, "Using an Online App in OneDrive," for details.

Note: This section uses an Excel workbook as an example.

2 Click the **Mode Menu** button.

3 Click **Open in Desktop App**.

A security dialog box appears to warn you that the web page is trying to run an app on your computer (Excel, in this example).

A If you want to skip this warning in the future, click the **Always allow** check box (☐ changes to ☑).

4 Click **Open**.

The document opens in the appropriate Microsoft 365 app.

From a OneDrive Folder

1 Open the OneDrive folder that contains the document you want to open.

2 Right-click the document.

3 Click Open in *App*, where *App* is the desktop app associated with the document type (such as Excel, as shown here).

The file opens in the appropriate Microsoft 365 app.

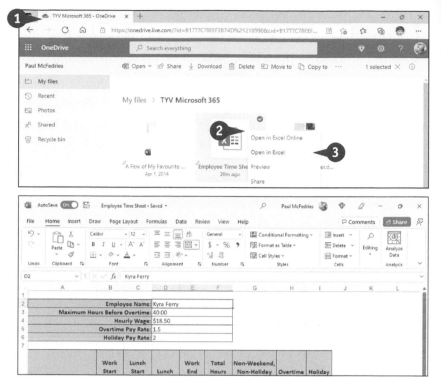

How can I tell that changes I have made are saved to my OneDrive space?

When you save your document in the Microsoft 365 program, watch the title bar in the app (A). When you see the message "Saving," it means that the app is uploading your changes to your OneDrive space. You see "Saved" when the upload is complete.

Upload a Document to OneDrive

You can upload any document from your computer to your OneDrive at any time. By default, Microsoft 365 saves all documents to the OneDrive folder on your computer and then, in the background, synchronizes the contents of the OneDrive folder with your online OneDrive space.

But suppose that you sign out of Microsoft 365 and choose to save documents locally on your computer. If you then find that you need a document in your OneDrive space to edit while you travel, you can place a document into your OneDrive folder on your computer and then upload it from your OneDrive space.

Upload a Document to OneDrive

1 Sign in to OneDrive using your browser.

Note: See the section "Sign In to OneDrive," earlier in this chapter, for details.

2 Click to display the folder where you want to place the document.

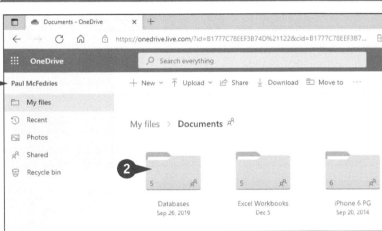

3 Click **Upload**.

4 Click **Files**.

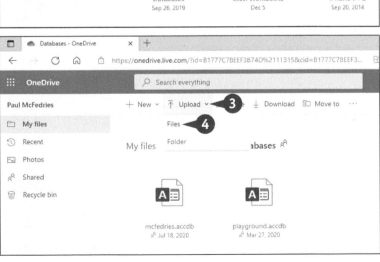

The Open dialog box appears.

5 Navigate to the folder containing the file you want to upload.

6 Click the file.

7 Click **Open**.

A The file appears in your OneDrive space.

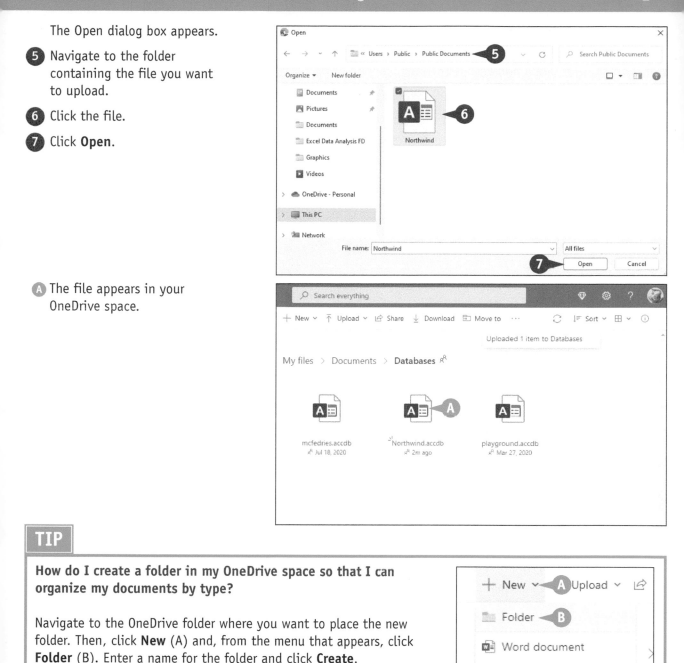

How do I create a folder in my OneDrive space so that I can organize my documents by type?

Navigate to the OneDrive folder where you want to place the new folder. Then, click **New** (A) and, from the menu that appears, click **Folder** (B). Enter a name for the folder and click **Create**.

Share a Document Using OneDrive

Y ou can use a Microsoft 365 online app to share a document stored on your OneDrive. Suppose that you finish the work on a document from your OneDrive space and you are ready for others to review it. You do not need to use the Microsoft 365 app installed on your computer to invite others to review the document; you can use commands available in OneDrive.

OneDrive offers three ways to share a document: You can send the document by email, share it using a social media service of your choice, or send a link to the document on your OneDrive.

Share a Document Using OneDrive

Open a Document to Share

1 In OneDrive, open the document you want to share.

2 Click **Share**.

The Send Link dialog box appears.

Note: Follow the steps in one of the following subsections to share the document.

Share via Email

1 For each person with whom you want to share the document, start typing the name or email address and then click the name when it appears.

A You can include a personal message here.

B You can click this ⌄ to control how recipients can edit.

2 Click **Send**.

Email messages are sent to the recipients you supplied, providing a link to the document.

Share via a Link

1 Click **Copy link**.

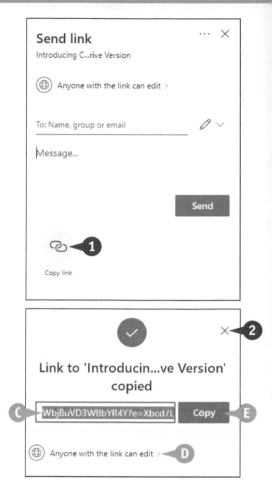

Send link

Introducing C...rive Version

🌐 Anyone with the link can edit ›

To: Name, group or email

Message...

Send

🔗—**1**

Copy link

C OneDrive generates a link and copies the link address to your computer's Clipboard; provide this link to anyone with whom you want to share the document.

D You can click here to customize how people who receive the link can work with the document.

E If you make changes to how link recipients can work with the document, the link address changes, so click **Copy** to copy the new address to the Clipboard.

2 Click **Close** (✕).

✓   ✕—**2**

Link to 'Introducin...ve Version' copied

C—| WbjBuVD3WBbYR4Y?e=Xbcd/L | **Copy**   —**E**

🌐 Anyone with the link can edit ›—**D**

TIP

Can I protect a shared document with a password?

Yes. Open the document and click **Share** to open the Send Link dialog box. Click **Anyone with the link can edit** to open the Link Settings dialog box. Enter the password in the **Set Password** text box (A), and then click **Apply** (B).

Link settings   ✕

Introducing C...rive Version

Who would you like this link to work for?

🌐 Anyone with the link   ⌄

👤 Specific people

Other settings

☑ Allow editing

📅 Set expiration date   ✕

🔒 ••••••••••••—**A**   👁

Strength: Strong

B— **Apply**   Cancel

PART II

Word

You can use Word to tackle any project involving text, such as correspondence, reports, and more. Word's versatile formatting features enable you to enhance your text documents and add elements such as tables or headers and footers. In this part, you learn how to build and format Word documents and tap into Word's tools to review and proofread your documents.

Chapter 5: Adding Text 54

Chapter 6: Formatting Text 62

Chapter 7: Adding Extra Touches 82

Chapter 8: Reviewing Documents 98

Change Word's Views

To help in your text adding and editing chores, you can control how you view your Word document in several ways. For example, you can use the Zoom feature to control the magnification of your document with either the Zoom slider or the Zoom buttons.

You can also choose from five different views: Print Layout, which displays margins, headers, and footers; Outline, which shows the document's outline levels; Web Layout, which displays a web page preview of your document; Read Mode, which optimizes your document for easier reading; and Draft, which omits certain elements such as headers and footers.

Change Word's Views

Using the Zoom Tool

1 Drag the **Zoom** slider on the Zoom bar.

A You can also click a magnification button to zoom in (+) or out (−).

B You can click the percentage to display the Zoom dialog box and precisely control zooming.

C Word magnifies the document, and the magnification percentage appears here.

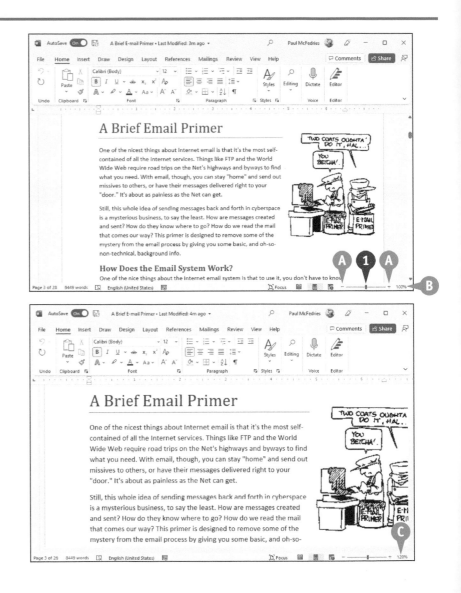

Switch Layout Views

1 Click the **View** tab on the Ribbon.

2 In the Views group, click a layout view button.

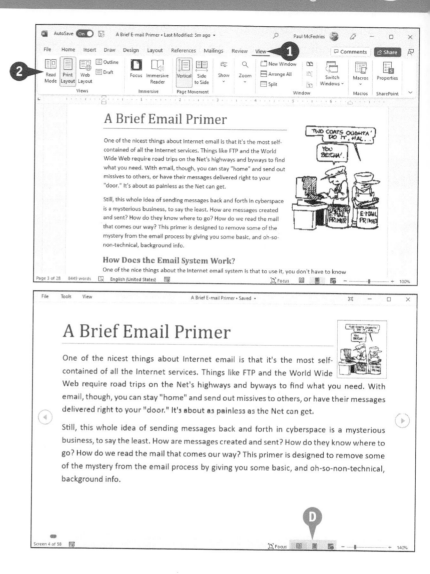

Word displays a new view of the document.

In this example, Read Mode view helps you focus on reading a document. See Chapter 8 for details on Read Mode.

D You can also switch views using the View buttons at the bottom of the program window.

How can I zoom an image?

While in Read Mode view, double-click an image. Word enlarges the image and displays a Zoom In icon (🔍) in the upper-right corner of the image. When you click 🔍 again, the image enlarges to fill your screen. You can click the Zoom Out icon (🔍) to return to the first zoom level, or you can press Esc or click anywhere outside the image to return to Read Mode. See Chapter 8 for more on Read Mode.

Type and Edit Text

You can use Word to quickly type and edit text for a letter, memo, or report. By default, Word is set to Insert mode; when you start typing, any existing text moves over to accommodate the new text. If you have set up Word to toggle between Insert mode and Overtype mode, you can press **Insert** to switch to Overtype mode. In Overtype mode, the new text overwrites the existing text.

Word makes typing easy; you do not need to worry about when to start a new line within a paragraph, and you can easily start new paragraphs and delete text.

Type and Edit Text

Type Text

1 Start typing your text.

A At the end of a line, Word automatically starts a new line, wrapping text to the next line for you.

B The insertion point marks your location in the document and moves to the right as you type. Text you type appears to the left of the insertion point.

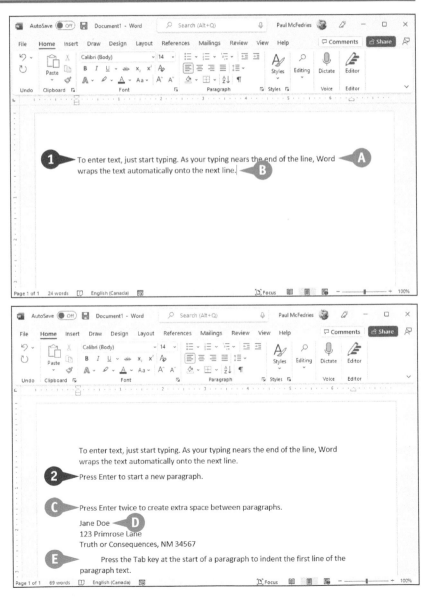

2 Press **Enter** to start a new paragraph.

C You can press **Enter** twice to add an extra space between paragraphs.

D You can press **Shift** + **Enter** to insert a line break and start a new line when your text does not fill the line. You often use line breaks when typing addresses.

E You can press **Tab** to quickly indent the first line of text in a paragraph.

Edit Text

F If you make a spelling mistake, Word either corrects the mistake as you type or underlines it in red.

1 Click to the right of a mistake in a document.

2 Press [Backspace] to delete characters to the left of the insertion point.

3 Click to the left of a mistake in a document.

4 Press [Delete] to delete characters to the right of the insertion point.

Note: You can delete larger quantities of text by selecting the text and pressing [Delete].

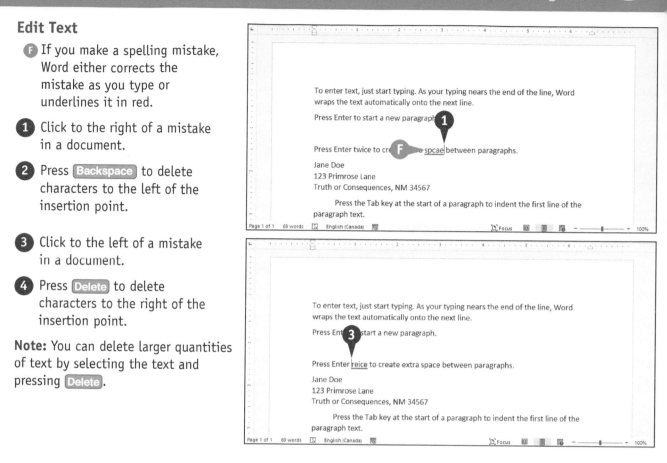

TIP

What is the difference between the Insert and Overtype modes?
By default, Word is set to Insert mode so that when you click to place the insertion point and start typing, any existing text moves to the right to accommodate new text. In Overtype mode, new text overwrites existing text. To toggle between these modes, enable [Insert] and then press it. To enable [Insert], click the **File** tab, click **Options**, and click **Advanced** in the window that appears. Under Editing Options, select **Use the Insert key to control Overtype mode** (☐ changes to ☑) and then click **OK**.

Insert Quick Parts

You can make working with Word faster and more efficient by taking advantage of Quick Parts. If you repeatedly type the same text in your documents — for example, your company name — you can add this text to the Quick Part Gallery. The next time you need to add the text to a document, you can select it from the gallery instead of retyping it.

You can also use any of the preset phrases included with Word. You access these preset Quick Parts from the Building Blocks Organizer. (See the first tip at the end of this section for more information.)

Insert Quick Parts

Create a Quick Parts Entry

1. Type the text that you want to store, including all formatting that should appear each time you insert the entry.

2. Select the text you typed.

3. Click the **Insert** tab.

4. Click the **Quick Parts** button (📓).

5. Click **Save Selection to Quick Part Gallery**.

The Create New Building Block dialog box appears.

6. Type a name that you want to use as a shortcut for the entry.

Ⓐ You can also assign a gallery, a category, and a description for the entry.

7. Click **OK**.

Word stores the entry in the Quick Part Gallery.

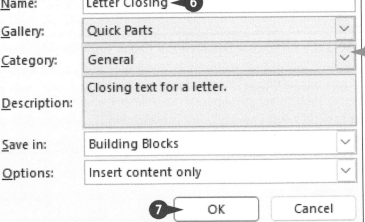

Insert a Quick Part Entry

1 Click in the text where you want to insert a Quick Part.

2 Click the **Insert** tab.

3 Click the **Quick Parts** button (📋).

All building blocks you define as Quick Parts appear in the Quick Part Gallery.

4 Click the entry that you want to insert.

B Word inserts the entry into the document.

How do I insert a preset Quick Part?
Click the **Insert** tab on the Ribbon, click the **Quick Parts** button (📋), and click **Building Blocks Organizer** to open the Building Blocks Organizer. Locate the Quick Part you want to insert (they are organized into galleries and categories), click it, and click **Insert**.

How do I remove a Quick Parts entry?
To remove a Quick Parts entry from the Building Blocks Organizer, open the Organizer (see the preceding tip for help), locate and select the entry you want to remove, click **Delete**, and click **Yes** in the dialog box that appears.

Insert Symbols

From time to time, you might need to insert a mathematical symbol or special character into your Word document. From the Symbol Gallery, you can insert many common symbols, including mathematical and Greek symbols, architectural symbols, and more.

If you do not find the symbol you need in the Symbol Gallery, you can use the Symbol dialog box. The Symbol dialog box displays a list of recently used symbols as well as hundreds of symbols in a variety of fonts. You can also use the Symbol dialog box to insert special characters.

Insert Symbols

1 Click the location in the document where you want the symbol to appear.

2 Click the **Insert** tab.

3 Click **Symbols**.

4 Click **Symbol**.

Ⓐ A gallery of commonly used symbols appears. If the symbol you need appears in the gallery, you can click it and skip the rest of these steps.

5 Click **More Symbols**.

The Symbol dialog box appears.

6 Click the symbol you want.

7 Click **Insert**.

Symbol																		?	×

Symbols | Special Characters

Font: (normal text) ∨ Subset: Latin-1 Supplement ∨

d	e	f	g	h	i	j	k	l	m	n	o	p	q	r	s	t	¦
u	v	w	x	y	z	{	|	}	~		¡	¢	£	¤	¥	¦
6 →	©	ª	«	¬	-	®	¯	°	±	²	³	´	µ	¶	·
¸	¹	º	»	¼	½	¾	¿	À	Á	Â	Ã	Ä	Å	Æ	Ç	È

Recently used symbols:

€	£	¥	©	®	™	±	≠	≤	≥	÷	×	∞	µ	α	β	π

Unicode name:
Copyright Sign   Character code: 00A9   from: Unicode (hex) ∨

AutoCorrect...   Shortcut Key...   Shortcut key: Alt+Ctrl+C

7 → Insert   Cancel

B The symbol appears at the current insertion point location in the document.

Note: You can control the size of the symbol the same way you control the size of text; see Chapter 6 for details on sizing text.

The dialog box remains open so that you can add more symbols to your document.

8 When finished, click **Close**.

Symbol														?	×

Symbols | Special Characters

Font: (normal text) ∨ Subset: Latin-1 Supplement ∨

d	e	f	g	h	i	j	k	l	m	n	o	p	q	r	s	t	¦
u	v	w	x	y	z	{	|	}	~		¡	¢	£	¤	¥	¦
§	¨	©	ª	«	¬	-	®	¯	°	±	²	³	´	µ	¶	·
¸	¹	º	»	¼	½	¾	¿	À	Á	Â	Ã	Ä	Å	Æ	Ç	È

Recently used symbols:

©	€	£	¥	®	™	±	≠	≤	≥	÷	×	∞	µ	α	β	π

Unicode name:
Copyright Sign   Character code: 00A9   from: Unicode (hex) ∨

AutoCorrect...   Shortcut Key...   Shortcut key: Alt+Ctrl+C

Insert   Close ← **8**

All text © Paul McFedries

B

How do I add a special character?

To add a special character, open the Symbol dialog box and click the **Special Characters** tab. Locate and click the character you want to add, and then click **Insert**. Click **Close** to close the dialog box.

Character:		Shortcut key:
—	Em Dash	Alt+Ctrl+Num -
–	En Dash	Ctrl+Num -
-	Nonbreaking Hyphen	Ctrl+Shift+_
¬	Optional Hyphen	Ctrl+-
	Em Space	
	En Space	
	1/4 Em Space	
°	Nonbreaking Space	Ctrl+Shift+Space
©	Copyright	Alt+Ctrl+C
®	Registered	Alt+Ctrl+R
™	Trademark	Alt+Ctrl+T
§	Section	
¶	Paragraph	
...	Ellipsis	Alt+Ctrl+.
'	Single Opening Quote	Ctrl+`,`
'	Single Closing Quote	Ctrl+`,`
"	Double Opening Quote	Ctrl+`,`
"	Double Closing Quote	Ctrl+`,`

Change the Font, Size, and Color

You can change the font (also called the *typeface*), text size, and color to alter the appearance of text in a document. For example, you might change the font, size, and color of your document's title text to emphasize it. You can also use Word's basic formatting commands — Bold, Italic, Underline, Strikethrough, Subscript, and Superscript — to quickly add formatting to your text. By default, when you type text in a Word document, the program uses an 11-point Calibri font, but you can change that font to one you prefer.

Change the Font, Size, and Color

Change the Font

1 Select the text that you want to format.

A If you drag to select, the Mini toolbar appears faded in the background, and you can use it by moving the mouse (⇖) over the Mini toolbar.

2 To use the Ribbon, click the **Home** tab.

3 Click the **Font** ⌄.

Word displays the Font list.

Note: When you point the mouse (⇖) at a font in the list, Word temporarily formats the selected text with a preview of the font.

4 Click the font you want to use.

B Word assigns the font to the selected text.

5 Click anywhere outside the selection to continue working.

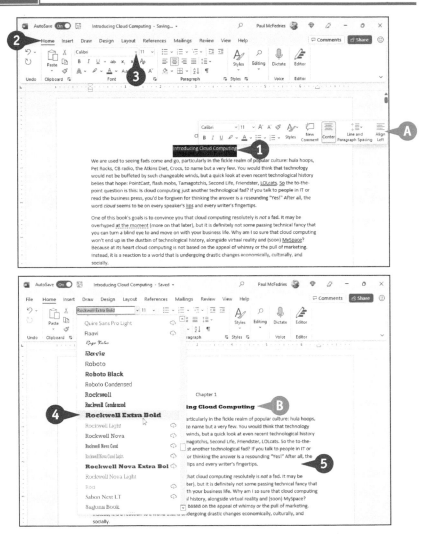

Change the Text Size

1 Select the text that you want to format.

2 Click the **Home** tab.

3 Click the **Font Size** ⌄.

Note: When you point the mouse (⌖) at a font size in the list, Word temporarily formats the selected text with a preview of the font size.

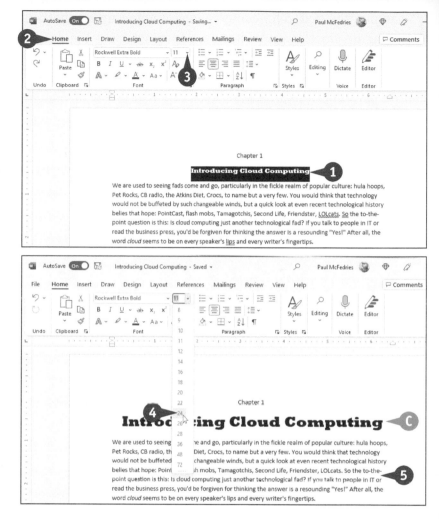

Word displays the Font Size list.

4 Click a size.

C Word changes the size of the selected text.

This example applies a 24-point font size to the text.

Note: You also can change the font size using the **Increase Font Size** (A^) and **Decrease Font Size** (A˅) buttons on the Home tab. Word increases or decreases the font size with each click of the button.

5 Click anywhere outside the selection to continue working.

TIPS

How do I apply formatting to my text?
To apply formatting to your text, select the text you want to format, click the **Home** tab, and click **Bold** (B) or press Ctrl+B, **Italic** (I) or press Ctrl+I, **Underline** (U) or press Ctrl+U, **Strikethrough** (ab), **Subscript** (X_2), or **Superscript** (x^2).

What is the toolbar that appears when I select text?
When you select text, the Mini toolbar appears, giving you quick access to common formatting commands. You can also right-click selected text to display the toolbar. To use any of the tools on the toolbar, click the desired tool; otherwise, continue working and the toolbar disappears.

continued ▶

Changing the text color can go a long way toward emphasizing the text on the page. For example, if you are creating an invitation, you might make the description of the event a different color to stand out from the other details. Likewise, if you are creating a report for work, you might make the title of the report a different color from the information contained in the report, or even color-code certain data in the report. When selecting text colors, avoid choosing colors that make your text difficult to read, such as light gray text on a white background.

Change the Font, Size, and Color (continued)

Change the Color

1 Select the text that you want to format.

2 Click the **Home** tab.

D To apply the currently selected color (red, in this example), click the **Font Color** button (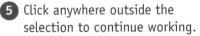), and then skip the rest of the steps in this subsection.

3 Click the **Font Color** ⌄.

Word displays the Font Color menu.

Note: When you point the mouse () at a font color in the menu, Word temporarily formats the selected text with a preview of the font color.

4 Click a color.

E Word assigns the color to the text.

This example applies a blue color to the text.

5 Click anywhere outside the selection to continue working.

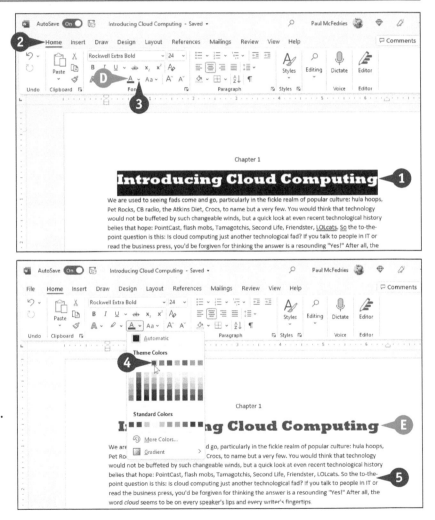

Using the Font Dialog Box

1. Select the text that you want to format.

2. Click the **Home** tab on the Ribbon.

3. Click the dialog box launcher (⌐) in the Font group.

   The Font dialog box appears.

4. Click the font, style, size, color, underline style, or effect that you want to apply.

F. A preview of your choices appears here.

5. Click **OK**.

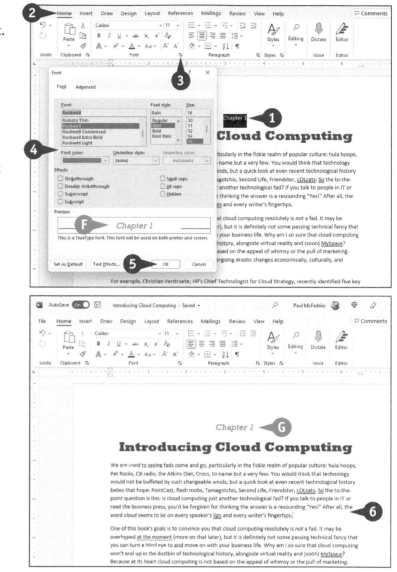

G. Word applies the font change.

6. Click anywhere outside the selection to continue working.

Can I change the default font and size?

Yes. To change the default font and size, follow these steps: Display the Font dialog box. Click the font and font size that you want to set as defaults. Click the **Set As Default** button. A new dialog box appears. Click **All documents based on the Normal template** (○ changes to ●) and then click **OK**. Click **OK** to close the Font dialog box. The next time you create a new document, Word applies the default font and size that you specified.

Align Text

You can use Word's alignment commands to change how text and objects are positioned horizontally on the page. By default, Word left-aligns text and objects. You can also choose to center text and objects on the page (using the Center command), align text and objects to the right side of the page (using the Right Align command), or justify text and objects so that they line up at both the left and right margins of the page (using the Justify command). You can change the alignment of all the text and objects in your document or change the alignment of individual paragraphs and objects.

Align Text

1 Click anywhere in the paragraph that you want to align or select the paragraphs and objects that you want to align.

2 Click the **Home** tab.

3 Click an alignment button.

The Align Left button (≡) aligns text with the left margin, the Center button (≡) centers text between the left and right margins, the Align Right button (≡) aligns text with the right margin, and the Justify button (≡) aligns text between the left and right margins.

Word aligns the text.

This example centers the text on the document page.

Ⓐ This text is aligned with the left margin.

Ⓑ This text is centered between both margins.

Ⓒ This text is aligned with the right margin.

Ⓓ This text is justified between both margins.

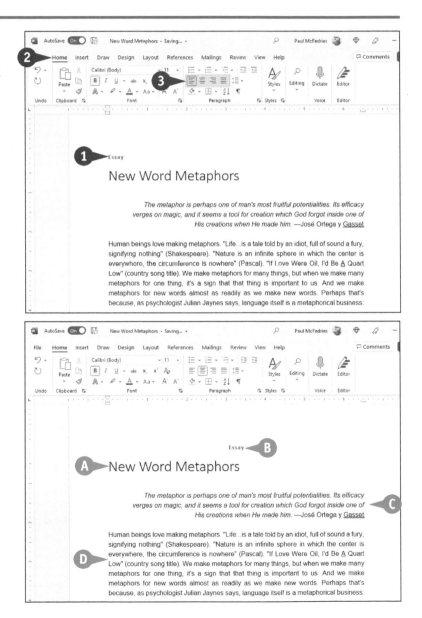

Set Line Spacing

You can adjust the amount of spacing that appears between lines of text in your paragraphs. For example, you might set 1.5 spacing to make paragraphs easier to read. By default, Word assigns 1.08 spacing for all new documents.

You can also control how much space appears before and after each paragraph in your document. You might opt to single-space the text within a paragraph, but to add space before and after the paragraph to set it apart from the paragraphs that precede and follow it.

Set Line Spacing

1 Click anywhere in the paragraph that you want to format.

Note: To format multiple paragraphs, select them.

2 Click the **Home** tab.

3 Click the **Line Spacing** button (‡≡).

4 Click a line spacing option.

A Word applies the new spacing.

This example applies 2.0 line spacing.

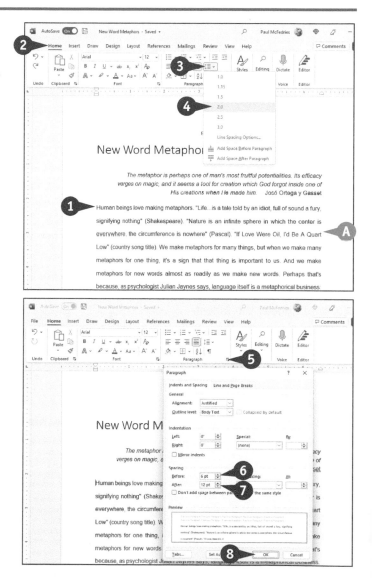

5 To control the spacing that surrounds a paragraph, click the dialog box launcher (⌐↓) in the Paragraph group.

The Paragraph dialog box opens.

6 Use the **Before** ⇳ to specify how much space should appear before the paragraph.

7 Use the **After** ⇳ to specify how much space should appear after the paragraph.

8 Click **OK** to apply the spacing settings.

Indent Text

You can use indents as a way to control the horizontal positioning of text in a document. Indents are margins that affect individual lines or entire paragraphs. You might use an indent to distinguish a particular paragraph on a page — for example, a long quote.

You can indent paragraphs in your document from the left and right margins. You also can indent only the first line of a paragraph or all lines *except* the first line of the paragraph. You can set indents using buttons on the Ribbon, the Paragraph dialog box, and the ruler.

Indent Text

Set Quick Indents

1 Click anywhere in the paragraph you want to indent.

2 Click **Home**.

3 Click an indent button.

A You can click the **Decrease Indent** button (⇤≡) to decrease the indentation.

B You can click the **Increase Indent** button (⇥≡) to increase the indentation.

C Word applies the indent change.

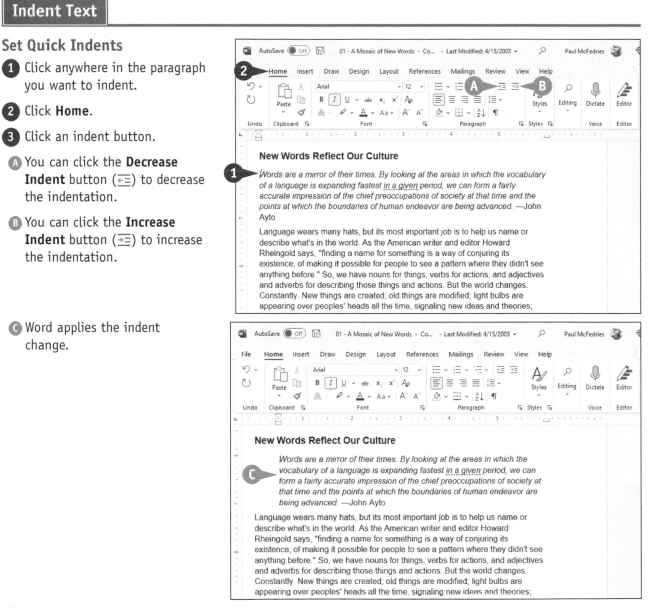

Set Precise Indents

1 Click anywhere in the paragraph you want to indent or select the text you want to indent.

2 Click **Home**.

3 Click the dialog box launcher (⌐∎) in the Paragraph group.

The Paragraph dialog box appears.

4 Type a specific indentation in the **Left** or **Right** indent box.

Ⓓ You can also click a spin arrow (⬍) to set an indent measurement.

Ⓔ To set a specific kind of indent, you can click the **Special** ⌄ and then click an indent.

Ⓕ The Preview area shows a sample of the indent.

5 Click **OK**.

Word applies the indent to the text.

TIP

How do I set indents using the Word ruler?
The ruler contains markers for changing the left indent, right indent, first-line indent, and hanging indent. Click the **View** tab and select **Ruler** (☐ changes to ☑) to display the ruler. On the left side of the ruler, drag the **Left Indent** button (▭) to indent all lines from the left margin, drag the **Hanging Indent** button (△) to create a hanging indent, or drag the **First Line Indent** button (▽) to indent the first line only. On the right side of the ruler, drag the **Right Indent** button (△) to indent all lines from the right margin.

Set Tabs

You can use tabs to create vertically aligned columns of text in your Word document. To insert a tab, press `Tab` on your keyboard; the insertion point moves to the next tab stop on the page.

By default, Word creates tab stops every 0.5 inch across the page and left-aligns the text on each tab stop. You can set your own tab stops using the ruler or the Tabs dialog box. You can also use the Tabs dialog box to change the tab alignment and specify an exact measurement between tab stops.

Set Tabs

Set Quick Tabs

1 Click here until the type of tab marker that you want to set appears.

Note: If you do not see the ruler, click **View** and then click **Ruler** (☐ changes to ☑).

   L sets a left-aligned tab.

   ⊥ sets a center-aligned tab.

   ⅃ sets a right-aligned tab.

   ⊥· sets a decimal tab.

   ▮ sets a bar tab (displays a vertical bar at the tab location).

2 Select the lines to which you want to add the tab.

3 Click the ruler at the tab location you want.

Ⓐ On each selected line, Word adds a tab at the location you clicked.

4 Click at the end of the text after which you want to add a tab.

5 Press `Tab`.

6 Type the text that should appear in the next column.

Set Precise Tabs

1. Select the lines to which you want to add the tab.

2. Click **Home**.

3. Click the dialog box launcher ( ) in the Paragraph group.

   The Paragraph dialog box appears.

4. Click **Tabs** on the Indents and Spacing tab.

   The Tabs dialog box appears.

5. Click in this box and type a new tab stop measurement.

6. Select a tab alignment (changes to).

B. You can also select a tab leader character (changes to).

7. Click **Set**.

   Word saves the new tab stop.

8. Click **OK**.

C. Word closes the dialog box and applies the new tab stops.

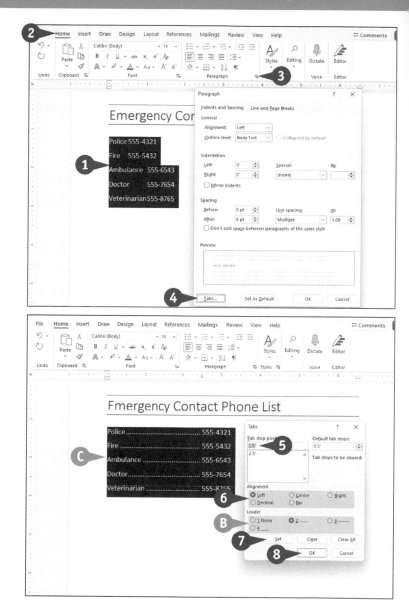

Can I remove tab stops that I no longer need?
Yes. To remove a tab stop from the ruler, drag the tab stop off the ruler. To remove a tab stop in the Tabs dialog box, select it and then click **Clear**. To clear every tab stop that you saved in the Tabs dialog box, click **Clear All**.

What are leader tabs?
You can use leader tabs to separate tab columns with dots, dashes, or lines. Leader tabs help readers follow the information across tab columns. You can set leader tabs using the Tabs dialog box, as shown in this section.

Set Margins

Word assigns a default 1-inch margin all the way around the page in every new document, but you can change these margin settings. For example, you can set wider margins to provide more room around the text or set smaller margins to fit more text on a page. You can apply your changes to the current document only or make them the new default setting for all new documents. Word applies the new margins to the entire document, but you can opt to apply the new margins only from the insertion point to the end of the document.

Set Margins

Set Margins Using Layout Tools

1. If you do not want to apply the new margins to the entire document, click at the point where you want to the new margin setting to begin (not shown).

2. Click **Layout**.

3. Click **Margins**.

   The Margins Gallery appears.

4. Click a margin setting.

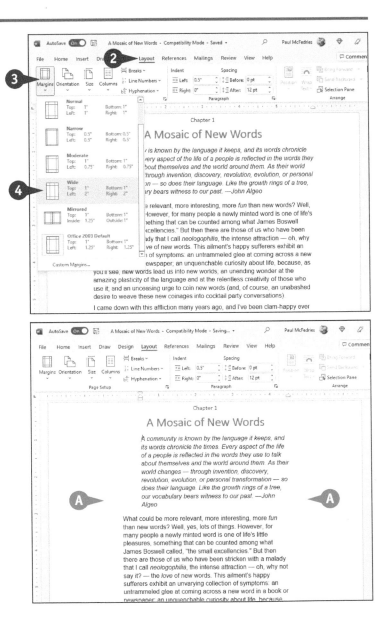

A. Word applies the new setting.

Set a Custom Margin

1 Click **Layout**.

2 Click **Margins**.

The Margins Gallery appears.

3 Click **Custom Margins**.

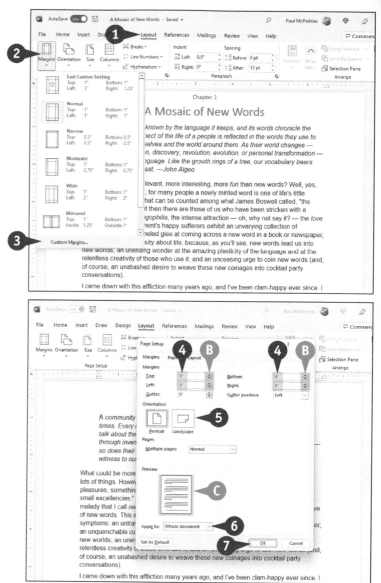

The Page Setup dialog box appears, displaying the Margins tab.

4 Type a specific margin in the **Top**, **Bottom**, **Left**, and **Right** boxes.

B You can also click a spin arrow (⬍) to set a margin measurement.

5 Choose a page orientation.

C Preview the margin settings here.

6 Click the **Apply to** ⌄ and specify whether the margin should apply to the whole document or from this point forward.

7 Click **OK**.

Word adjusts the margins in the document.

TIPS

How do I set new default margins?
Make the desired changes to the Margins tab of the Page Setup dialog box and click **Set As Default** before clicking **OK**. Click **Yes** in the dialog box that appears, asking if you want to change the default settings for every new document.

Why is my printer ignoring my margin settings?
In most cases, printers have a minimum margin setting of 0.25 inch. If you set your margins smaller than your printer's minimum margin setting, you place text in an unprintable area. Check your printer documentation for more information.

Create Lists

You can draw attention to lists of information by using bullets or numbers. Bulleted and numbered lists can help you present your information in an organized way. A bulleted list adds dots or other similar symbols in front of the list items, whereas a numbered list adds sequential numbers or letters in front of the list items. Use bullets when the items in your list do not follow any particular order and use numbers when the items in your list are sequential. You can create a list as you type it or after you have typed the items.

Create Lists

Create a List as You Type

1 Type **1.** to create a numbered list or ***** to create a bulleted list.

2 Press `Spacebar` or `Tab`.

A Word automatically formats the entry as a list item and displays the AutoCorrect Options button (📝) so that you can undo or stop automatic numbering.

3 Type a list item.

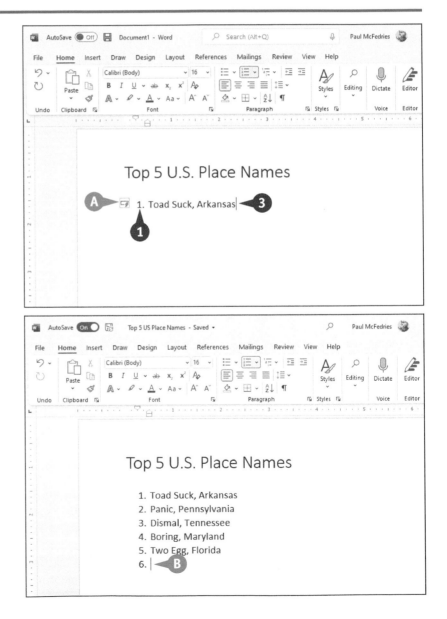

4 Press `Enter` to prepare to type another list item.

B Word automatically adds a bullet or number for the next item. In this example, `Enter` was pressed after item 5 and Word automatically created item 6.

5 Repeat steps **3** and **4** for each list item.

To stop entering items in the list, press `Enter` twice.

Create a List from Existing Text

1. Select the text to which you want to assign bullets or numbers.

2. Click **Home**.

3. Click the **Numbering** button (≔) or the **Bullets** button (≔).

   This example uses bullets.

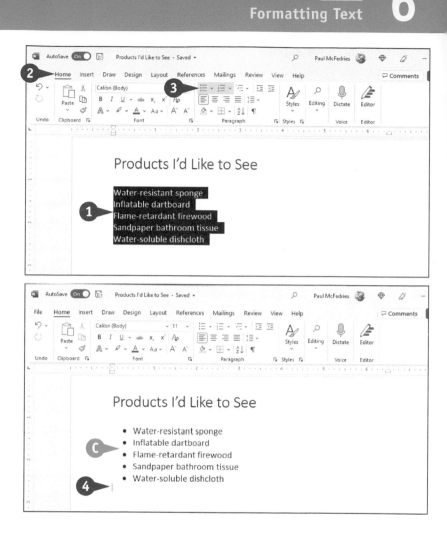

C Word applies numbers or bullets to the selection.

4. Click anywhere outside the selection to continue working.

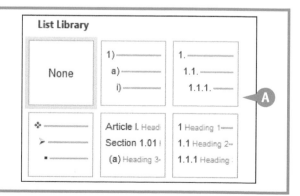

TIP

Can I create a bulleted or numbered list with more than one level, like the type of list you use when creating an outline?

Yes. Click the **Multilevel List** button (⸻). Click a format (A) from the menu that appears and then type your list. You can press Enter to enter a new list item at the same list level. Each time you press Tab, Word indents a level in the list. Each time you press Shift+Tab, Word outdents a level in the list.

List Library

None	1) ── a) ── i) ──	1. ── 1.1. ── 1.1.1. ── **A**
✤ ── ➤ ── ▪ ──	Article I. Head Section 1.01 I (a) Heading 3	1 Heading 1── 1.1 Heading 2─ 1.1.1 Heading

Copy Formatting

Suppose you have applied a variety of formatting options to a paragraph to create a certain look — for example, you changed the font, the size, the color, and the alignment. If you want to re-create the same look elsewhere in the document, you do not have to repeat the same steps as when you applied the original formatting, again changing the font, size, color, and alignment. Instead, you can use the Format Painter feature to "paint" the formatting to the other text in one swift action.

Copy Formatting

1. Select the text containing the formatting that you want to copy.

2. Click **Home**.

3. Click the **Format Painter** button (🖌).

A. The mouse (⇖) changes to 🖌I when you move the mouse over your document.

4. Click and drag over the text to which you want to apply the same formatting.

B. Word copies the formatting from the original text to the new text.

To copy the same formatting multiple times, you can double-click the Format Painter button (🖌).

You can press Esc to cancel the Format Painter feature at any time.

Clear Formatting

Sometimes, you may find that you have applied too much formatting to your text, making it difficult to read. Or perhaps you applied the wrong formatting to your text. In that case, instead of undoing all your formatting changes manually, you can use the Clear Formatting command to remove any formatting you have applied to the document text. When you apply the Clear Formatting command, Word removes all formatting applied to the text and restores the default settings.

Clear Formatting

1 Select the text from which you want to remove formatting.

Note: If you do not select text, Word removes text formatting from the entire document.

2 Click **Home**.

3 Click the **Clear All Formatting** button (A◇).

A Word removes all formatting from the selected text.

Format with Styles

You can make formatting faster and easier by using styles. A *style* is a set of text-formatting characteristics that you can apply all at once. These characteristics can include the text font, size, color, alignment, spacing, and more. Instead of assigning multiple formatting settings repeatedly, you can create a style with the required formatting settings and apply it whenever you need it.

In addition to creating your own styles for use in your documents, you can apply any of the preset styles that Word supplies. These include styles for headings, normal text, quotes, and more.

Format with Styles

Create a New Quick Style

1 Format the text as desired and then select the text.

2 Click **Home**.

3 Click the **More** button (▼) in the Styles group.

4 Click **Create a Style**.

The Create New Style from Formatting dialog box appears.

5 Type a name for the style.

6 Click **OK**.

Word adds the style to the list of Quick Styles.

Apply a Style

1. Select the text that you want to format.

2. Click **Home**.

3. Click a style from the Styles list.

Ⓐ You can click the **More** button (▼) to see the full gallery of available styles.

Ⓑ Word applies the style.

TIPS

How do I remove a style that I no longer need?

Click **Home**, click **More** (▼) in the Styles group to display the Styles gallery, right-click the style that you want to remove, and then click **Remove from Style Gallery**. Word immediately removes the style from the Styles list.

How do I customize an existing style?

Click **Home**, click **More** (▼) in the Styles group to display the Styles gallery, right-click the style, and then click **Modify** to display the Modify Style dialog box. Click the type of change that you want to make. For example, to switch fonts, click the **Fonts** option and then select another font.

Using a Template

template is a special file that stores styles and other Word formatting options. When you create a Word document using a template, the styles and options in that template become available for you to use with that document. Word comes with several templates preinstalled, and you can also create your own.

Pre-existing templates come typically with boilerplate text you can use as a model for your document. Select the boilerplate text and replace it with your own text. Use the template's styles in the Styles gallery to format headings and other text.

Using a Template

1 From any document, click **File**.

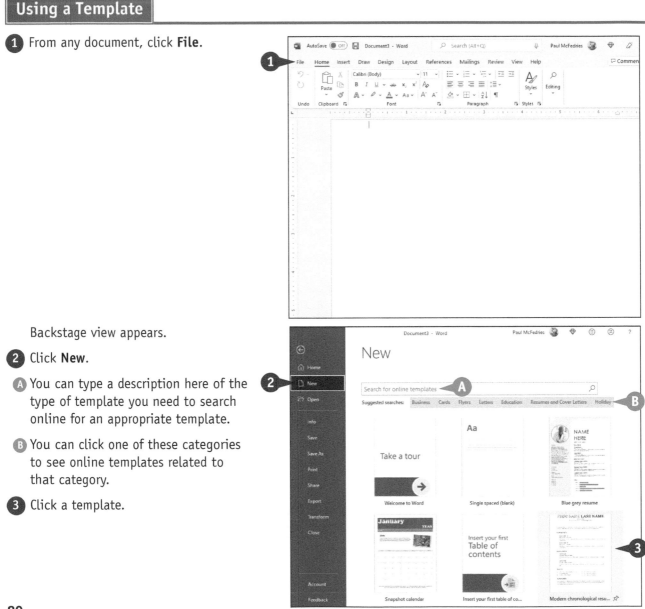

Backstage view appears.

2 Click **New**.

A You can type a description here of the type of template you need to search online for an appropriate template.

B You can click one of these categories to see online templates related to that category.

3 Click a template.

Word displays a window like this one that describes and shows a preview of the template you selected.

④ Click **Create**.

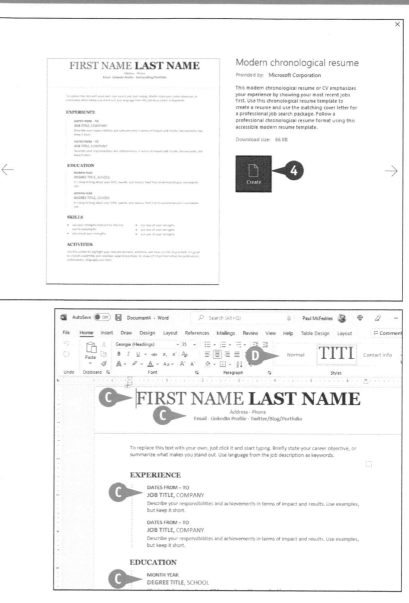

A document containing the template's styles appears.

ⓒ You can replace boilerplate text with your own text.

ⓓ You can use styles in the Styles Gallery to continue formatting the document.

Note: See the previous section, "Format with Styles," for details on using and creating styles.

TIP

How can I create my own templates?

The easiest way to create a template is to base it on an existing Word document that uses styles. Open the document on which you want to base your template, click the **File** tab, and click **Save As**. Select a location and click a folder, or click **Browse**. The Save As dialog box opens; locate and select the folder in which you want to save the template, type a name for it in the **File Name** box, click the **Save as type** ⌄, and choose **Word Template**. Click **Save** and Word saves the template in the folder you chose.

Insert an Online Video

You can insert a video available on the Internet into a Word document. After you have inserted the video, you can play it directly from the Word document.

You can insert videos you find using an Internet search site (such as Google or Bing) or videos available on YouTube, or you can insert a video embed code — an HTML code that uses the src attribute to define the video file you want to embed. Most videos posted on the Internet are public domain, but, if you are unsure, do some research to determine whether you can use the video freely.

Insert an Online Video

1 Use your web browser to locate the video you want to insert.

2 Select the address.

3 Right-click the address and then click **Copy**.

4 In the Word document, click where you want the video to appear.

5 Click **Insert**.

6 Click **Online Videos**.

The Insert a Video dialog box appears.

7 Right-click the text box and then click **Paste**.

A The copied address appears in the text box.

8 Click **Insert**.

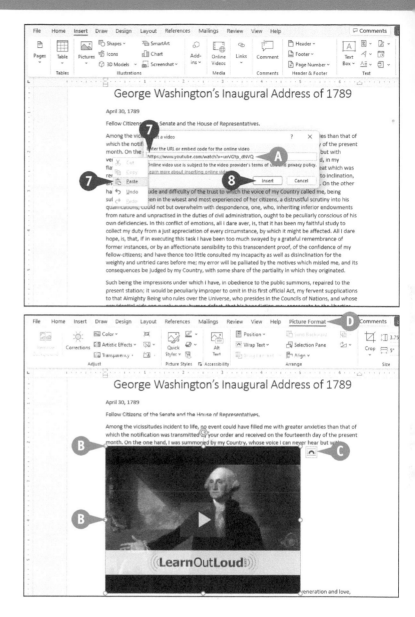

B The video appears in your document, selected and surrounded by handles (○).

C The Layout Options button (⌐) controls text flow around the video; see the section "Insert an Online Picture" in Chapter 3 for more information.

D The Picture Format contextual tab appears on the Ribbon; you can use the tools on this tab to format the video.

TIP

How do I play an inserted video?
From Print Layout view or Read Mode view, click the video **Play** button (▷). The video appears in its own window; the document appears behind a shaded, translucent background; and the Play button appears red. Click anywhere on the video — not just on the Play button — to start the video; as you slide the mouse over the video, the Play button changes to red. To stop the video and return to the document, click anywhere outside the video on the shaded translucent background of the document window or press Esc.

Assign a Theme

A *theme* is a predesigned set of styles, color schemes, fonts, and other visual attributes. Applying a theme to a document is a quick way to add polish to it. And, because themes are shared among the Office programs, you can use the same theme in your Word document that you have applied to worksheets in Excel or slides in PowerPoint.

Word also offers several *style sets*, each of which is a predefined collection of styles for document titles, headings, and text. The look applied by each style set depends on the selected theme.

Assign a Theme

Apply a Theme

1. Click **Design**.
2. Click **Themes**.

   Word displays the Themes gallery.

3. Click a theme.

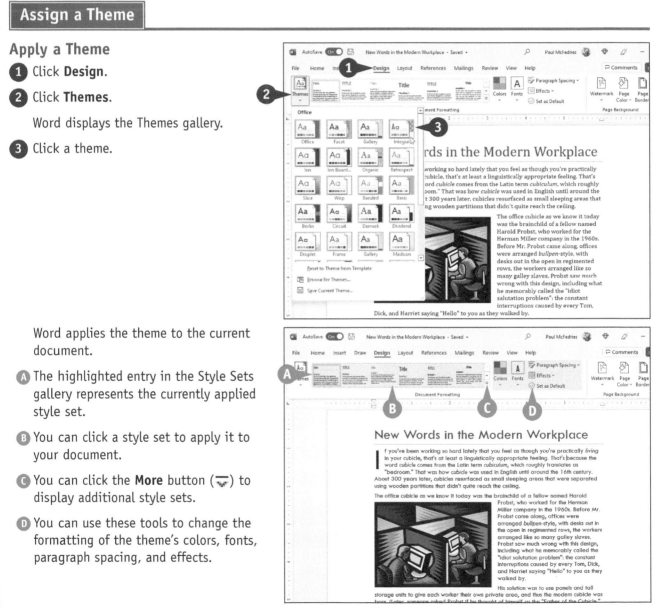

Word applies the theme to the current document.

Ⓐ The highlighted entry in the Style Sets gallery represents the currently applied style set.

Ⓑ You can click a style set to apply it to your document.

Ⓒ You can click the **More** button (▼) to display additional style sets.

Ⓓ You can use these tools to change the formatting of the theme's colors, fonts, paragraph spacing, and effects.

Create a Custom Theme

1. Click the **Design** tab.

2. Use the tools in the Document Formatting section of the Ribbon to apply a theme and edit the formatting to create the theme that you want to save.

3. Click the **Themes** button.

4. Click **Save Current Theme**.

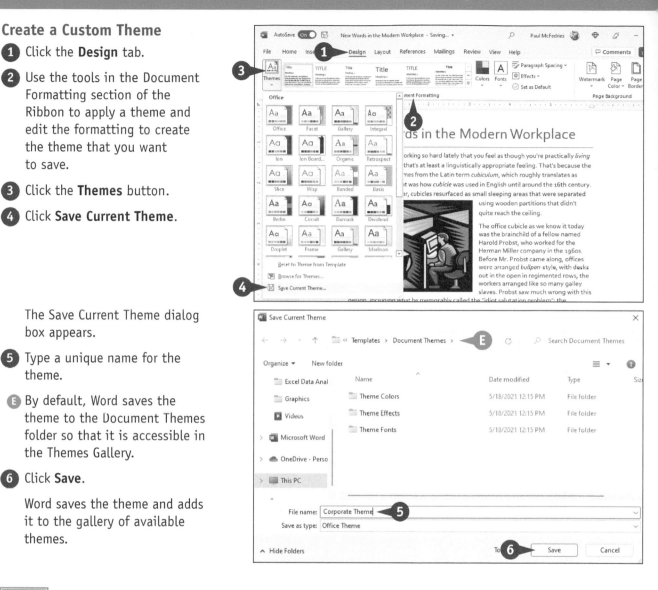

The Save Current Theme dialog box appears.

5. Type a unique name for the theme.

E. By default, Word saves the theme to the Document Themes folder so that it is accessible in the Themes Gallery.

6. Click **Save**.

Word saves the theme and adds it to the gallery of available themes.

TIP

How do I change the background color of the page?

To apply a page color, click the **Design** tab on the Ribbon, click the **Page Color** button in the Page Background group, and click a color in the palette; Word applies the color you selected to the background of the page. Although you can apply a background color to the pages of your document, be aware that Word does not save page colors as part of themes. Remember that themes are most effective in helping you establish a set of predefined styles available in a document. For help applying a style, see the section "Format with Styles" in Chapter 6.

Add Borders

You can apply borders around your text to separate sections of text or make the document aesthetically appealing. You can add borders around a single paragraph, multiple paragraphs, or each page in the document. (Be aware that you should not add too many effects, such as borders, to your document because it will become difficult to read.)

Word comes with several predesigned borders, which you can apply to your document. Alternatively, you can create your own custom borders — for example, making each border line a different color or thickness. Another option is to apply shading to your text to set it apart.

Add Borders

Add a Paragraph Border

1 Select the text to which you want to add a border.

2 Click **Home**.

3 Click **Borders** (⊞).

4 Click a border.

Ⓐ Word applies the border to the text.

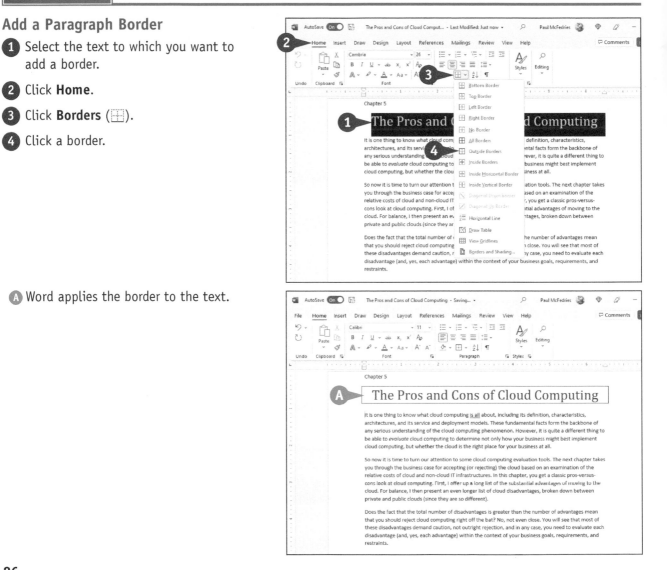

Add a Page Border

1. Click the **Design** tab.

2. Click the **Page Borders** button.

   The Borders and Shading dialog box appears and displays the Page Border tab.

3. Click the type of border that you want to add.

   B You can use these settings to select a different border line style, color, and width.

   C You can click the **Apply to** ⌄ to specify whether to apply the border to each page of your entire document, a section, the first page of a section, or all pages of a section except the first.

   D The Preview area displays a sample of the selections.

4. Click **OK**.

   E Word applies the page border.

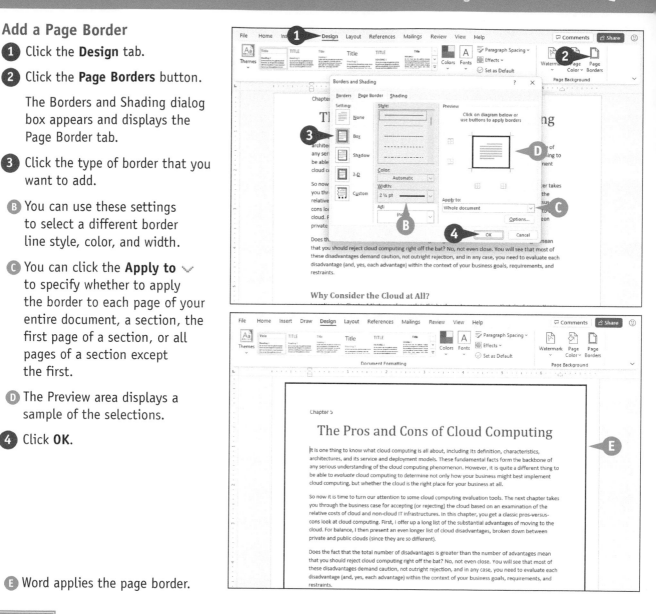

TIPS

How do I add shading to my text?

To add shading behind a block of text, select the text, click the **Home** tab on the Ribbon, click the **Shading** button (🖊) in the Paragraph group, and click a color.

How do I create a custom border?

Select the text to which you want to add a border, open the **Borders and Shading** dialog box, click the **Borders** tab, and choose **Custom**. Choose the settings to apply to the first line of the border; then click in the **Preview** area where you want the line to appear. Repeat for each line you want to add, and then click **OK**.

Create Columns

You can create columns in Word to present your text in a format similar to a newspaper or magazine. For example, if you are creating a brochure or newsletter, you can use columns to make text flow from one block to the next.

If you simply want to create a document with two or three columns, you can use one of Word's preset columns. Alternatively, you can create custom columns, choosing the number of columns you want to create in your document, indicating the width of each column, specifying whether a line should appear between them, and more.

Create Columns

Create Quick Columns

1 Select the text that you want to place into columns (not shown).

Note: If you want to apply columns to all text in your document, skip step **1**.

2 Click the **Layout** tab.

3 Click the **Columns** button.

4 Click the number of columns that you want to assign.

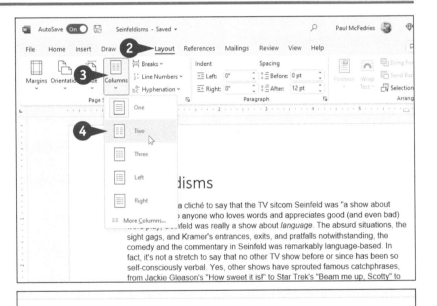

A Word displays the selected text, or your document if you skipped step **1**, across the number of columns that you specified.

Seinfeldisms

It has become a cliché to say that the TV sitcom Seinfeld was "a show about nothing." But to anyone who loves words and appreciates good (and even bad) word play, Seinfeld was really a show about *language*. The absurd situations, the sight gags, and Kramer's entrances, exits, and pratfalls notwithstanding, the comedy and the commentary in Seinfeld was remarkably language-based. In fact, it's not a stretch to say that no other TV show before or since has been so self-consciously verbal. Yes, other shows have sprouted famous catchphrases, from Jackie Gleason's "How sweet it is!"

While discussing a serial killer called "The Lopper" because he cuts peoples' heads off, Kramer tells us that the police have had "some internal dissension about the name," with an alternative being "The Denogginizer" (The Frogger, Apr. 23, 1998). Then there's the following exchange (The Abstinence, Nov. 21, 1996):

JERRY: I thought the whole dream of dating a doctor was debunked.

ELAINE: No, it's not debunked, it's totally bunk.

JERRY: Isn't bunk bad? Like, "that's a lot of bunk."

GEORGE: No, something is bunk

Create Custom Columns

1 Select the text that you want to place into columns (not shown).

Note: If you want to apply columns to all text in your document, skip step **1**.

2 Click the **Layout** tab.

3 Click the **Columns** button.

4 Click **More Columns**.

The Columns dialog box appears.

B You can click a preset for the type of column style that you want to apply.

5 Use the **Number of columns** ⬍ to set the number of columns.

6 Deselect the **Equal column width** check box to set separate widths for each column (☑ changes to ☐).

7 Set an exact column width and spacing here.

C You can specify whether the columns apply to the selected text or the entire document.

8 Click **OK**.

D Word applies the column format to the selected text, or to your document if you skipped step **1**.

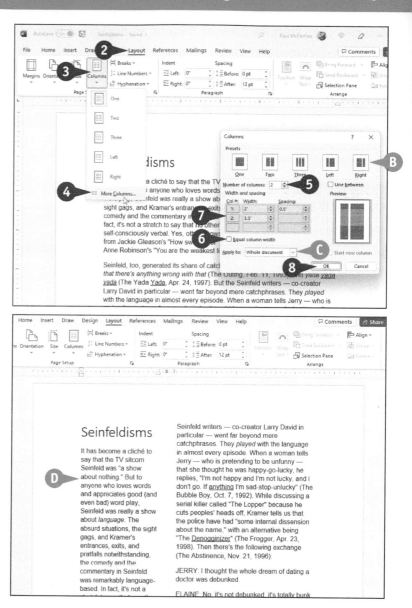

TIPS

Can I add a vertical line between the columns?
Yes. Adding vertical lines between columns is often a good idea because it helps the reader by creating a more prominent visual break between each column. Follow steps **1** to **4** in the "Create Custom Columns" subsection to open the Columns dialog box. Click **Line between** (☐ changes to ☑).

Can I create a break within a column?
Yes. To add a column break, click where you want the break to occur and then press [Ctrl]+[Shift]+[Enter]. To remove a break, select it and press [Delete]. To return to a one-column format, click the **Columns** button on the Layout tab, and then click **One** to select the single-column format.

Insert a Table

You can use tables to present data in an organized fashion. For example, you might add a table to your document to display a simple database of items or a roster of classes. Tables contain columns and rows, which intersect to form cells. You can insert all types of data in cells, including text and graphics.

To enter text in a cell, click in the cell and then type your data. As you type, Word wraps the text to fit in the cell. Press Tab to move from one cell to another. You can select table cells, rows, and columns to perform editing tasks and apply formatting.

Insert a Table

Insert a Table

1. Click in the document where you want to insert a table (not shown).

2. Click **Insert**.

3. Click **Table**.

A. Word displays a table grid.

4. Slide the mouse (↖) across the squares that represent the number of rows and columns you want in your table.

B. Word previews the table as you drag over cells.

5. Click the square representing the lower-right corner of your table.

Word adds the table to your document.

C The Table Design and Layout contextual tabs appear on the Ribbon.

6 Click in a table cell and type information.

D If necessary, Word expands the row size to accommodate the text.

Note: To change the width of a column, drag the column's left border; to change the height of a row, drag the row's bottom border.

You can press Tab to move the insertion point to the next cell.

Delete a Table

1 Click anywhere in the table you want to delete.

2 Click the **Layout** contextual tab.

3 Click **Delete**.

4 Click **Delete Table**.

Word removes the table and its contents from your document.

TIPS

Can I add rows to a table?

Yes. To add a row to the bottom of the table, place the insertion point in the last cell and press Tab. To add a row anywhere else, use the buttons in the Layout tab's Rows & Columns group.

What, exactly, is a table cell?

A *cell* refers to the intersection of a row and column in a table. In spreadsheet programs, columns are named with letters, rows with numbers, and cells using the column letter and row number. For example, the cell at the intersection of Column A and Row 2 is called A2.

Apply Table Styles

When you click within a table you have added to your document, two contextual tabs appear on the Ribbon: Table Design and Layout. You can use the styles found in the Table Design tab to add instant formatting to your Word tables. Word offers numerous predefined table styles, each with its own unique set of formatting characteristics, including shading, color, borders, and fonts.

The Table Design tab also includes settings for creating custom borders and applying custom shading. You can also use check boxes in the Table Style Options group to add a header row, emphasize the table's first column, and more.

Apply Table Styles

1 Click anywhere in the table that you want to format.

2 Click **Table Design**.

3 Click the **More** button (▼) in the lower-right corner of the Table Styles group.

Word displays the Table Styles gallery.

4 Click the style you want to apply.

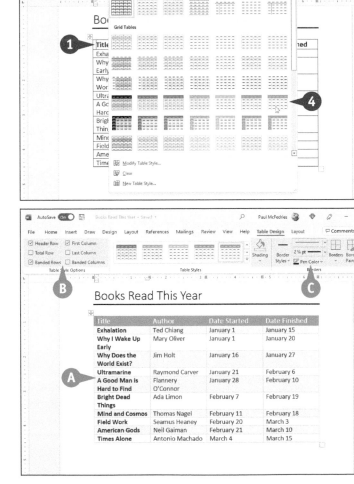

Ⓐ Word applies the style.

Ⓑ You can toggle table parts on or off using the Table Style Options check boxes.

Ⓒ You can click these options to change the shading and borders.

Insert Table Rows or Columns

You can quickly insert rows or columns into a table after you create it. You can insert rows at the top of, the bottom of, or within the table, and you can insert columns to the left of, the right of, or within the table.

If you applied a table style to your table, Word adjusts the appearance of the table to maintain the table style when you add a row or column to the table. For example, if your table style includes alternating shaded rows, Word adjusts the shading when you insert a row.

Insert Table Rows or Columns

1 Click in the row next to the row where you want to add a new row.

Note: To add a column, click in the column next to the column where you want to add a new column.

2 Click **Layout**.

3 Click **Insert Above** or **Insert Below**.

Note: To add a column, click **Insert Left** or **Insert Right**.

Ⓐ Word inserts the new row (or column) at the location you specified and selects the new row (or column).

Note: This section inserts a row above another within the table.

Ⓑ Word adjusts any table style you applied.

Note: To quickly add a row to the bottom of your table, click in the cell at the end of the last cell in the table and press Tab.

Add Headers and Footers

To include text at the top or bottom of every page, such as page numbers, your name, or the date, you can use a header or footer. Header text appears at the top of the page above the margin; footer text appears at the bottom of the page below the margin.

Word comes with several predefined header and footer layouts, which add placeholder text that you edit as needed. Word also offers tools for inserting page numbers and other document information into a header or footer. To view header or footer text, you must display the document in Print Layout view.

Add Headers and Footers

Insert a Header or Footer

1 Click **Insert**.

2 Click the **Header** button to add a header, or click the **Footer** button to add a footer.

This example adds a footer.

A The header or footer gallery appears.

3 Click a header or footer style.

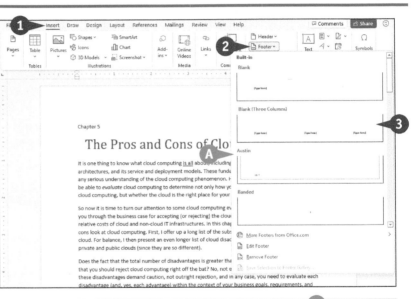

Word adds the header or footer.

B The text in your document appears dimmed.

C The insertion point appears in the Footer area.

D The Header & Footer contextual tab appears on the Ribbon.

E Some footers contain placeholder text that you can click to select and then type your own text.

Add a Page Number Field

1. Click to select the text placeholder where you want the page number field to appear.

2. Click **Page Number**.

3. Click **Current Position**.

4. Click the page number style you want.

   Word adds a field that shows the current number of each page.

Add Other Information Fields

1. Click to select the text placeholder where you want the information field to appear.

2. Use a button in the Insert group to add the type of field you want.

3. When you have completed your header and footer tasks, click **Close Header and Footer**.

   Word closes the Header & Footer tab and displays the header or footer on the document page.

Note: To edit a header or footer, click **Insert**; then either click **Header** and then click **Edit Header** or click **Footer** and then click **Edit Footer**.

TIPS

Can I omit the header or footer from the first page?
Yes. Click the **Insert** tab, click the **Header** or **Footer** button, and click **Edit Header** or **Edit Footer**. Next, select **Different First Page** (☐ changes to ☑) in the Options group. If you want to remove the header or footer for odd or even pages, select **Different Odd & Even Pages** (☐ changes to ☑).

How do I remove a header or footer?
Click the **Insert** tab, click the **Header** or **Footer** button, and click **Remove Header** or **Remove Footer**. Word removes the header or footer from your document.

Insert Footnotes and Endnotes

Y ou can include footnotes or endnotes in your document to identify sources or references to other materials or to add explanatory information. When you add a footnote or endnote, a small numeral or other character appears alongside the associated text, with the actual footnote or endnote appearing at the bottom of a page or the end of the document, respectively.

When you insert footnotes or endnotes in a document, Word automatically numbers them for you. As you add, delete, and move text in your document, any associated footnotes or endnotes are likewise added, deleted, or moved, as well as renumbered.

Insert Footnotes and Endnotes

Insert a Footnote

1 Click where you want to insert the footnote reference.

2 Click the **References** tab.

3 Click **Insert Footnote**.

A Word displays the footnote number in the body of the document and in the note at the bottom of the current page.

4 Type the footnote text.

You can double-click the footnote number or press Shift + F5 to return the insertion point to the place in your document where you inserted the footnote.

Insert an Endnote

1 Click where you want to insert the endnote reference.

B In this example, the endnote number appears on Page 2.

2 Click the **References** tab.

3 Click **Insert Endnote**.

Word inserts the endnote number in the body of your document (not shown).

C Word inserts the endnote number at the end of your document and displays the insertion point in the endnote area at the bottom of the last page of the document.

D In this example, the endnote appears on Page 20.

4 Type your endnote text.

You can double-click the endnote number or press Shift + F5 to return the insertion point to the place in your document where you inserted the endnote.

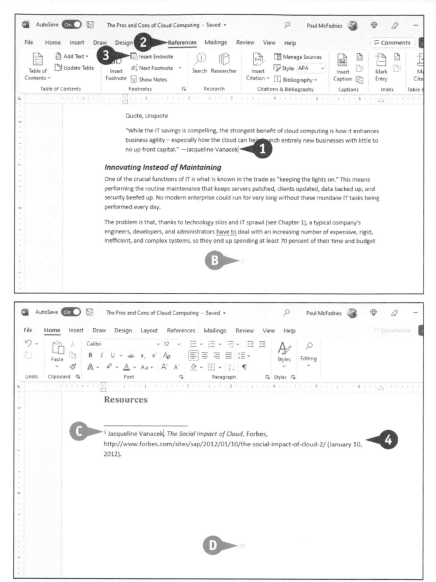

How can I change the starting number for footnotes or endnotes in my document?
If you need to change the starting footnote or endnote number in your document — for example, if you are working on a new chapter, but you want the numbering to continue from the previous one — click the **References** tab and click the dialog box launcher (⌐⃗) in the Footnotes group. The Footnote and Endnote dialog box appears; click in the **Start at** box and type a number or use the spin arrow (⇅) to set a new number. Click **Apply** to apply the changes to the document.

Work in Read Mode View

Read Mode view optimizes your document for easier reading and helps minimize eye strain when you read the document on-screen. This view removes most toolbars and supports mouse, keyboard, and tablet motions. To move from page to page in a document using your mouse, you can click the arrows on the left and right sides of the pages or use the scroll wheel. To navigate using the keyboard, you can press the Page Up, Page Down, spacebar, and Backspace keys on the keyboard, or you can press any arrow key. If you use a tablet or other touchpad device, swipe left or right with your finger.

Work in Read Mode View

Look Up Information

1 Click 📖 to display the document in Read Mode view.

2 Select the word you want to look up and right-click.

3 From the menu that appears, click **Search "word"**, where word is the word you selected in step **2**.

A The Search task pane appears and displays web search results for the word.

4 To close the Search task pane, you can click the **Close** button (✕).

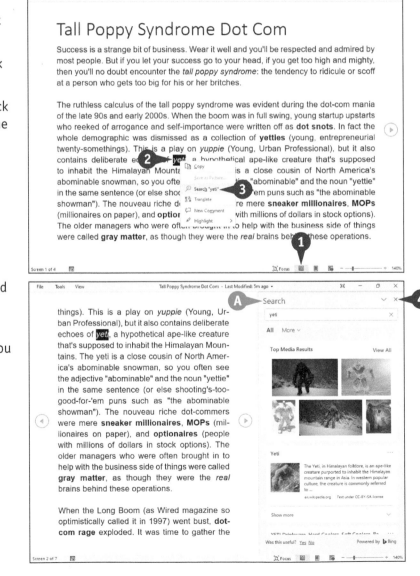

Translate a Word or Phrase

1 Click 📖 to display the document in Read Mode view.

2 Select the word or phrase you want to translate and right-click.

3 From the menu that appears, click **Translate**.

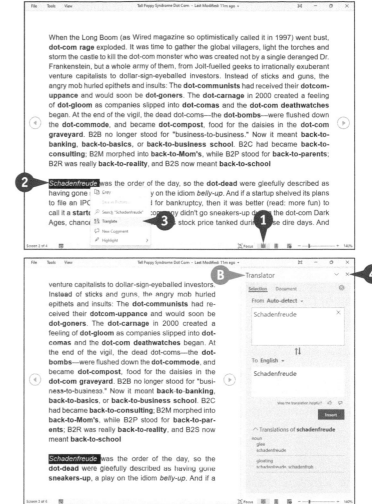

B The Translator task pane opens, displaying a translation of the word or phrase you selected in step **2**.

4 To close the Translator task pane, click ✕ in the upper-right corner of the pane.

Can I change the color of the page?

Yes. Follow these steps:

1 Click **View** (not shown).

2 Click **Page Color**.

3 Choose a page color.

This example uses Sepia.

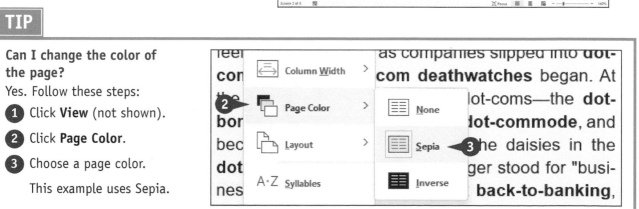

continued ▶

Read Mode view offers more than just minimized eye strain; while you work in Read Mode view, you can look up words on the Web, translate a word or phrase, highlight important text, and insert comments in documents you are reviewing. If you are viewing a long document in Read Mode view, you can also use the Navigation pane to move around the document. You can open the Navigation pane from the Tools menu in Read Mode view; for details on using the Navigation pane, see the section "Navigate Document Content," later in this chapter.

Work in Read Mode View (continued)

Highlight Important Text

1 Click 📖 to display the document in Read Mode view.

2 Select the words you want to highlight and right-click.

3 From the menu that appears, hover the mouse (▷) over ❯.

Word displays the color palette.

C Alternatively, click **Highlight** to apply the default or most recently used color and skip step **4**.

4 Click a highlight color.

D Word highlights the selected text in the color you chose.

5 Click anywhere outside the highlight to see its full effect and continue working.

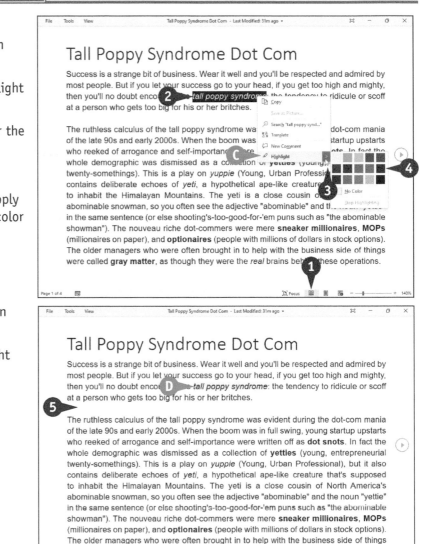

Insert a Comment

1 Click 📖 to display the document in Read Mode view.

2 Select the words about which you want to comment, and right-click.

3 From the menu that appears, click **New Comment**.

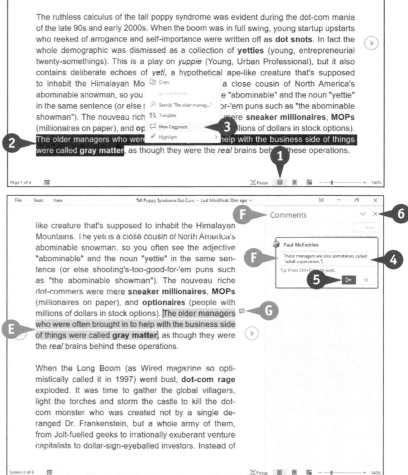

E Word changes the color used to select the text.

F Word displays the Comments task pane and adds a new comment box containing the insertion point.

4 Type your comment.

5 Click **Post comment** (▶).

Note: You can also post your comment by pressing **Ctrl** + **Enter**.

6 Click ✕ to close the Comments task pane.

G This symbol represents your comment; click it at any time to view the comment.

TIPS

What are some of the different views available in Read Mode?
To display all comments in the document, click **View** and then click **Show Comments**. To view your document as if it were printed on paper, click **View** and then click **Layout**. From the menu that appears, click **Paper Layout**.

Can I change the column width?
Yes. Click **View** and then click **Column Width**. From the menu that appears, choose **Narrow** or **Wide**; click **Default** to return to the original column view. Note that on a standard monitor, Default and Wide look the same; Wide takes effect on widescreen monitors.

Find and Replace Text

Vou can use Word's Find tool to search for a word or phrase instead of scrolling through your document to locate that text. Find is useful when you are working with a long document and you want to edit a paragraph that contains a specific word or phrase.

You can use the Replace tool to replace instances of a word or phrase with other text. For example, suppose you complete a long report and then realize that you have misspelled the name of a person or product; you can use the Replace tool to quickly correct the misspellings.

Find and Replace Text

Find Text

1 Click at the beginning of your document.

2 Click **Home**.

3 Click **Find**.

Note: You can also run the Find command by pressing Ctrl + F.

Ⓐ The Navigation pane appears.

4 Type the text that you want to find.

Ⓑ Word searches the document and highlights occurrences of the text.

Ⓒ Word also lists occurrences of the text in the Navigation pane.

5 Click an entry in the Navigation pane.

Ⓓ Word selects the corresponding text in the document.

6 When finished, click the Navigation pane's **Close** button (✕).

Replace Text

1 Click at the beginning of your document.

2 Click **Home**.

3 Click **Replace**.

Note: You can also run the Replace command by pressing Ctrl + H.

The Find and Replace dialog box opens with the Replace tab shown.

4 In the **Find what** box, type the text that you want to find.

5 Type the replacement text in the **Replace with** box.

6 Click **Find Next**.

E Word locates the first occurrence.

7 Click **Replace** to replace the occurrence.

F To replace every occurrence in the document, you can click **Replace All**.

Note: When Word finds no more occurrences, a message appears; click **OK**, and the Cancel button in the Find and Replace dialog box changes to Close.

8 Click **Close** (not shown).

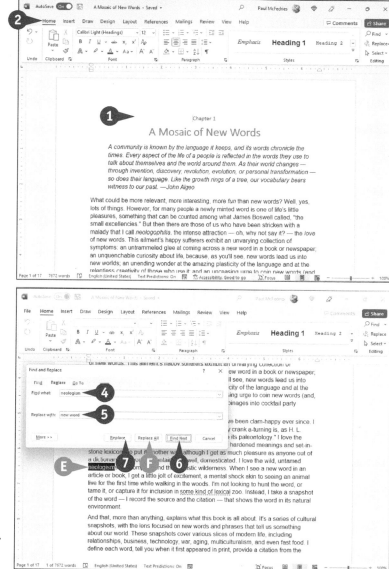

TIPS

Where can I find detailed search options?
Click **More** in the Find and Replace dialog box to reveal additional search options. For example, you can search for matching text case, whole words, and more. You can also search for specific formatting or special characters by clicking **Format** and **Special**.

How can I search for and delete text?
Start by typing the text you want to delete in the **Find what** box; then leave the **Replace with** box empty. When you search and click **Replace**, Word looks for the text and replaces it with nothing, effectively deleting the text for which you searched.

Navigate Document Content

If you are working with a very long document, using the scroll bar on the right side of the screen or the Page Up and Page Down keys on your keyboard to locate a particular page in that document can be time-consuming. To rectify this, you can use the Navigation pane to navigate through a document. This pane can display all the headings in your document or a thumbnail image of each page in your document. You can then click a heading or a thumbnail image in the Navigation pane to view the corresponding page.

Navigate Document Content

Navigate Using Headings

Note: To navigate using headings, your document must contain text styled with Heading styles. See Chapter 6 for details on styles.

1 Click **View**.

2 Click **Navigation Pane** (☐ changes to ☑).

The Navigation pane appears.

Ⓐ Heading 1 styles appear at the left edge of the Navigation pane.

Ⓑ Word indents Heading 2 styles slightly and each subsequent heading style a bit more.

Ⓒ This icon (▲) represents a heading displaying subheadings; you can click it to hide subheadings.

Ⓓ This icon (▷) represents a heading that is hiding subheadings; you can click it to display the subheadings.

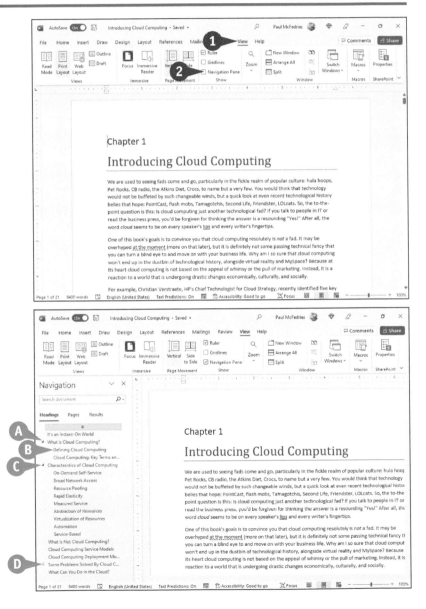

3 Click any heading in the Navigation pane to select it.

E Word moves the insertion point to this heading in your document.

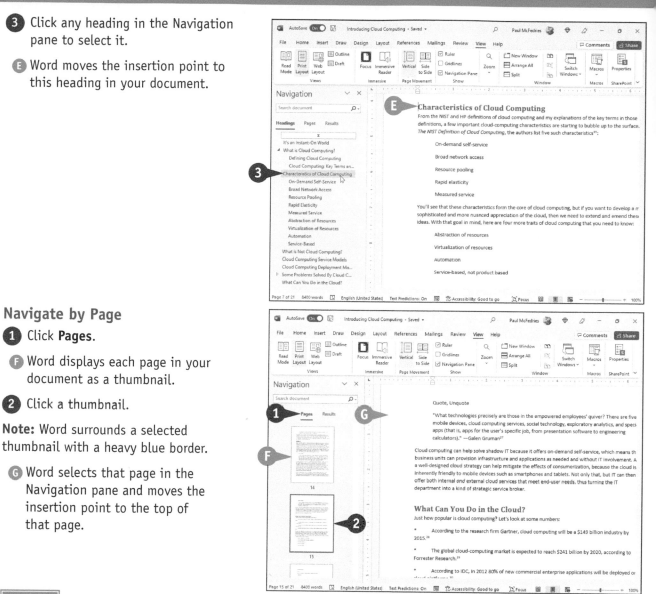

Navigate by Page

1 Click **Pages**.

F Word displays each page in your document as a thumbnail.

2 Click a thumbnail.

Note: Word surrounds a selected thumbnail with a heavy blue border.

G Word selects that page in the Navigation pane and moves the insertion point to the top of that page.

What can I do with the Search Document box?
You can use the Search Document box to find text in your document; see the "Find Text" subsection of the section "Find and Replace Text" for details on using this box and on other ways you can search for information in your document.

Can I control the headings that appear?
Yes. While viewing headings, right-click any heading in the Navigation pane. From the menu that appears, point at **Show Heading Levels** and, from the submenu that appears, click the heading level you want to display (for example, **Show Heading 1**, **Show Heading 2**, and so on, up to **Show Heading 9**).

Check Spelling and Grammar

Word automatically checks for spelling and grammar errors. Misspellings appear underlined with a red wavy line, and grammar errors are underlined with a blue wavy line. If you prefer, you can turn off Word's automatic Spelling and Grammar checking features.

Alternatively, you can use Word's Editor feature to review your entire document for spelling and grammatical errors, as well as writing refinements such as clarity, conciseness, and formality.

Check Spelling and Grammar

Correct a Mistake

1 When you encounter a spelling or grammar problem, right-click the underlined text.

A A menu appears, showing possible corrections. Click one, if applicable.

B To ignore the error, click **Ignore All**.

C To make Word stop flagging a word as misspelled, click **Add to Dictionary**.

Correct Errors Via the Editor

1 Open the document you want to check.

2 Click **Review**.

3 Click **Editor**.

D Word displays the Editor task pane.

E This box gives your overall Editor Score. Accurate and readable documents have scores of 85% or higher.

F Each box tells you the number of errors Editor found in each category.

4 Click the category you want to work with.

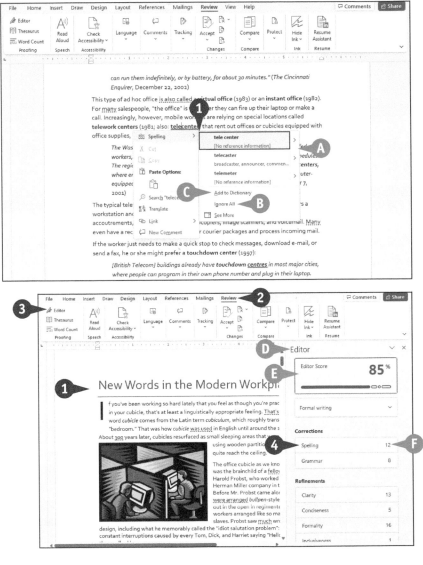

Ⓖ The error appears here.

Ⓗ Suggestions to correct the error appear here.

5 Click the suggestion you want to use.

Ⓘ To correct all misspellings of the same word, you can click ⌄ and then click **Change All**.

Ⓙ You can click **Ignore Once** to leave this instance unchanged; click **Ignore All** to leave all instances in the document unchanged; click **Add to Dictionary** to tell Word this instance is not an error.

6 Repeat step **5** for each error.

7 Click **Back** (←).

Ⓚ Editor shows the updated Editor Score.

Ⓛ Editor displays ✓ beside a category that has no outstanding errors.

8 Repeat steps **4** to **7** to fix errors in each of the Editor categories.

9 When you are done, click **Close** (✕) to close the Editor task pane.

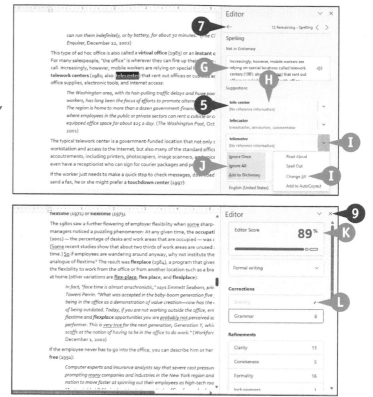

TIP

How do I turn the automatic spelling and grammar checking off?

To turn off the automatic checking features, follow these steps:

1 Click the **File** tab and then click **Options** (not shown).

2 In the Word Options dialog box, click **Proofing**.

3 In the When Correcting Spelling and Grammar in Word section, click **Check spelling as you type** (☑ changes to ☐).

4 Click **Mark grammar errors as you type** (☑ changes to ☐).

5 Click **OK**.

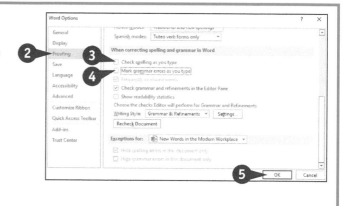

Customize AutoCorrect

As you may have noticed, Word automatically corrects your text as you type. It does this using its AutoCorrect feature, which works from a preset list of misspellings.

To speed up your text-entry tasks, you can add your own problem words — ones you commonly misspell — to the list. The next time you mistype the word, AutoCorrect fixes your mistake for you. If you find that AutoCorrect consistently changes a word that is correct as is, you can remove that word from the AutoCorrect list. If you would prefer that AutoCorrect not make any changes to your text as you type, you can disable the feature.

Customize AutoCorrect

1 Click the **File** tab (not shown).

Backstage view appears.

2 Click **Options**.

The Word Options dialog box appears.

3 Click **Proofing** to display proofing options.

4 Click **AutoCorrect Options**.

The AutoCorrect dialog box appears.

Ⓐ If you want to disable AutoCorrect, click **Replace text as you type** (☑ changes to ☐) and skip to step **8**.

Ⓑ The corrections Word already makes automatically appear in this area.

⑤ In the Replace text box, type the word you typically mistype or misspell.

⑥ In the With text box, type the correct version of the word.

⑦ Click **Add**.

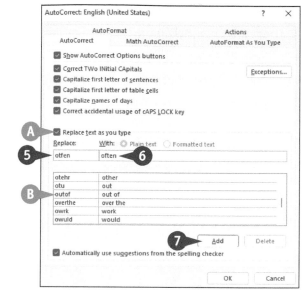

Ⓒ Word adds the entry to the list to automatically correct.

You can repeat steps **5** to **7** for each automatic correction you want to add.

⑧ Click **OK** to close the AutoCorrect dialog box.

⑨ Click **OK** to close the Word Options dialog box.

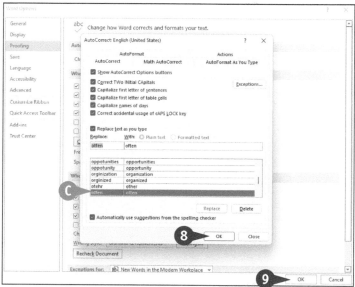

TIPS

How does the automatic correction work?

As you type, if you mistype or misspell a word stored as an AutoCorrect entry, Word corrects the entry when you press `Spacebar`, `Tab`, or `Enter`.

What should I do if Word automatically replaces an entry that I do not want replaced?

Position the insertion point at the beginning of the AutoCorrected word and click the **AutoCorrect Options** button (▭). From the list that appears, click **Change back to**. To make Word permanently stop correcting an entry, follow steps **1** to **4** in this section, click the stored AutoCorrect entry in the list, and then click **Delete**.

Using Word's Thesaurus and Dictionary

If you are having trouble finding just the right word or phrase, you can use Word's Thesaurus. The Thesaurus can help you find a synonym — a word with a similar meaning — for the word you originally chose, as well as an antonym, which is a word with an opposite meaning.

You also can, through the Search feature, use Bing to explore the Web using a word in your document. Bing returns a variety of entries found on the Web and can provide you with a definition of the word using the Oxford University Press Dictionaries.

Using Word's Thesaurus and Dictionary

Using Word's Thesaurus

1 Click anywhere in the word for which you want to find a substitute or opposite.

2 Click **Review**.

3 Click **Thesaurus**.

Note: You can also press 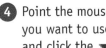 **Shift** + **F7** to run the Thesaurus command.

The Thesaurus task pane appears.

A The word you selected appears here.

B Each word with an arrow on its left and a part of speech on its right represents a major heading.

Note: You cannot substitute major headings for the word in your document.

C Each word listed below a major heading is a synonym or antonym for the major heading.

4 Point the mouse (⌖) at the word you want to use in your document and click the ▼ that appears.

5 Click **Insert**.

Word replaces the word in your document with the one in the Thesaurus pane.

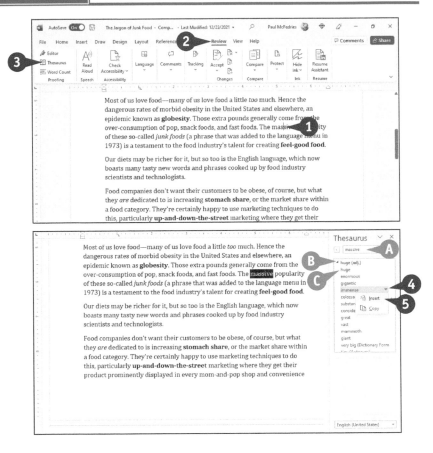

Display a Definition

1 Use your mouse to select the word for which you want a definition.

Note: You can also select a word by double-clicking it.

Word displays the Mini toolbar.

2 Click **Define "*word*"**, where *word* is the term you selected in step **1**.

D The Search task pane appears on the right side of the screen.

E Word displays the main definition for the word, as well as other information about the word.

F You can click **Show more definitions** to see the complete list of definitions for the word.

3 When you are done, click ✕ to close the Search task pane.

TIP

Is there a faster way I can display synonyms?
Yes. Follow these steps:

1 Right-click the word for which you want a synonym (not shown).

2 Click **Synonyms**.

3 To replace the word in your document, click a choice in the list that appears.

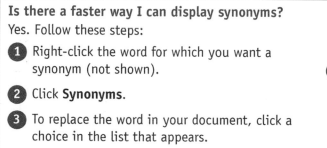

Translate Text

You can translate a word from one language to another using language dictionaries installed on your computer. If you are connected to the Internet, the Translation feature searches the dictionaries on your computer as well as online dictionaries.

Although the feature is capable of complex translations, it may not grasp the tone or meaning of your text. You can choose Translate Document from the Translate drop-down menu to send the document over the Internet for translation, but be aware that Word sends documents as unencrypted HTML files. If security is an issue, do not choose this route; instead, consider hiring a professional translator.

Translate Text

Translate a Word or Phrase

1 Select a word or phrase to translate.

2 Click **Review**.

3 Click **Translate**.

4 Click **Translate Selection**.

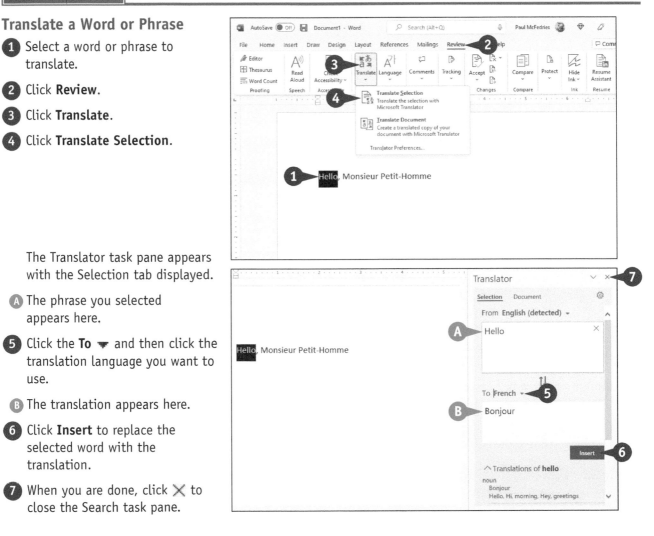

The Translator task pane appears with the Selection tab displayed.

Ⓐ The phrase you selected appears here.

5 Click the **To** ▼ and then click the translation language you want to use.

Ⓑ The translation appears here.

6 Click **Insert** to replace the selected word with the translation.

7 When you are done, click ✕ to close the Search task pane.

Translate a Document

1 Open the document you want to translate.

2 Click the **Review** tab.

3 Click **Translate**.

4 Click **Translate Document**.

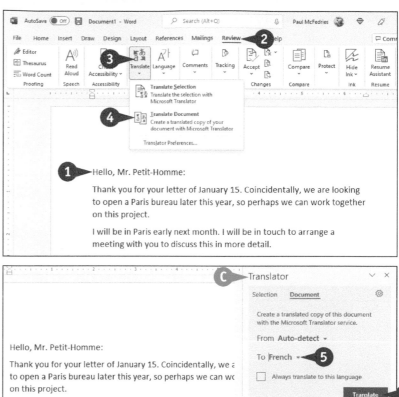

C The Translator task pane appears with the Document tab displayed.

5 Click the **To** ▼ and then click the translation language you want to use.

6 Click **Translate**.

Word closes the Translator task pane and then displays the translated document.

TIP

The document translation is incorrect. Why did it not work?
Occasionally, the Microsoft Translator service misidentifies the original language of the document. To ensure that Microsoft Translator knows the correct original language, follow steps **1** to **4** in the "Translate a Document" subsection to open the Translator task pane, click the **From** ▼ (A), and then select the original language of the document (B).

Track and Review Document Changes

If you share your Word documents with others, you can use the program's Track Changes feature to identify the edits others have made, including formatting changes and text additions or deletions. The Track Changes feature uses different colors for each person's edits, so you can easily distinguish edits made by various people. By default, Word displays changes in Simple Markup view, which indicates, in the left margin, areas that have changes. This section demonstrates how to track and interpret changes.

When you review the document, you decide whether to accept or reject the changes.

Track and Review Document Changes

Turn On Tracking

1 Click **Review**.

2 Click **Track Changes** to start monitoring document changes.

3 Edit the document.

Ⓐ A red vertical bar appears in the left margin area to indicate that changes were made to the corresponding line.

Note: When you open a document containing tracked changes, Simple Markup is the default view.

Ⓑ The displayed value in this drop-down list tells you the current markup view.

Review Changes

1 Click any vertical bar in the left margin.

All vertical bars turn gray, and Word changes the view to All Markup and displays all changes in the document.

C Additions to the text appear underlined and in color.

D Deleted text appears in color with strikethrough formatting.

2 Place the insertion point at the beginning of the document.

3 Click **Next Change** (🖹).

E Word highlights the first change.

4 Click **Accept** to add the change to the document.

F Alternatively, click the **Reject and Move to Next** button (🖹) to revert the text to its original state.

Note: To accept all changes in the document, click ▼ under the **Accept** button and choose **Accept All Changes**.

5 Repeat steps **3** and **4** until you have reviewed all changes.

6 When you complete the review, click **Track Changes** to turn the feature off.

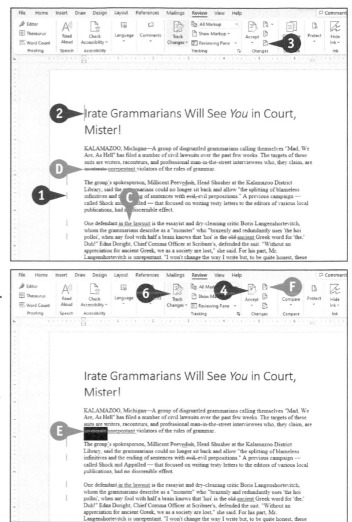

TIP

Can I see who made each change?
Yes. You can use the Reviewing pane. Follow these steps: Click the **Review** tab on the Ribbon, and then click **Reviewing Pane**. The Reviewing pane opens, summarizing the types of edits and showing each person's edits.

Lock and Unlock Tracking

You can control who can turn tracking on and off using the Lock Tracking feature. This feature requires a password to turn off tracking. You no longer need to deal with the situation where you turn on tracking and send out a document for review, and when you get the document back, it contains no change markings because the reviewer turned the Track Changes feature off.

In the past, you needed to use the Compare Documents feature to determine how the reviewed document differed from the original. Now, you can lock tracking.

Lock and Unlock Tracking

Lock Tracked Changes

1 In the document for which you want to lock tracked changes, click **Review**.

2 Click **Track Changes** to turn on tracking.

3 Click ▼ at the bottom of the **Track Changes** button.

4 Click **Lock Tracking**.

The Lock Tracking dialog box appears.

5 Type a password here.

6 Retype the password here.

7 Click **OK**.

Note: Make sure you remember the password or you will not be able to turn off the Track Changes feature.

Word saves the password and disables the Track Changes button.

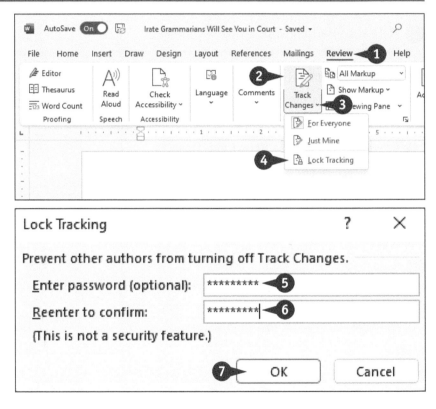

Unlock Tracked Changes

1 Open a document with tracked changes locked.

2 Click **Review**.

3 Click ▼ at the bottom of the **Track Changes** button.

4 Click **Lock Tracking**.

The Unlock Tracking dialog box appears.

5 Type the password.

6 Click **OK**.

Word enables the Track Changes button so that you can click it and turn off the Track Changes feature.

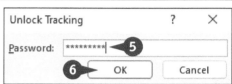

TIP

What happens if I supply the wrong password?

This message box appears. You can retry as many times as you want. If you cannot remember the password, you can create a new version that contains all revisions already accepted, which you can then compare to the original to identify changes. Press Ctrl+A to select the entire document. Then press Shift+← to unselect just the last paragraph mark in the document. Then press Ctrl+C to copy the selection. Start a new blank document and press Ctrl+V to paste the selection.

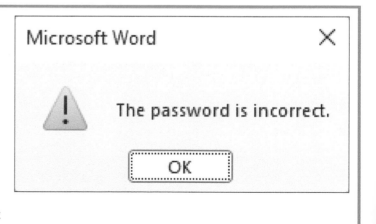

Combine Reviewers' Changes

Suppose that two different people review a document, but they review simultaneously using the original document. When they each return the reviewed document, you have two versions of the original document, each containing potentially different changes. Fortunately, you can combine the documents so that you can work from the combined changes of both reviewers.

When you combine two versions of the same document, Word creates a third file that flags any discrepancies between the versions using revision marks like you see when you enable the Track Changes feature. You can then work from the combined document and evaluate each change.

Combine Reviewers' Changes

Note: To make your screen as easy to understand as possible, close all open documents.

1. Click **Review**.

2. Click **Compare**.

3. Click **Combine**.

   The Combine Documents dialog box appears.

4. Click the **Open** button (📁) for the first document you want to combine.

   The Open dialog box appears.

5. Navigate to the folder containing the first file you want to combine.

6. Click the file.

7. Click **Open**.

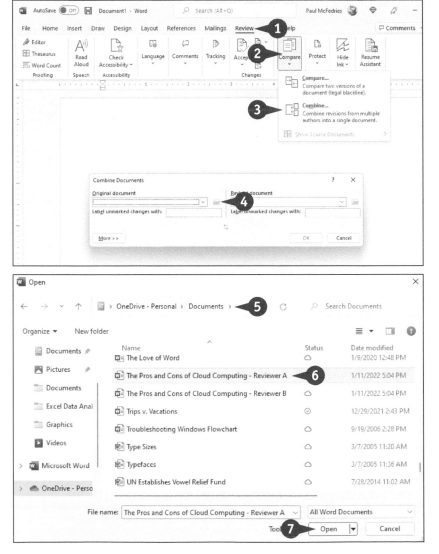

The Combine Documents dialog box reappears.

8 Repeat steps **4** to **7**, clicking the Open button ( ) for the second document you want to combine.

Ⓐ You can type a label for changes to each document in these boxes.

9 Click **OK**.

Word displays four panes.

Ⓑ The left pane contains a summary of revisions.

Ⓒ The center pane contains the result of combining both documents.

Ⓓ The top-right pane displays the document you selected in step **6**.

Ⓔ The bottom-right pane displays the document you selected in step **8**.

TIPS

Two reviewers reviewed the same document, but they forgot to track changes; can I somehow see their changes?

Yes. Follow the steps in this section, but, in step **3**, click **Compare**. Word again displays four panes: The summary appears in the left pane; results of comparing the two documents appear in the center pane; the document you select in step **6** appears in the top right pane; and the document you select in step **8** appears in the bottom-right pane.

How do I save the combined document?

The same way you save any Word document; see Chapter 2 for details.

Work with Comments

You can add comments to your documents. For example, when you share a document with other users, you can use comments to leave feedback about the text without typing directly in the document, and others can do the same.

To indicate that a comment was added, Word displays a balloon in the right margin near the commented text. When you review comments, they appear in a block. Your name appears in comments you add, and you can easily review, reply to, or delete a comment, or, instead of deleting the comment, you can indicate that you have addressed the comment.

Work with Comments

Add a Comment

1 Click or select the text about which you want to comment.

2 Click **Review**.

3 Click **New Comment**.

Ⓐ A comment balloon and block appear, marking the location of the comment.

4 Type your comment.

5 Click anywhere outside the comment to continue working.

Review a Comment

1 While working in Simple Markup view, click a comment balloon.

Ⓑ Word highlights the text associated with the comment.

Ⓒ Word displays the Comments block and the text it contains.

Ⓓ To view all comments along the right side of the document, you can click **Show Comments**.

2 Click anywhere outside the comment to hide the Comments block and its text.

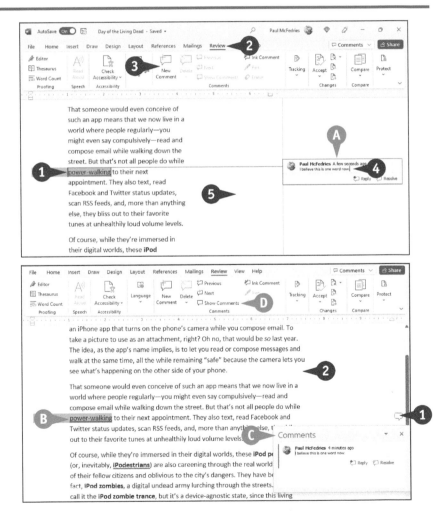

Reply to a Comment

1 While working in Simple Markup view, click a comment balloon to display its text.

2 Click **Reply**.

E Word starts a new comment, indented under the first comment.

3 Type your reply.

4 Click anywhere outside the comment to continue working.

Delete a Comment

1 Click the comment that you want to remove.

2 Click **Review**.

3 Click **Delete**.

Note: You can also right-click a comment and click **Delete Comment**.

F You can delete all comments in the document by clicking ▼ at the bottom of the **Delete** button and then clicking **Delete All Comments in Document**.

Word deletes the comment.

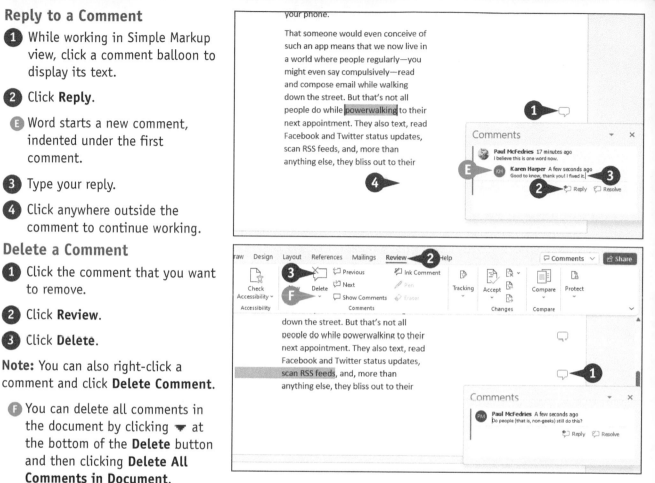

TIP

Can I indicate that I have addressed a comment without deleting it?

Yes, you can mark the comment as resolved. Click the comment to open its comment box, move the mouse ⬧ over the text of the comment, and then click **Resolve** (A). Word fades the comment text to light gray.

PART III

Excel

Excel is a powerful spreadsheet program. You can use Excel strictly as a program for manipulating numerical data, or you can use it as a database program to track and manage large quantities of data. You also can chart mathematical data and create PivotTables and PivotCharts that summarize large quantities of data. In this part, you learn how to enter data into worksheets and tap into the power of Excel's formulas, functions, and charting capabilities to analyze data.

Chapter 9: Building Spreadsheets 124

Chapter 10: Worksheet Basics 152

Chapter 11: Working with Formulas and Functions 168

Chapter 12: Working with Charts 180

Enter Cell Data

You can enter data into any cell in an Excel worksheet. You can type data directly into the cell, or you can enter data using the Formula bar. Data can be text, such as row or column labels, or numbers, which are called *values*. Values also include formulas. Excel automatically left-aligns text data in a cell and right-aligns values.

Long text entries appear truncated if you type additional data into adjoining cells. Values too large to fit in a cell might be represented by a series of pound signs. However, Excel offers features to help you remedy these situations.

Enter Cell Data

Type into a Cell

1 Click the cell into which you want to enter data.

The cell you clicked is called the *active cell*. It has a thicker border around it than the other cells.

A To magnify your view of the worksheet, click and drag the **Zoom** slider.

2 Type your data.

B The data appears both in the cell and in the Formula bar.

3 To store the data in the cell, press Enter or click the **Enter** button (✓).

Note: If you press Enter, the cell pointer moves down one row. If you click the **Enter** button (✓), the cell pointer remains in the cell you clicked in step **1**.

Type Data in the Formula Bar

 Click the cell into which you want to enter data.

 Click in the Formula bar.

③ Type your data.

Ⓒ The data appears both in the Formula bar and in the cell.

④ Click the **Enter** button (✓) or press Enter to enter the data.

Ⓓ To cancel an entry, you can click the **Cancel** button (✕) or press Esc.

TIP

What if the data that I type is too long to fit in the cell?

For text entries, if the cell to the right is empty, Excel extends your text into that cell; if the cell to the right is not empty, Excel truncates the display of your text (the text itself remains intact, however).

For numeric and date entries, Excel expands the column to accommodate your entry. If Excel cannot expand the column, then your entry appears as a series of pound signs (#; again, the actual data in the cell is unaffected).

You can force Excel to display your entry in full by resizing the column; see the later section "Resize Columns and Rows." Alternatively, you can activate the Wrap Text feature to increase the cell's height; see the later section "Turn On Text Wrapping."

Select Cells

To edit data or perform mathematical or formatting operations on data in an Excel worksheet, you must first select the cell or cells that contain that data. For example, you might apply formatting to data in a single cell or to data in a group, or *range*, of cells.

To select a single cell, you just click the cell. To select a range of cells, you can use your mouse or keyboard. Besides selecting cells or ranges of cells, you can also select the data contained in a cell, as described in the tip.

Select Cells

Select a Range of Cells

1 Click the cell representing the upper-left corner of the range of cells that you want to select.

A The cell pointer (⊕) appears as you move the mouse.

2 Click and drag down and to the right across the cells that you want to include in the range.

3 Release the mouse button.

B Excel highlights the selected cells in gray.

C The Quick Analysis button (📊) appears. See Chapter 10 for details about data analysis choices.

D To select all the cells in the worksheet, you can click here (   ).

You can select multiple noncontiguous cells by pressing and holding **Ctrl** while clicking cells.

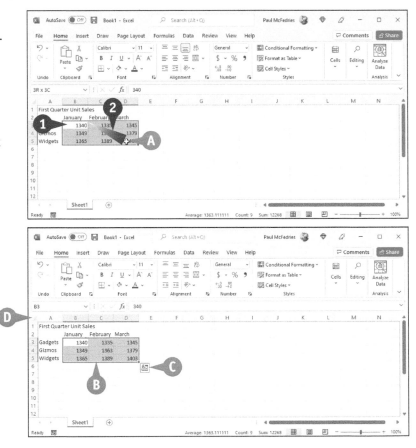

Select a Column or Row

1 Position the mouse (⬉) over the column letter or row number that you want to select.

The cell pointer changes from ⬧ to ⬇ if you position the mouse over a column, or ➡ if you position the mouse over a row.

2 Click the column or row.

E Excel selects the entire column or row.

To select multiple contiguous columns or rows, you can click and drag across the column or row headings.

You can select multiple noncontiguous columns or rows by pressing and holding Ctrl while clicking column or row headings.

TIPS

How do I select data inside a cell?
Click the cell; then click in the Formula bar and drag over the characters or numbers you want to select. Alternatively, double-click the cell and drag to select the data.

Can I use my keyboard to select a range?
Yes. Use the arrow keys to navigate to the first cell in a range. Next, press and hold Shift while using the arrow keys (◄ or ► and ▼ or ▲) to select the remaining cells in the range.

Using AutoFill for Faster Data Entry

You can use Excel's AutoFill feature to add a data series to your worksheet or to duplicate a single entry in your worksheet to expedite data entry. You can create numeric series and, using Excel's built-in lists of common entries, you can enter text series such as a list containing the months in the year. You can also create your own custom data lists, as described in the tip.

When you click a cell, a green square called the *fill handle* appears in the lower-right corner of the cell; you use the fill handle to create a series.

Using AutoFill for Faster Data Entry

AutoFill a Text Series

1 Type the first entry in the text series.

2 Click and drag the cell's fill handle across or down the number of cells that you want to fill.

A changes to ✛.

If you type an entry that Excel does not recognize as part of a list, AutoFill copies the selection to every cell that you drag over.

3 Release the mouse button.

B AutoFill fills in the text series and selects the series.

C The AutoFill Options button (📋) may appear, offering additional options that you can assign to the data.

AutoFill a Number Series

1 Type the first entry in the number series.

2 In an adjacent cell, type the next entry in the number series.

3 Select both cells.

Note: See the previous section, "Select Cells," to learn more.

4 Click and drag the Fill handle across (if the selected cells are in a row) or down (if the selected cells are in a column) the number of cells that you want to fill.

Ⓓ 🕂 changes to **+**.

5 Release the mouse button.

Ⓔ AutoFill fills in the number series and selects the series.

Ⓕ The AutoFill Options button (🔳) may appear, offering additional options that you can assign to the data.

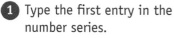

TIP

How do I create a custom list?
To add your own custom list to AutoFill's list library, first create the custom list in your worksheet cells. Then select the cells containing the list that you want to save. Click the **File** tab and then click **Options**. In the Options dialog box, click the **Advanced** tab. In the General section, click the **Edit Custom Lists** button. In the Custom Lists dialog box, click **Import**. Excel adds your list to the Custom Lists box. The entries in the list appear in the List Entries box. Click **OK** to close the Custom Lists dialog box. Click **OK** again to close the Options dialog box.

Turn On Text Wrapping

By default, long lines of text appear on one line in an Excel table. If you type additional data into adjoining cells, long lines of text appear truncated, but the text itself is not affected. If you select the cell and look at the Formula bar, you see all the text.

You can display all the text in a cell by resizing the column width (see the section "Resize Columns and Rows," later in this chapter). Alternatively, you can wrap text within the cell so that some text appears on the next line. When you wrap text, Excel maintains column width and increases row height to accommodate the number of lines that wrap.

Turn On Text Wrapping

1 Click the cell in which you want to wrap text.

Note: You can also apply text wrapping to multiple cells. See the section "Select Cells," earlier in this chapter, to learn how to select multiple cells for a task.

2 Click **Home**.

3 Click the **Wrap Text** button (ab).

Ⓐ Excel wraps the text in the cell.

Note: See the section "Resize Columns and Rows," later in this chapter, to learn how to adjust cell depth and width to accommodate your data.

Center Data Across Columns

You can center data across a range of selected cells in your worksheet. You can use Excel's Merge and Center command to quickly merge and center a title above multiple columns.

Click ▼ beside the Merge and Center button (⊞) for additional options. Merge Across merges each selected row of cells into a larger cell. Merge Cells merges selected cells in multiple rows and columns into a single cell. Unmerge Cells splits a cell into multiple cells.

Center Data Across Columns

1 Select the cell containing the data that you want to center, along with the adjacent cells over which you want to center the data.

Note: When you merge and center, Excel deletes any data in selected adjacent cells.

2 Click **Home**.

3 Click the **Merge and Center** button (⊞).

A You can also click the **Merge and Center** ▼ to select from several merge options.

B Excel merges the cells and centers the data.

Adjust Cell Alignment

By default, Excel automatically aligns text to the left and numbers to the right of a cell. It also vertically aligns all data to sit at the bottom of the cell. If you want, however, you can change the horizontal and vertical alignment of data within cells — for example, you can center data vertically and horizontally within a cell to improve the appearance of your worksheet data.

Besides controlling the alignment of data within a cell, you can also indent data and change its orientation in a cell.

Adjust Cell Alignment

Set Horizontal Alignment

1. Select the cells that you want to format.

2. Click **Home**.

3. Click an alignment button:

   Click the **Align Left** button (≡) to align data to the left.

   Click the **Center** button (≡) to center-align the data.

   Click the **Align Right** button (≡) to align data to the right.

Note: To justify cell data, click the dialog box launcher (⌐▣) in the Alignment group. In the Format Cells dialog box that appears, click the **Horizontal** ⌄ and click **Justify**.

Excel applies the alignment to your cells.

Ⓐ This example aligns the data to the right.

Set Vertical Alignment

1. Select the cells that you want to format.

2. Click **Home**.

3. Click an alignment button:

   Click the **Top Align** button ($\equiv$) to align data to the top.

   Click the **Middle Align** button ($\equiv$) to align data in the middle.

   Click the **Bottom Align** button ($\equiv$) to align data to the bottom.

   Excel applies the alignment to your cells.

B. This example aligns the data to the middle of the cell.

TIPS

How do I indent cell data?

To indent data, click **Home** and then click the **Increase Indent** button ($\overrightarrow{\equiv}$). To decrease an indent, click the **Decrease Indent** button ($\overleftarrow{\equiv}$).

Can I change the orientation of data in a cell?

Yes. For example, you might angle column labels to make them easier to distinguish from one another. To do so, select the cells you want to change, click **Home**, click $\vee$ next to the **Orientation** button ($\gg$), and click an orientation. Excel applies the orientation to the data in the selected cell or cells.

Change the Font and Size

You can change the font or font size for any cell or range in your worksheet. For example, you can make the worksheet title larger than the rest of the data, or you might resize the font for the entire worksheet to make the data easier to read. You can apply multiple formats to a cell or range — for example, you can change both the font and the font size.

If you particularly like the result of applying a series of formatting options to a cell, you can copy the formatting and apply it to other cells in your worksheet.

Change the Font and Size

Change the Font

1 Select the cell or range for which you want to change fonts.

2 Click **Home**.

3 Click the **Font** ⏷.

Ⓐ You can use ⏶ and ⏷ to scroll through all the available fonts.

You can also begin typing a font name to choose a font.

4 Click a font.

Ⓑ Excel applies the font.

Change the Font Size

1 Select the cell or range for which you want to change font size.

2 Click **Home**.

3 Click the **Font Size** ▼.

4 Click a size.

C Excel applies the new size to the selected cell or range.

Can I apply multiple formatting options at the same time?

Yes. The Format Cells dialog box enables you to apply a new font, size, or any other basic formatting options to selected data. Click **Home** and then click the dialog box launcher (🖳) in the Font group.

How can I copy cell formatting?

Select the cell or range that contains the formatting you want to copy. Click **Home** and then click the **Format Painter** button (🖌) in the Clipboard group. Click and drag over the cells to which you want to apply the formatting and release the mouse button to copy the formatting.

Change Number Formats

You can use number formatting to control the appearance of numerical data in your worksheet. For example, if you have a column of prices, you can format the data as numbers with dollar signs and decimal points. If prices listed are in a currency other than dollars, you can indicate that as well.

Excel offers several different number categories, or styles, to choose from. These include Currency styles, Accounting styles, Date styles, Time styles, Percentage styles, and more. You can apply number formatting to single cells, ranges, columns, rows, or an entire worksheet.

Change Number Formats

1. Select the cell, range, or data that you want to format.

2. Click **Home**.

3. Click the **Number Format** ▼.

4. Click a number format.

Excel applies the number format to the data.

Ⓐ You can click the **Accounting Number Format** button ($) to quickly apply dollar signs to your data. Click the button's ▼ to specify a different currency symbol, such as Euro.

Ⓑ You can click the **Percent Style** button (%) to quickly apply percent signs to your data.

Ⓒ You can click the **Comma Style** button (,) to quickly display commas in your number data.

Ⓓ You can click the dialog box launcher (⬛) in the Number group to open the Format Cells dialog box and display additional number-formatting options.

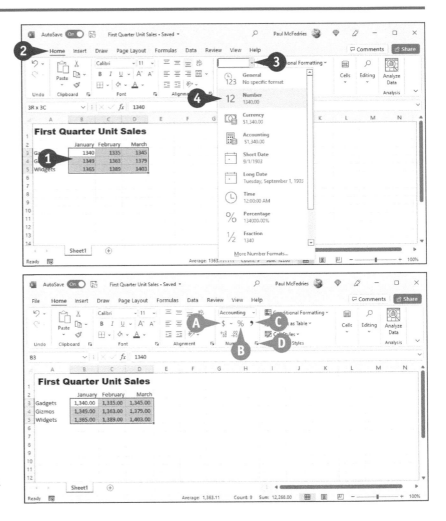

Increase or Decrease Decimals

You can control the number of decimal places that appear in numbers using the Increase Decimal and Decrease Decimal buttons. You may want to increase the number of decimal places shown in a cell if your worksheet contains data that must be precise to be accurate, as with worksheets containing scientific data. If the data in your worksheet is less precise or does not measure fractions of items, you might reduce the number of decimal places shown to two decimal places or no decimal places.

Increase or Decrease Decimals

1 Select the cell or range for which you want to adjust the number of decimal places displayed.

2 Click **Home**.

3 Click a decimal button:

You can click the **Increase Decimal** button ( ) to increase the number of decimal places displayed.

You can click the **Decrease Decimal** button ( ) to decrease the number of decimal places displayed.

Excel adjusts the number of decimals that appear in the cell or cells.

A In this example, the Decrease Decimal button ( ) was clicked twice to display no decimal places.

Add Cell Borders and Shading

By default, Excel displays gridlines separating each cell to help you enter data, but the gridlines do not print (also by default). You can print gridlines or hide them from view.

Alternatively, you can add printable borders to selected worksheet cells to help define the contents or more clearly separate the data from surrounding cells. You can add borders to all four sides of a cell or to just one, two, or three sides. You also can apply shading to help set apart different data.

Add Cell Borders and Shading

Add Quick Borders

1 Select the cell or range around which you want to place a border.

2 Click **Home**.

3 Click ▼ beside the **Borders** button (⊞).

Ⓐ To apply the current border selection shown on the button, click the **Borders** button (⊞).

4 Click a border style.

Ⓑ Excel assigns the borders to the cell or range.

Add a Fill Color

1. Select the cells to which you want to apply a fill color.

2. Click **Home**.

3. Click ▼ beside the **Fill Color** button (◇).

C. To apply the current fill color selection shown on the button, click the **Fill Color** button (◇).

4. Select a fill color.

Note: Remember, if the color you select is too dark, your data can become difficult to read.

D. Excel applies the fill color to the selected cell or range.

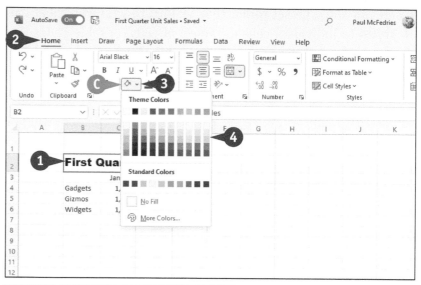

TIP

Can I turn worksheet gridlines on and off?

Yes. Printing gridlines makes worksheet data easier to read on paper. On the other hand, you might want to turn off gridlines on-screen during a presentation. To control the appearance of gridlines, click the **Page Layout** tab. In the Sheet Options group, under Gridlines, deselect **View** (A) to hide gridlines on-screen (☑ changes to ☐). Select **Print** (B) to print gridlines (☐ changes to ☑).

	Gridlines	Headings
A	☐ View	☑ View
B	☑ Print	☐ Print
	Sheet Options	↘

Format Data with Styles

You can apply preset formatting designs to your worksheet data using styles. You can apply cell styles to individual cells or ranges of cells, or table styles to a range of worksheet data. When you apply a table style, Excel converts the range into a table. Tables help you manage and analyze data independent of other data in the worksheet. For example, beside each column heading in a table, an AutoFilter ▼ appears that you can use to show only certain information in the table.

You can also apply a *theme* — a predesigned set of formatting attributes — to a worksheet. See the tip at the end of this section for more details.

Format Data with Styles

Apply a Cell Style

1. Select the cell or range that you want to format.

2. Click **Home**.

3. Click **Cell Styles**.

4. Click a style.

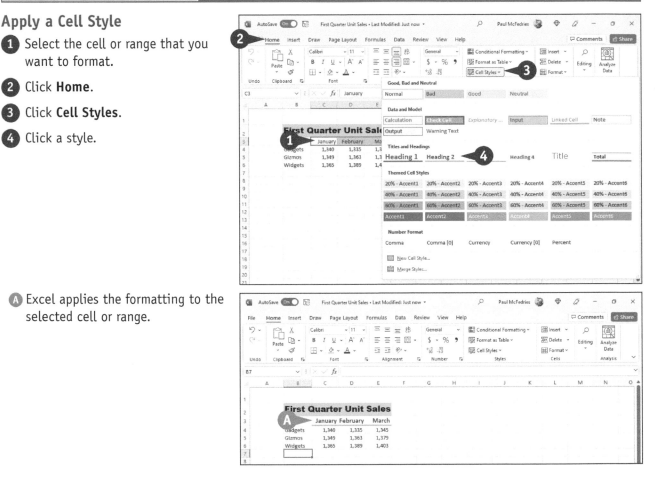

Ⓐ Excel applies the formatting to the selected cell or range.

Format as a Table

1. Select the cells that you want to format.

2. Click **Home**.

3. Click **Format as Table**.

4. Click a table style.

   The Create Table dialog box appears.

5. Verify the selected cells.

6. Click **OK**.

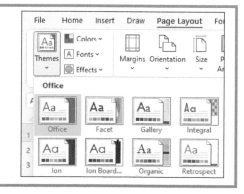

Ⓑ Excel applies the formatting style.

Ⓒ AutoFilter down arrows (▼) appear in the column headings.

How do I apply a theme?

You can use themes to create a similar appearance among all the Office documents that you create. To apply a theme, click the **Page Layout** tab, click the **Themes** button, and select a theme from the list.

Apply Conditional Formatting

You can use Excel's Conditional Formatting tool to apply certain formatting attributes, such as bold text or a fill color, to a cell when the value of that cell meets a required condition. For example, if your worksheet tracks weekly sales, you might set up Excel's Conditional Formatting tool to alert you if a sales figure falls below what is required for you to break even.

Besides using preset conditions, you can also create your own. To help you distinguish the degree to which various cells meet your conditional rules, you can also use color scales and data bars.

Apply Conditional Formatting

Apply a Conditional Rule

① Select the cell or range to which you want to apply conditional formatting.

② Click **Home**.

③ Click **Conditional Formatting**.

④ Click **Highlight Cells Rules** or **Top/Bottom Rules**.

This example uses Top/Bottom Rules.

⑤ Click the type of rule that you want to create.

A rule dialog box appears.

⑥ Specify the values that you want to assign for the condition.

⑦ Click **OK**.

Ⓐ If the value of a selected cell meets the condition, Excel applies the conditional formatting.

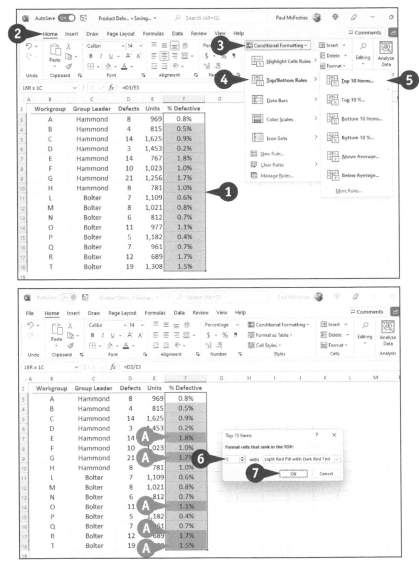

Apply Data Bars

1 Select the cell or range that contains the conditional formatting.

2 Click **Home**.

3 Click **Conditional Formatting**.

4 Click **Data Bars**.

5 Click a data bar fill option.

Ⓑ You can apply a color scale or an icon set instead by clicking **Color Scales** or **Icon Sets**.

Ⓒ Excel applies the data bars to the selection. Longer data bars represent higher values in your selection.

How do I create a new rule for conditional formatting?

Click **Home**, click the **Conditional Formatting** button, and then click **New Rule** to open the New Formatting Rule dialog box. Here, you define the condition of the rule as well as what formatting you want to apply when the condition is met.

How do I remove conditional formatting from a cell?

Select the range that contains the formatting you want to remove, click **Home**, click the **Conditional Formatting** button, and then click **Manage Rules**. Next, click the rule you want to remove, click **Delete Rule**, and then click **OK**.

Insert Rows and Columns

You can insert rows and columns into your worksheets to include more data. For example, you may have typed product names in the rows of a worksheet that shows product sales over a period of time, but you forgot to include a particular product. Now you need to insert a new row so that you can add the product and its sales.

You are not limited to inserting new rows and columns one at a time; if need be, you can insert multiple new rows and columns simultaneously.

Insert Rows and Columns

Insert a Row

1 Click the number of the row that should appear below the new row you want to insert.

2 Click **Home**.

3 Click **Insert**.

You can also right-click a row number and click **Insert**.

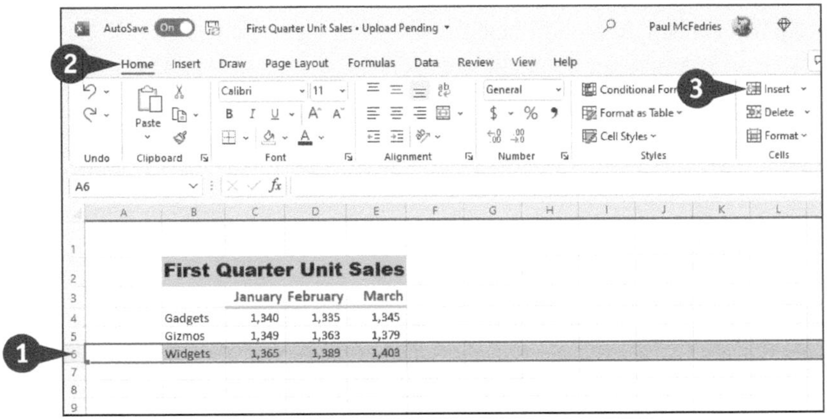

A Excel inserts a row.

B The Insert Options button (✐) appears, and you can click it to view a list of options that you can assign to the new row.

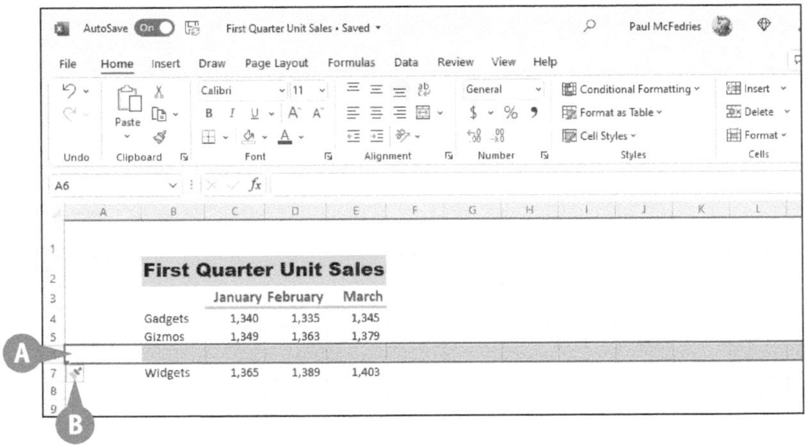

Insert a Column

1 Click the letter of the column that should appear to the right of the new column you want to insert.

2 Click **Home**.

3 Click **Insert**.

You can also right-click a column heading and click **Insert**.

C Excel inserts a column.

D The Insert Options button (🖌️) appears when you insert a column; click it to view a list of options that you can apply to the new column.

Workgroup	Group Leader	Defects	Units	% Defective
A	Hammond	8	969	0.8%
B	Hammond	4	815	0.5%
C	Hammond	14	1,625	0.9%
D	Hammond	3	1,453	0.2%
E	Hammond	14	767	1.8%
F	Hammond	10	1,023	1.0%

TIPS

How can I insert multiple columns and rows?

First, select two or more columns or rows in the worksheet; then click **Home** and then **Insert**. Excel adds the same number of new columns or rows as the number you originally selected.

What options appear when I click the Insert Options button?

For a new row, you can select **Format Same As Above**, **Format Same As Below**, or **Clear Formatting** (○ changes to ◉). For a new column, you can select **Format Same As Left**, **Format Same As Right**, or **Clear Formatting** (○ changes to ◉).

Resize Columns and Rows

A numeric value that is too large to fit into its cell might appear as pound signs (#). A text entry that is too long for its cell will appear truncated if the cell to the right contains data. To display longer numeric or text entries fully, you can increase the width of the column.

Similarly, some tall cell entries might appear cut off on the top and/or bottom if the row is not high enough. To see the full cell entry, you can increase the height of the row.

Resize Columns and Rows

1 Position the mouse (⟍) on the right edge of the column letter or the bottom edge of the row number that you want to resize.

The mouse (⟍) changes to ↔ (for a column) or to ↕ (for a row).

2 Click and drag the edge to the desired size (not shown).

A A solid line marks the new edge of the column or row as you drag.

B Excel displays the new column width or row height.

3 Release the mouse button.

C Excel resizes the column or row, and previously truncated values now appear.

D You can also select a column or row, click the **Format** button, and from the menu that appears, click **AutoFit Column Width** or **AutoFit Row Height** to resize the column or row to fit existing text.

Freeze Column and Row Titles On-Screen

In a worksheet that contains more information than will fit on one screen, you can freeze one or more columns and/or rows to keep information in those columns and rows on-screen, regardless of where you place the cell pointer. Freezing the top row or the leftmost column of your worksheet is very useful when the column or row contains headings or titles.

Freezing columns and rows affects only on-screen work; it does not affect printing.

Freeze Column and Row Titles On-Screen

1 To freeze one or more rows, select a cell below the rows you want to freeze.

To freeze one or more columns, select a cell to the right of the columns you want to freeze.

Note: To freeze both a column and a row, click the cell to the right of the column and below the row that you want visible on-screen at all times.

2 Click **View**.

3 Click **Freeze Panes**.

4 Click **Freeze Panes**.

Alternatively, you can skip step **1** and choose either **Freeze Top Row** or **Freeze First Column**.

This example freezes the top two rows.

Excel freezes the areas you identified.

5 Scroll down (for rows) or to the right (for columns).

A The frozen rows or columns remain on-screen.

B The scrolled data changes.

C To unlock the columns and rows, click **View**, click **Freeze Panes**, and then click **Unfreeze Panes**.

Name a Range

You can assign a distinctive name to a cell or to a range in a worksheet. Assigning these so-called *range names* to cells and ranges can help you more easily identify their contents. You can also use range names in formulas, which can help you decipher a formula. (Formulas are discussed in Chapter 11.) Note that each name you assign must be unique in the workbook. When it comes to naming ranges, you must follow a few other rules, as discussed in the tip at the end of this section.

Name a Range

Assign a Range Name

1. Select the cells comprising the range that you want to name.

2. Click **Formulas**.

3. Click **Define Name**.

   The New Name dialog box opens.

Note: Excel suggests a name using a label near the selected range. If you like the suggested name, skip step **4**.

4. Type a name for the selected range in the **Name** field.

   Ⓐ You can add a comment or note about the range here. For example, you might indicate what data the range contains.

5. Click **OK**.

Excel assigns the name to the cells.

Ⓑ When you select the range, its name appears in the Name box.

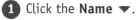

Select a Named Range

① Click the **Name** ▼.

② Click the name of the range of cells you want to select.

Ⓒ Excel selects the cells in the range.

Note: You can use the Name Manager to make changes to your range names. Click **Formulas**; then click the **Name Manager** button. You can edit existing range names, change the cells referenced by a range, or remove ranges to which you no longer need names assigned in the worksheet.

TIP

What are the rules for naming ranges?

Besides being unique in the workbook, each name can be no more than 255 characters. You can use uppercase and lowercase letters in a range name, but Excel ignores case — sales and SALES are the same name. The first character must be a letter, an underscore (_), or a backslash (\). You cannot use spaces in a range name; instead, substitute the underscore or the dash. You cannot name a range using cell references such as A1 or $F$6, nor can you name a range using either the uppercase or lowercase forms of the letters *C* and *R*.

Clear or Delete Cells

You can clear the formatting applied to a cell, the contents of the cell, any comments you assigned to the cell, any hyperlink formatting in the cell, or all these elements. Clearing a cell is useful when you want to return the cell to its original state in Excel and you do not want to remove all of the applied formatting manually.

You can also delete rows or columns of data. When you delete rows or columns, Excel adjusts the remaining cells in your worksheet, shifting them up or to the left to fill any gap in the worksheet structure.

Clear or Delete Cells

Clear Cells

1. Select the cell or range containing the data or formatting that you want to remove.

2. Click **Home**.

3. Click the **Clear** button (◇).

4. Choose an option to identify what you want to clear.

   This example clears formats.

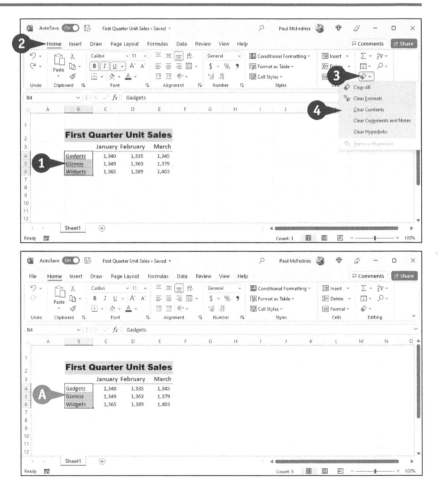

Ⓐ Excel clears the cell using the option you selected in step **4**.

In this example, Excel clears the formatting but retains the cell data.

Delete Rows or Columns

1 Click the number of the row or the letter of the column that you want to delete.

This example deletes a column.

2 Click **Home**.

3 Click **Delete**.

You can also right-click a row number or column heading and click **Delete**.

B Excel deletes the row or column and moves remaining data up or to the left to fill the resulting gap in the worksheet structure.

TIP

What is the difference between Clear Formats and Clear Contents?
Clear Formats removes just the formatting of a cell or range and leaves the contents of the cell or range. You retain the data and can reformat the cell or range; this command is most useful when you have applied several different formats and do not like the results. In a sense, Clear Formats lets you start over. Clear Contents, on the other hand, deletes the data in the cell but retains the cell's formatting. In this case, you can enter new data and it displays the same formatting as the data you cleared.

Add a Worksheet

By default, when you create a new blank workbook in Excel, it contains one worksheet, which is often all you need. In some cases, however, your workbook might require additional worksheets. For example, if your workbook contains data about products your company sells, you might want to add worksheets related to the product data, such as calculations, data analysis, charts, or PivotTables.

When you add a new worksheet, Excel gives it a default name. To help you better keep track of your data, you can rename your new worksheet. For more information, see the next section, "Rename a Worksheet."

Add a Worksheet

1 Click the **New Sheet** button (⊕).

A You can also right-click a worksheet tab, click **Insert** to open the Insert dialog box, click **Worksheet**, and then click **OK**.

B Excel adds a new blank worksheet and gives it a default worksheet name.

Rename a Worksheet

When you create a new workbook, Excel assigns the default name Sheet1 to the worksheet. Likewise, Excel assigns default names (Sheet2, Sheet3, and so on) to each worksheet you add to an existing workbook. To help you identify their content, you can change the names of your Excel worksheets to something more descriptive. For example, if your workbook contains four worksheets, each detailing a different sales quarter, then you can give each worksheet a unique name, such as Quarter 1, Quarter 2, and so on.

Rename a Worksheet

1 Double-click the worksheet tab that you want to rename.

A Excel opens the name for editing and highlights the current name.

B You can also right-click the worksheet name and click **Rename**.

2 Type a new name for the worksheet.

Note: Worksheet names must be 1 to 31 characters long, must be unique in the workbook, and cannot contain any of the following characters: / \ ? * : [or].

3 Press Enter.

Excel assigns the new worksheet name.

Change Page Setup Options

You can change worksheet settings related to page orientation, margins, and more. For example, suppose that you want to print a worksheet that has a few more columns than will fit on a page in Portrait orientation. (Portrait orientation accommodates fewer columns but more rows on the page and is the default page orientation that Excel assigns.) You can change the orientation of the worksheet to Landscape, which accommodates more columns but fewer rows on a page.

You can also use Excel's page setup settings to insert page breaks and set margins to control the placement of data on a printed page.

Change Page Setup Options

Change the Page Orientation

1 Click the **Page Layout** tab.

2 Click **Orientation**.

3 Click **Portrait** or **Landscape**.

Note: Portrait is the default orientation.

Ⓐ Vertical and horizontal (not shown) dotted lines identify page breaks that Excel inserts after you change the orientation at least once.

4 Excel applies the new orientation. This example applies Landscape.

Ⓑ Excel moves the page break indicators based on the new orientation.

Ⓒ You can click the **Margins** button to set up page margins.

Insert a Page Break

① Select a cell in the row above which you want to insert a page break.

② Click the **Page Layout** tab.

③ Click **Breaks**.

④ Click **Insert Page Break**.

Ⓓ Excel inserts a solid line representing a user-inserted page break.

How do I print just part of a worksheet?
To print only a part of a worksheet, select the cells that you want to print, click the **Page Layout** tab on the Ribbon, click the **Print Area** button, and then click **Set Print Area**. Then print as usual.

Can I set different margins for different pages that I print?
Yes. Excel assigns the same margins to all pages of a worksheet. If you need different margins for different sections that you plan to print, place each section for which you need different margins on separate worksheets. Then, for each worksheet, click **Page Layout**, click **Margins**, and set the margin you want.

Move or Copy Worksheets

You can move or copy a worksheet to a new location within the same workbook or to an entirely different workbook. For example, moving a worksheet is helpful if you insert a new worksheet and the worksheet tab names appear out of order.

Besides moving worksheets, you can also copy them. Copying a worksheet is helpful when you plan to make major changes to the worksheet and you want a backup copy. Or you might want to copy a worksheet if you need a new worksheet that uses much of the same structure or data as an existing worksheet.

Move or Copy Worksheets

1 If you plan to move or copy a worksheet to a different workbook, open the other workbook.

2 Click the tab of the worksheet you want to move or copy to make it the active worksheet.

3 Click **Home**.

4 Click **Format**.

5 Click **Move or Copy Sheet**.

A You can also right-click the worksheet tab and then click **Move or Copy**.

6 The Move or Copy dialog box appears.

B You can click the **To book** ∨ to select a destination workbook.

7 Click the worksheet before which you want the moved or copied worksheet to appear.

C You can copy a worksheet by selecting **Create a copy** (☐ changes to ☑).

8 Click **OK**.

Excel moves or copies the worksheet to the new location.

Delete a Worksheet

You can delete a worksheet that you no longer need. For example, you might delete a worksheet that contains outdated data or information about a product that your company no longer sells.

When you delete a worksheet, Excel prompts you to confirm the deletion unless the worksheet is blank, in which case it deletes the worksheet immediately. When you delete a worksheet, Excel permanently removes it from the workbook and displays the worksheet to the right of the one you deleted unless you deleted the last worksheet. In that case, Excel displays the worksheet to the left of the one you deleted.

Delete a Worksheet

① Click the tab of the worksheet you want to delete.

② Click **Home**.

③ Click the **Delete** ∨.

④ Click **Delete Sheet**.

Ⓐ You can also right-click the worksheet tab and then click **Delete**.

If the worksheet is blank, Excel deletes it immediately.

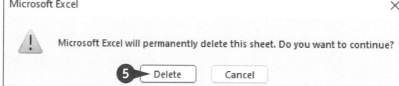

If the worksheet contains any data, Excel prompts you to confirm the deletion.

⑤ Click **Delete**.

Excel deletes the worksheet.

Find and Replace Data

Y ou can search for information in your worksheet and replace it with other information. For example, suppose that you want to change the product category Confections to Sweets. You can search for Confections and replace each occurrence with Sweets. Be aware that Excel finds all occurrences of information as you search and replace it, so be careful when replacing all occurrences at once. You can search and then skip occurrences that you do not want to replace.

You can search the entire worksheet or you can limit the search to a range of cells that you select before you begin the search.

Find and Replace Data

1 Click the **Home** tab.

2 Click **Find & Select**.

3 Click **Replace**.

A To only search for information, click **Find** instead.

Excel displays the Replace tab of the Find and Replace dialog box.

4 Use the Find What text box to type the text that you want to find and replace.

5 Use the Replace With text box to type the text that you want Excel to use to replace the text you typed in step **4**.

6 Click **Find Next**.

B Excel finds the first occurrence of the text.

7 Click **Replace**.

Excel replaces the information in the cell and finds the next occurrence.

8 Repeat step **7** as needed.

C If you find an occurrence that you do not want to replace, click **Find Next** instead.

D You can click **Replace All** if you do not want to review each occurrence before Excel replaces it.

Excel displays a message when it cannot find any more occurrences.

9 Click **OK** (not shown) and then click **Close**.

TIPS

Where can I find detailed search options?
Click the **Options** button in the Find and Replace dialog box. For example, you can search the entire workbook or the selected worksheet, search just rows or columns, and more. You can also search for specific formatting or special characters using Format options.

How can I search for and delete data?
In the Find and Replace dialog box, type the text you want to delete in the **Find what** box; leave the **Replace with** box empty. When you click **Replace**, Excel looks for the data and deletes it without adding new data to the worksheet.

Create a Table

You can create a table from any rectangular range of related data in a worksheet. A *table* is a collection of related information. Table rows — called *records* — contain information about one element, and table columns divide the element into *fields*. In a table containing name and address information, a record would contain all the information about one person, and all first names, last names, addresses, and so on would appear in separate columns.

When you create a table, Excel identifies the information in the range as a table and simultaneously formats the table and adds AutoFilter arrows to each column.

Create a Table

1 Set up a range in a worksheet that contains similar information for each row.

2 Click anywhere in the range.

3 Click **Insert**.

4 Click **Table**.

The Create Table dialog box appears, displaying a suggested range for the table.

Ⓐ You can click **My table has headers** (☑ changes to ☐) if labels for each column do *not* appear in the first row of the range.

Ⓑ You can click the **Range selector** button (⬆) to select a new range for the table boundaries by dragging in the worksheet.

⑤ Click **OK**.

Excel creates a table and applies a table style to it.

Ⓒ The Table Design contextual tab appears on the Ribbon.

Ⓓ ▼ appears in each column header.

Ⓔ Excel assigns the table a generic name.

Create Table	? ✕
Where is the data for your table?	
$A$1:$G$46	⬆ Ⓑ
Ⓐ ☑ M**y** table has headers	
⑤ OK	Cancel

	A	B	C	D	E	F	G	H	I
1	Product Name ▼	Category ▼	On Hold ▼	On Hand ▼	Unit Cost ▼	List Price ▼	Value ▼		Ⓓ
2	Chai	Beverages	25	25	$13.50	$18.00	$337.50		
3	Syrup	Confections	0	50	$7.50	$10.00	$375.00		
4	Cajun Seasoning	Confections	0	0	$16.50	$22.00	$0.00		
5	Olive Oil	Condiments	0	15	$16.01	$21.35	$240.19		
6	Boysenberry Spread	Condiments	0	0	$18.75	$25.00	$0.00		
7	Dried Pears	Fruits	0	0	$22.50	$30.00	$0.00		
8	Curry Sauce	Sauces/Soups	0	0	$30.00	$40.00	$0.00		
9	Walnuts	Produce	0	40	$17.44	$23.25	$697.50		
10	Fruit Cocktail	Produce	0	0	$29.25	$39.00	$0.00		
11	Chocolate Biscuits Mix	Confections	0	0	$6.90	$9.20	$0.00		
12	Marmalade	Condiments	0	0	$60.75	$81.00	$0.00		
13	Scones	Grains/Cereals	0	0	$7.50	$10.00	$0.00		
14	Beer	Beverages	33	33	$10.50	$14.00	$341.50		

TIP

When should I use a table?

If you need to identify common information, such as the largest value in a range, or you need to select records that match a criterion, use a table. Tables make ranges easy to navigate. When you press **Tab** with the cell pointer in a table, the cell pointer stays in the table, moving directly to the next cell and to the next table row when you tab from the last column. When you scroll down a table so that the header row disappears, Excel replaces the column letters with the labels that appear in the header row.

Filter or Sort Table Information

When you create a table, Excel automatically adds AutoFilter arrows to each column; you can use these arrows to quickly and easily filter and sort the information in the table.

When you filter a table, you display only those rows that meet conditions you specify, and you specify those conditions by making selections from the AutoFilter lists. You can also use the AutoFilter arrows to sort information in a variety of ways. Excel recognizes the type of data stored in table columns and offers you sorting choices that are appropriate for the type of data.

Filter or Sort Table Information

Filter a Table

① Click ▼ next to the column heading you want to use for filtering.

Ⓐ Excel displays a list of the unique values in the selected column.

② To exclude all instances of a particular value, deselect that value's check box (☑ changes to ☐).

③ To include all instances of a particular value, select that value's check box (☐ changes to ☑).

④ Repeat steps 2 and 3 until you have selected all the filters you want to use.

⑤ Click **OK**.

Ⓑ Excel displays only the data meeting the criteria you selected in step 2.

Ⓒ The AutoFilter ▼ changes to ◥ to indicate the data in the column is filtered.

Ⓓ To clear the filter, click **Data** and then click **Clear** (🔽).

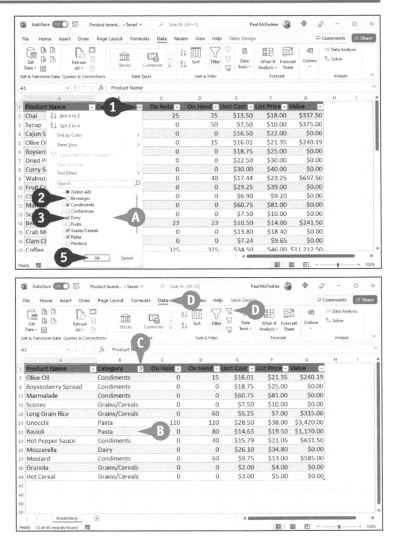

Sort a Table

1 Click ▼ next to the column heading you want to use for sorting

E Excel displays a list of possible sort orders.

2 Click a sort order.

This example sorts from largest to smallest.

F Excel re-orders the information.

G ▼ changes to ⊞ to indicate the data in the column is sorted.

Note: You cannot clear a sort the way you can a filter. To remove a sort, you can click **Home** and then click **Undo** ↺.

How does the Sort by Color option work?

If you apply font colors, cell colors, or both to some cells in the table, you can then sort the table information by the colors you assigned. You can manually assign colors, or you can assign colors using conditional formatting; see Chapter 9 for details on using conditional formatting.

I do not see the AutoFilter down arrow beside my table headings. What should I do?

Click inside the table, click the **Data** tab, and then click **Filter**. This button toggles on and off the table's AutoFilter buttons.

Analyze Data Quickly

You can easily analyze data in a variety of ways using the Quick Analysis button. You can apply various types of conditional formatting; create different types of charts, including line and column charts; or add miniature graphs called *sparklines* (see Chapter 12 for details on sparkline charts). You can also sum, average, and count occurrences of data as well as calculate percent of total and running total values. In addition, you can apply a table style and create a variety of different PivotTables.

The choices displayed in each analysis category are not always the same; the ones you see depend on the type of data you select.

Analyze Data Quickly

1 Select a range of data to analyze.

A The Quick Analysis button (⊞) appears.

2 Click the **Quick Analysis** button (⊞).

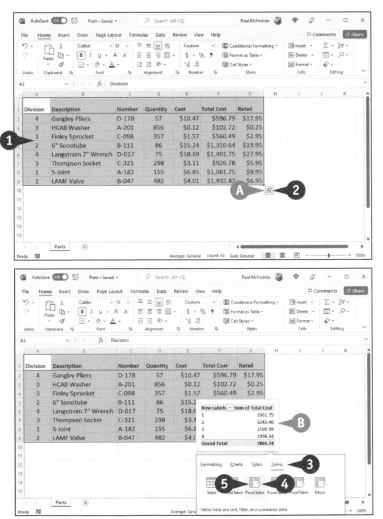

Quick Analysis categories appear.

3 Click each category heading to view the options for that category.

4 Point the mouse (⤢) at a choice under a category.

B A preview of that analysis choice appears.

Note: For an explanation of the Quick Analysis choices, see the next section, "Understanding Data Analysis Choices."

5 When you find the analysis choice you want to use, click it and Excel creates it.

Understanding Data Analysis Choices

The Quick Analysis button () offers a variety of ways to analyze selected data. This section provides an overview of the analysis categories and the choices offered in each category.

Formatting

Use formatting to highlight parts of your data. With formatting, you can add data bars, color scales, and icon sets. You can also highlight values that exceed a specified number and cells that contain specified text.

Formatting	Charts	Totals	Tables	Sparklines

Data Bars Color... Icon Set Greater... Text... Clear...

Conditional Formatting uses rules to highlight interesting data.

Charts

Pictures often get your point across better than raw numbers. You can quickly chart your data; Excel recommends different chart types, based on the data you select. If you do not see the chart type you want to create, you can click **More**.

Formatting	Charts	Totals	Tables	Sparklines

Clustere... Clustere... Clustere... Stacked... Stacked... More...

Recommended Charts help you visualize data.

Totals

Using the options in the Totals category, you can easily calculate sums — of both rows and columns — as well as averages, percent of total, and the number of occurrences of the values in the range. You can also insert a running total that grows as you add items to your data.

Formatting	Charts	Totals	Tables	Sparklines

Sum Average Count % Total Running... Sum

Formulas automatically calculate totals for you.

Tables

Using the choices under the Tables category, you can convert a range to a table, making it easy to filter and sort your data. You can also quickly and easily create a variety of PivotTables — Excel suggests PivotTables you might want to consider and then creates any you might choose.

Formatting	Charts	Totals	Tables	Sparklines

Table PivotTable PivotTable PivotTable PivotTable More

Tables help you sort, filter, and summarize data.

Sparklines

Sparklines are tiny charts that you can display beside your data that provide trend information for selected data. See Chapter 12 for more information on sparkline charts.

Formatting	Charts	Totals	Tables	Sparklines

Line Column Win/Loss

Sparklines are mini charts placed in single cells.

Insert a Note

You can add notes to your worksheets. You might add a note to make a comment or reminder to yourself about a particular cell's contents, or you might include a note for other users to see. For example, if you share your workbooks with other users, you can use notes to leave feedback about the data without typing directly in the worksheet.

When you add a note to a cell, Excel displays a small red triangle in the upper-right corner of the cell until you choose to view it. Notes you add are identified with your username.

Insert a Note

Add a Note

1. Click the cell to which you want to add a note.

2. Click **Review**.

3. Click **Notes**.

4. Click **New Note**.

   You can also right-click the cell and choose **Insert Note**.

A note balloon appears.

5. Type your note text.

6 Click anywhere outside the note balloon to deselect the note.

A Cells that contain notes display a tiny red triangle in the upper-right corner.

View a Note

1 Position the mouse (✥) over a cell containing a note.

B The note balloon appears, displaying the note.

How do I view all the notes in a worksheet?
If a worksheet contains several notes, you can view them one after another by clicking **Review**, then **Notes**, and then **Next Note** or **Previous Note**. Alternatively, display all notes simultaneously by clicking the **Show All Notes** button.

How do I remove a note?
To remove a note, right-click the cell containing the note and choose **Delete Note** from the shortcut menu that appears.

Understanding Formulas

You can use formulas, which you build using mathematical operators, values, and cell references, to perform all kinds of calculations on your Excel data. For example, you can add the contents of a column of monthly sales totals to determine the cumulative sales total. If you are new to writing formulas, this section explains the basics of building your own formulas in Excel. You learn about the correct way to structure formulas in Excel, how to reference cell data in your formulas, which mathematical operators are available for your use, and more.

Formula Structure

Ordinarily, when you write a mathematical formula, you write the values and the operators, followed by an equal sign, such as 2+2=. In Excel, formula structure works a bit differently. All Excel formulas begin with an equal sign (=), such as =2+2. The equal sign tells Excel to recognize any subsequent characters you enter as a formula rather than as a regular cell entry.

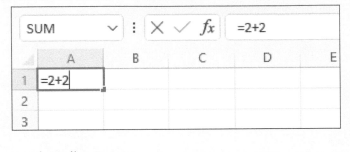

Reference a Cell

Every cell in a worksheet has a unique address, composed of the cell's column letter and row number, and that address appears in the Name box to the left of the Formula bar. Cell B3, for example, identifies the third cell down in column B. Although you can enter specific values in your Excel formulas, you can make your formulas more versatile if you include — that is, *reference* — a cell address rather than the value in that cell. Then, if the data in the cell changes but the formula remains the same, Excel automatically updates the result of the formula.

Cell Ranges

A group of related cells in a worksheet is called a *range*. You specify a range using the cells in the upper-left and lower-right corners of the range, separated by a colon. For example, range A1:B3 includes cells A1, A2, A3, B1, B2, and B3. You can also assign names to ranges to make it easier to identify their contents. Range names must start with a letter, underscore, or backslash, and can include uppercase and lowercase letters. Spaces are not allowed.

Mathematical Operators

You use mathematical operators in Excel to build formulas. Basic operators include the following:

Operator	Operation
+	Addition
-	Subtraction
*	Multiplication
/	Division
%	Percentage
^	Exponentiation

Operator	Operation
=	Equal to
<	Less than
<=	Less than or equal to
>	Greater than
>=	Greater than or equal to
<>	Not equal to

Operator Precedence

Excel performs operations in a formula from left to right, but gives some operators precedence over others, following the rules you learned in high school math:

Order	Operation
First	All operations enclosed in parentheses
Second	Exponential operations
Third	Multiplication and division
Fourth	Addition and subtraction

When you are creating equations, the order of operations determines the results. For example, suppose you want to determine the average of values in cells A2, B2, and C2. If you enter the equation =A2+B2+C2/3, Excel first divides the value in cell C2 by 3 and then adds that result to A2+B2 — producing the wrong answer. The correct way to write the formula is =(A2+B2+C2)/3. By enclosing the values in parentheses, you are telling Excel to perform the addition operations in the parentheses before dividing the sum by 3.

Reference Operators

You can use Excel's reference operators to control how a formula groups cells and ranges to perform calculations. For example, if your formula needs to include the cell range D2:D10 and cell E10, you can instruct Excel to evaluate all the data contained in these cells using a reference operator. Your formula might look like this: =SUM(D2:D10,E10).

Operator	Example	Operation
:	=SUM(D3:E12)	Range operator. Evaluates the reference as a single reference, including all the cells in the range from both corners of the reference.
,	=SUM(D3:E12,F3)	Union operator. Evaluates the two references as a single reference.
[space]	=SUM(D3:D20 D10:E15)	Intersect operator. Evaluates the cells common to both references.
[space]	=SUM(Totals Sales)	Intersect operator. Evaluates the intersecting cell or cells of the column labeled Totals and the row labeled Sales.

Create a Formula

You can write a formula to perform a calculation on data in your worksheet. In Excel, all formulas begin with an equal sign (=) and contain the values or references to the cells that contain the relevant values. For example, the formula for multiplying the contents of cells D2 and E2 together is =D2*E2. Formulas appear in the Formula bar; formula results appear in the cell to which you assign a formula.

Note that, in addition to referring to cells in the current worksheet, you can build formulas that refer to cells in other worksheets.

Create a Formula

1 Click the cell where you want to place a formula.

2 Type =.

A Excel displays the formula in the Formula bar and in the active cell.

3 Click the first cell that you want to include in the formula.

B Excel inserts the cell reference into the formula.

4 Type an operator for the formula.

5 Click the next cell that you want to include in the formula.

C Excel inserts the cell reference into the formula.

6 Repeat steps **4** and **5** until all the necessary cells and operators have been added.

7 Press Enter.

D You can also click the **Enter** button (✓) on the Formula bar to accept the formula.

E You can click the **Cancel** button (✕) to cancel the formula.

F The result of the formula appears in the cell.

G The formula appears in the Formula bar; you can view it by clicking the cell containing the formula.

Note: If you change a value in a cell referenced in your formula, Excel automatically updates the formula result to reflect the change.

TIPS

How do I edit a formula?
To edit a formula, click in the cell containing the formula and make any corrections in the Formula bar. Alternatively, double-click in the cell to make edits to the formula from within the cell. When finished, press Enter or click the **Enter** button (✓) on the Formula bar.

How do I reference cells in other worksheets?
To reference a cell in another worksheet, specify the worksheet name followed by an exclamation mark and then the cell address (for example, Sheet2!D12 or Sales!D12). If the worksheet name includes spaces, enclose the sheet name in single quote marks, as in 'Sales Totals'!D12.

Apply Absolute and Relative Cell References

By default, Excel uses relative cell referencing. If you copy a formula containing a relative cell reference to a new location, Excel adjusts the cell addresses in that formula to refer to the cells at the formula's new location. In cell B8, if you enter the formula =B5+B6 and then copy that formula to cell C8, Excel adjusts the formula to =C5+C6.

When a formula must always refer to the value in a particular cell, use an absolute cell reference. Absolute references are preceded with dollar signs. If your formula must always refer to the value in cell D2, enter **$D$2** in the formula.

Apply Absolute and Relative Cell References

Copy Relative References

1. Click the cell containing the formula you want to copy.

   Ⓐ In the Formula bar, the formula appears with a relative cell reference.

2. Click **Home**.

3. Click **Copy** (📋).

4. Select the cells where you want the formula to appear.

5. Click **Paste** (📋).

   Ⓑ Excel copies the formula to the selected cells.

   Ⓒ The adjusted formula appears in the Formula bar and in the selected cells.

Note: You can press Esc to stop copying.

Copy Absolute References

1 Enter the formula, including dollar signs ($) for absolute addresses as needed.

2 Click the cell containing the formula you want to copy.

D In the Formula bar, the formula appears with an absolute cell reference.

3 Click **Home**.

4 Click **Copy** (📋).

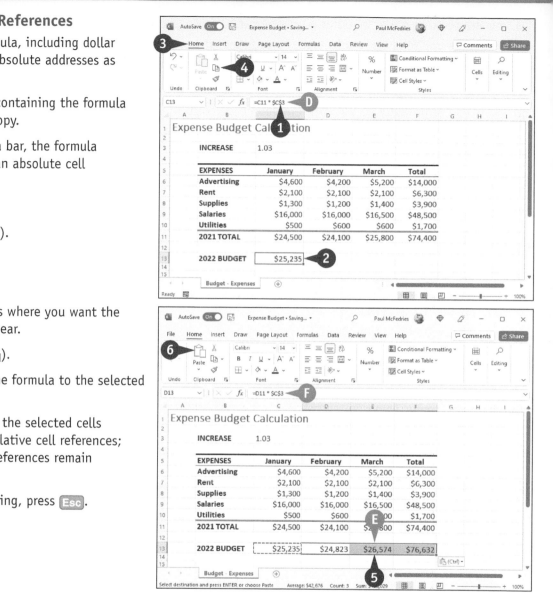

5 Select the cells where you want the formula to appear.

6 Click **Paste** (📋).

E Excel copies the formula to the selected cells.

F The formula in the selected cells adjusts only relative cell references; absolute cell references remain unchanged.

Note: To stop copying, press Esc.

When would I use absolute cell referencing?

Use absolute cell referencing to always refer to the same cell in a worksheet. For example, suppose your worksheet contains pricing information that refers to a discount rate in cell G10. When you create a formula that involves the discount rate, that formula must always reference cell G10, even if you move or copy the formula to another cell. In this case, use $G$10. You can also combine absolute and relative references, creating *mixed references* that allow either the row or column to change while the other remains static if you copy the formula.

Understanding Functions

If you are looking for a speedier way to enter formulas, you can use any one of a wide variety of functions. *Functions* are ready-made formulas that perform a series of operations on a specified set of values. Excel offers more than 400 functions, grouped into 13 categories, that you can use to perform various types of calculations.

Functions use arguments to identify the cells that contain the data you want to use in your calculations. Function arguments can refer to individual cells or to ranges of cells. This section explains the basics of working with functions.

Using Functions

Functions are distinct in that each one has a unique name. For example, the function that adds values is called SUM, and the function for averaging values is called AVERAGE. You use functions as part of your worksheet formulas. You can insert a function by typing the function name and arguments directly into your formula; alternatively, you can use the Insert Function dialog box to select and apply functions to your data.

Construct an Argument

Functions use *arguments* to indicate which values you want to calculate. Arguments can be numbers, cell or range references, range names, or even other functions. Arguments are enclosed in parentheses after the function name. For functions that require multiple arguments, you use a comma to separate the values, as in =AVERAGE(A5,C5,F5). If your range has a name, you can insert the name, as in =AVERAGE(Sales).

Types of Functions

Excel groups functions into 13 categories, not including functions installed with Excel add-in programs:

Category	Description
Financial	Includes functions for calculating loans, principal, interest, yield, and depreciation.
Date & Time	Includes functions for calculating dates, times, and minutes.
Math & Trig	Includes a wide variety of functions for calculations of all types.
Statistical	Includes functions for calculating averages, probabilities, rankings, trends, and more.
Lookup & Reference	Includes functions that enable you to locate references or specific values in your worksheets.
Database	Includes functions for counting, adding, and filtering database items.
Text	Includes text-based functions to search and replace data and other text tasks.
Logical	Includes functions for logical conjectures, such as if-then statements.
Information	Includes functions for testing your data.
Engineering	Offers many kinds of functions for engineering calculations.
Cube	Enables Excel to fetch data from SQL Server Analysis Services, such as members, sets, aggregated values, properties, and key performance indicators (KPIs).
Compatibility	Use these functions to keep your workbook compatible with earlier versions of Excel.
Web	Use these functions when you work with web pages, services, or XML content.

Common Functions

The following table lists some of the more popular Excel functions that you might use with your own spreadsheet work.

Function	Category	Description	Syntax
SUM	Math & Trig	Adds values	=SUM(number1, number2, . . .)
ROUND	Math & Trig	Rounds a number to a specified number of digits	=ROUND(number, number_digits)
ROUNDDOWN	Math & Trig	Rounds a number down	=ROUNDDOWN(number, number_digits)
INT	Math & Trig	Rounds down to the nearest integer	=INT(number)
COUNT	Statistical	Counts the number of cells in a range that contain data	=COUNT(value1, value2, . . .)
AVERAGE	Statistical	Averages a series of arguments	=AVERAGE(number1, number2, . . .)
MIN	Statistical	Returns the smallest value in a series	=MIN(number1, number2, . . .)
MAX	Statistical	Returns the largest value in a series	=MAX(number1, number2, . . .)
MEDIAN	Statistical	Returns the middle value in a series	=MEDIAN(number1, number2, . . .)
PMT	Financial	Finds the periodic payment for a fixed loan	=PMT(interest_rate, number_of_periods, present_value, future_value, type)
RATE	Financial	Returns an interest rate	=RATE(number_of_periods, payment, present_value, future_value, type, guess)
TODAY	Date & Time	Returns the current date	=TODAY()
IF	Logical	Returns one of two results that you specify based on whether the value is true or false	=IF(logical_text, value_if_true, value_if_false)
AND	Logical	Returns true if all the arguments are true, and false if any argument is false	=AND(logical1, logical2, . . .)
OR	Logical	Returns true if any argument is true, and false if all arguments are false	=OR(logical1, logical2, . . .)

Insert a Function

Although you can insert functions directly into your formulas, it is often easier and more accurate to use the Insert Function feature. This feature enables you to look for a particular function from among Excel's 400-plus available functions and to guide you through successfully entering the function. After you select your function, the Function Arguments dialog box opens to help you build the formula by describing the arguments you need for the function you chose. Functions use arguments to identify the cells that contain the data you want to use in your calculation.

Insert a Function

1 Enter your formula up to the point where you want to insert the function.

Note: If you are using the function by itself, then you only need to enter the equal sign (=).

2 Click **Formulas**.

3 Click **Insert Function**.

Ⓐ Alternatively, click **Insert Function** (*fx*) on the Formula bar.

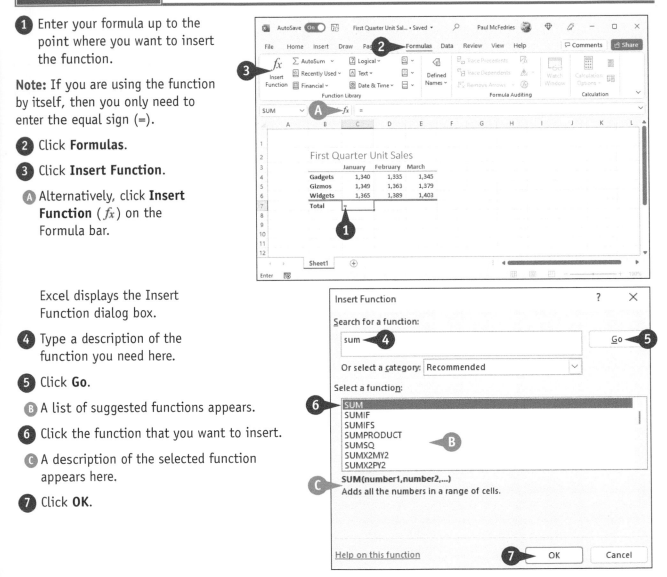

Excel displays the Insert Function dialog box.

4 Type a description of the function you need here.

5 Click **Go**.

Ⓑ A list of suggested functions appears.

6 Click the function that you want to insert.

Ⓒ A description of the selected function appears here.

7 Click **OK**.

The Function Arguments dialog box appears.

8 In the worksheet, select the cell or range for the first argument required by the function.

D Excel adds the cell or range address as the argument to the function.

9 Repeat step **8** as needed.

E When you have specified all the required arguments, Excel displays the function result here.

10 When you finish specifying the arguments, click **OK**.

F Excel displays the function results in the cell.

G The function appears in the Formula bar.

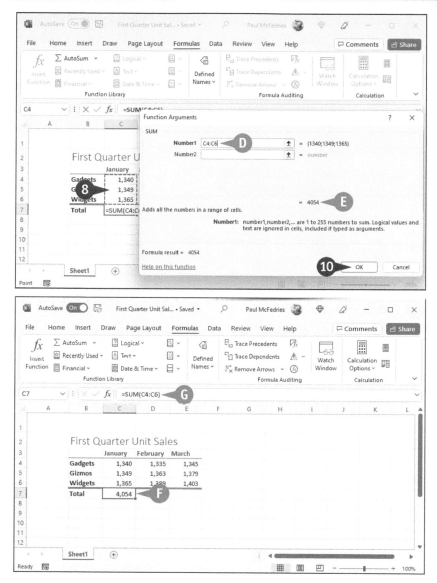

Can I edit a function?

Yes. Click the cell containing the function, click the **Formulas** tab, and then click the **Insert Function** button. Excel displays the function's Function Arguments dialog box, where you can change the cell references or values as needed. You can also edit directly in the cell.

Do I need to specify a value for all the function's arguments?

Not necessarily. Most functions support two types of argument: required and optional. Required arguments, which appear in bold type in the Function Arguments dialog box, must be specified before the function will return a result. Optional arguments, which appear in regular type in the Function Arguments dialog box, can be omitted, and the function will still return a result.

Total Cells with AutoSum

One of the most popular Excel functions is AutoSum. AutoSum automatically totals the contents of selected cells. For example, you can quickly total a column of sales figures. One way to use AutoSum is to select a cell and let the function guess which surrounding cells you want to total. Alternatively, you can specify exactly which cells to sum.

In addition to using AutoSum to total cells, you can select a series of cells in your worksheet; Excel displays the total of the cells' contents in the status bar, along with the number of cells you selected and an average of their values.

Total Cells with AutoSum

Using AutoSum to Total Cells

1 Click the cell in which you want to store a total.

2 Click **Formulas**.

3 Click **AutoSum**.

Ⓐ If you click the **AutoSum** ▼, you can select other common functions, such as Average or Max.

You can also click the **AutoSum** button (∑) on the **Home** tab.

Ⓑ AutoSum generates a formula to total the adjacent cells.

4 Press **Enter** or click the **Enter** button (✓).

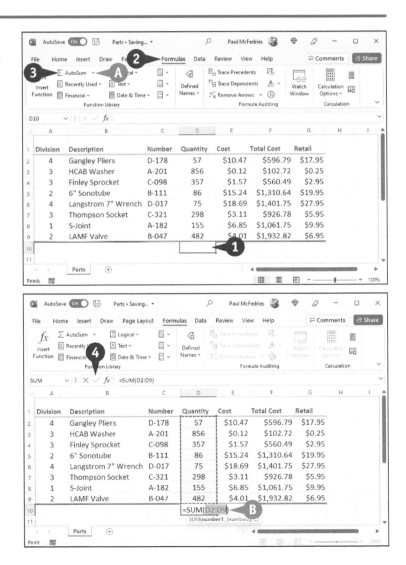

C Excel displays the result in the cell.

D You can click the cell to see the function in the Formula bar.

Total Cells Without Applying a Function

1 Select a range of cells whose values you want to total.

Note: To sum noncontiguous cells, click the first cell; then press and hold `Ctrl` while clicking the other cells.

E Excel sums the contents of the cells, displaying the total in the status bar.

F Excel also counts the number of cells you have selected.

G Excel also displays an average of the values in the selected cells.

TIPS

Can I select a different range of cells to sum?

Yes. AutoSum takes its best guess when determining which cells to total. If it guesses wrong, select the correct range of cells you want to add together before pressing `Enter` or clicking the **Enter** button ($\checkmark$).

Can I display any other calculations in the status bar?

Yes. Excel displays the Sum, Count, and Average by default, but there are three other calculations you can display: Minimum (the lowest value in the range), Maximum (the highest value in the range), and Numerical Count (the count of the cells that contain numeric values). To display any of these calculations, right-click the status bar and then click the calculation you want.

Create a Chart

You can quickly convert your spreadsheet data into easy-to-read charts. You can create column, line, pie, bar, area, scatter, stock, surface, doughnut, bubble, and radar charts. Excel even recommends the type of chart that works best for your data. If you do not like Excel's recommendations, you can select the chart of your choice.

You can create charts using the Ribbon or using the Quick Analysis button. After you create a chart, you can use buttons beside the chart or on the Chart Design and Format contextual tabs to fine-tune the chart to best display and explain the data.

Create a Chart

Using the Ribbon

1 Select the range of data that you want to chart.

You can include any headings and labels, but do not include subtotals or totals.

2 Click **Insert**.

3 Click **Recommended Charts**.

The Insert Chart dialog box appears.

A A preview of your data appears in the selected chart type.

B If you do not see the chart you want to use, click **All Charts**.

4 Click a chart type.

5 Click **OK**.

C Excel creates a chart and places it in the worksheet.

D Whenever you select the chart, Chart Tools tabs appear on the Ribbon.

E You can use the **Chart Elements** (⊞), **Chart Styles** (✎), and **Chart Filters** (▽) buttons to add chart elements such as axis titles, customize the look of your chart, or change the data in the chart.

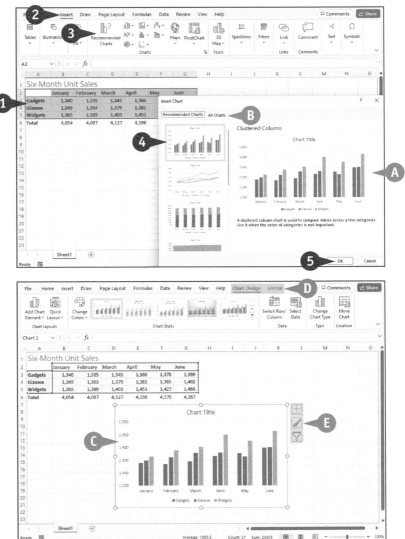

Using the Quick Analysis Button

1 Select the range of data that you want to chart.

You can include any headings and labels, but do not include subtotals or totals.

2 Click the **Quick Analysis** button (📋).

3 From the categories that appear, click **Charts**.

4 Slide the mouse ↳ over a recommended chart type.

F Excel displays a preview of your data using that chart type.

G If you do not see the chart you want to use, click **More**.

5 Click a chart type to insert it.

Excel inserts the chart type you selected.

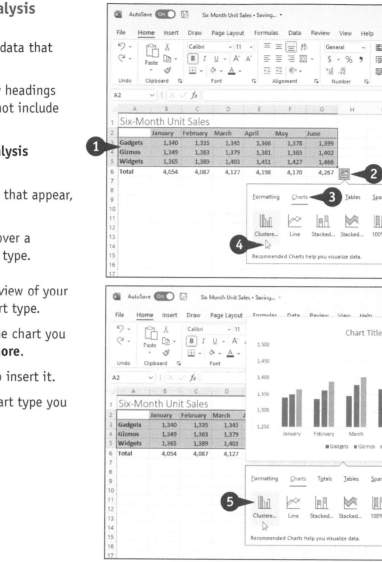

Can I select noncontiguous data to include in a chart?

Yes. To select noncontiguous cells and ranges, select the first cell or range and then press and hold Ctrl while selecting additional cells and ranges.

In my column chart, I want bars for the elements appearing in the legend; is there an easy way to make that happen?

Yes. The legend displays the row headings in your selected data, whereas the bars represent the column headings. So, you should switch the rows and columns in the chart. Click the chart to select it. Then, click the **Chart Design** contextual tab and, in the Data group, click **Switch Row/Column**.

Move and Resize Charts

After creating a chart, you may decide that it would look better if it were a different size or located elsewhere on the worksheet. For example, you may want to reposition the chart at the bottom of the worksheet or make the chart larger so it is easier to read.

Moving or resizing a chart is like moving or resizing any other type of Office object. When you select a chart, handles appear around that chart; you use these handles to make the chart larger or smaller. Moving the chart is a matter of selecting it and then dragging it to the desired location.

Move and Resize Charts

Resize a Chart

1 Click any edge of the chart.

A Excel selects the chart and surrounds it with handles.

B ⊞, ✐, and ▽ appear.

2 Position the mouse pointer over a (↖ changes to ⬂, ↕, ⬈, or ⬌).

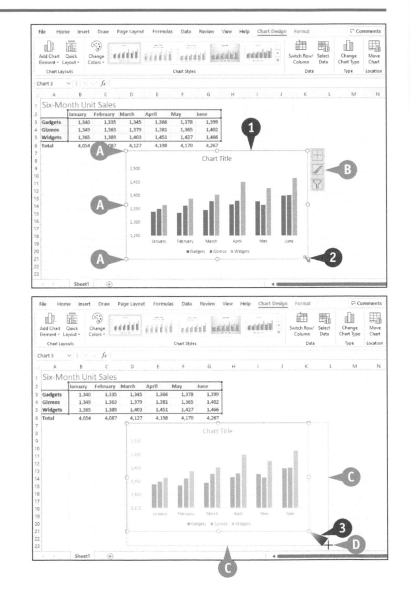

3 Click and drag a handle to resize the chart.

C A frame appears, representing the chart as you resize it on the worksheet.

D ⬂, ↕, ⬈, or ⬌ changes to +.

4 Release the mouse button.

Excel resizes the chart.

Move a Chart

1 Click any edge of the chart.

E Excel selects the chart and surrounds it with handles.

F ⊞, ✎, and ▽ appear.

2 Position the mouse pointer over an empty area of the chart (✛ changes to ⬚).

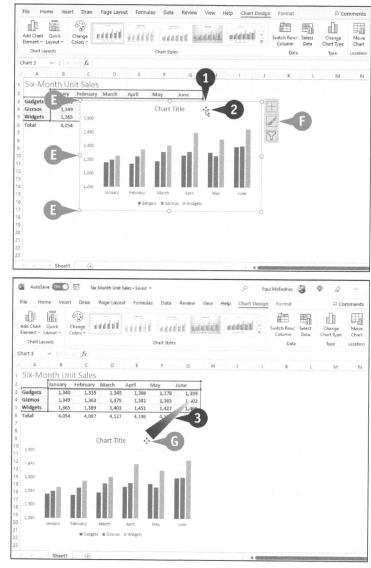

3 Click and drag the chart to a new location on the worksheet.

G ⬚ changes to ✛, and ⊞, ✎, and ▽ disappear.

4 Release the mouse button.

Excel moves the chart.

TIP

Can I delete a chart or move it to its own worksheet?

Yes. To delete a chart, click its edge and press Delete. To move a chart to its own worksheet, click its edge, click **Chart Design**, and click **Move Chart** to display the Move Chart dialog box. Select **New sheet** (A) (○ changes to ◉) and click **OK**. Excel adds a new worksheet called Chart1 to the workbook and places the chart in that worksheet.

Change the Chart Type

Excel makes it easy to change the chart type. When you create a chart, Excel recommends chart types that are suitable for your data, but you are not limited to the chart type you choose. For example, you might create a column chart but then realize your data would be better presented in a line chart.

You select a new chart type using the Chart Design contextual tab. To make this tab available, you select the chart. You click the edge of the chart to select the entire chart; you can select individual elements of the chart by clicking them. As long as you click anywhere inside the chart, the Chart Design tab appears on the Ribbon.

Change the Chart Type

1 Click an edge of the chart to select it.

A Handles surround the chart.

2 Click **Chart Design**.

3 Click **Change Chart Type**.

The Change Chart Type dialog box appears.

B To view Excel's recommendations for chart types for your data, click this tab.

4 Click a chart type.

5 Click a chart variation.

C A preview of your chart appears here; point the mouse at the preview to enlarge it.

6 Click **OK**.

D Excel changes the chart to the chart type that you selected.

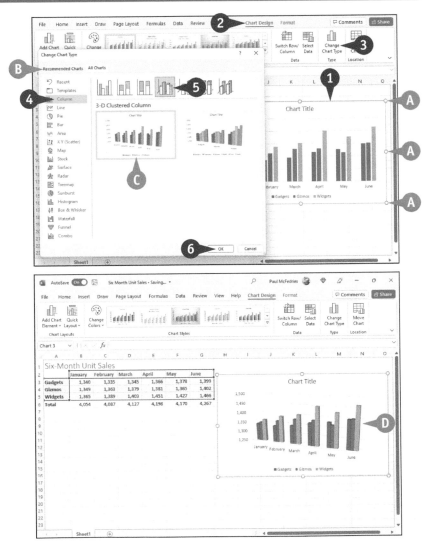

Change the Chart Style

You can change the chart style to enhance the appearance of a chart. You can choose from a wide variety of preset styles to find just the look you want. For example, you might prefer a brighter color scheme for the chart to make it stand out.

You can access various preset chart styles from the Chart Design tab or from the Chart Styles button that appears along the right edge of a selected chart. To select a chart, click along its edge.

Change the Chart Style

1 Click an edge of the chart to select it.

2 Click the **Chart Styles** button (✐).

Ⓐ The Chart Styles pane appears.

3 Click **Style** to view available chart styles.

Ⓑ You can click ▲ and ▼ to scroll through available styles.

You can point the mouse at a style to preview it.

4 Click a new style.

Ⓒ You can also click **Chart Design** and then click a style in the **Chart Styles** gallery.

Excel applies the new style to your chart.

5 Click **Color** to view color schemes for your chart.

6 Click a color scheme.

Ⓓ Excel applies the new color scheme to your chart.

Ⓔ You can also click **Chart Design** and then click a style in the **Change Colors** gallery.

Ⓕ You can click the **Chart Styles** button (✐) again to close the Chart Styles pane.

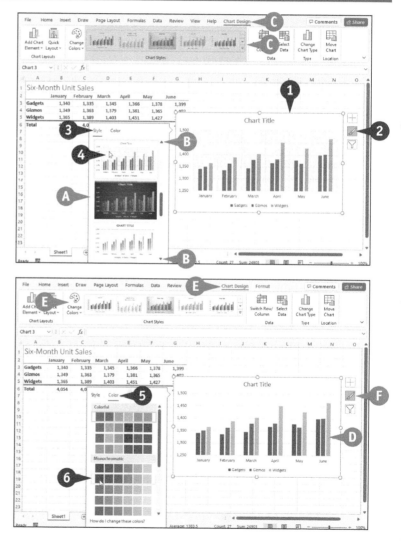

Change the Chart Layout

You can customize your chart's appearance by applying one of Excel's preset chart layout options. The chart layout determines how Excel positions chart elements such as the title and legend. For example, many chart layouts include a legend that appears either to the right of or above or below the chart.

The main chart elements affected by most chart layouts are the chart title, legend (which identifies each chart data series), data table (a summary of the chart values), horizontal gridlines (lines across the chart that can make it easier to read the values), and axis titles.

Change the Chart Layout

1 Click an edge of the chart to select it.

2 Click **Chart Design**.

3 Click **Quick Layout**.

A A gallery of layouts appears.

You can point the mouse at each layout to preview its appearance.

4 Click a layout.

B Excel applies the new layout to the chart.

C You can right-click the chart title and then click **Edit Text** to change the default title.

D You can right-click an axis title and then click **Edit Text** to change the default title.

E In this layout, the legend appears to the right of the chart.

F This layout includes horizontal gridlines.

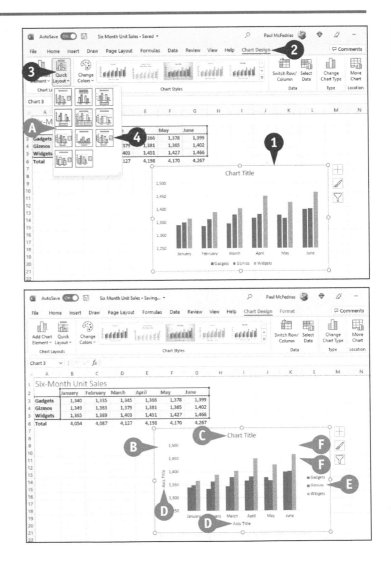

Add Chart Elements

You can add a variety of elements to your chart. For example, you can include or exclude axes, axis titles, a chart title, data labels, a data table, error bars, gridlines, a legend, and a trendline. Remember that displaying too many elements on a chart can make it hard to understand. This section shows you how to add axis titles; you use the same technique to add any chart element.

Add Chart Elements

1 Click an edge of the chart to select it.

2 Click the **Chart Elements** button (⊞).

Ⓐ The Chart Elements pane appears.

You can point the mouse at an element to preview it.

3 Click the element you want to add to the chart (☐ changes to ☑).

You can also click an existing element to remove it from the chart (☑ changes to ☐).

Ⓑ Alternatively, you can click **Chart Design** and then click **Add Chart Element**.

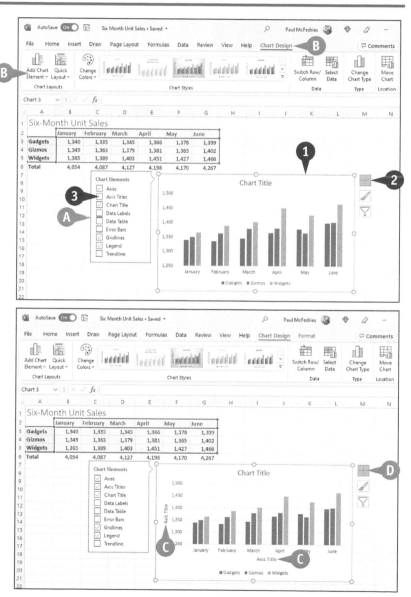

Ⓒ Excel applies the change to your chart.

Ⓓ You can click the **Chart Elements** button (⊞) again to close the Chart Elements pane.

Note: If you add any type of title, Excel inserts dummy text representing the title. You can replace the dummy text by right-clicking the title box and then clicking **Edit Text**. Then, type your replacement title.

Format Chart Elements

Y ou can change the formatting of any element in a chart, such as the background pattern for the plot area or the color of a data series. You use the Format pane to apply formatting to the selected element. The pane appears automatically when you format an element.

The available settings in the Format pane change, depending on the element you select. This section shows you how to add a fill color to the chart area, which is the area behind your data in the chart. You can apply these same techniques to format other chart elements.

Format Chart Elements

1 Click an edge of the chart to select it.

2 Click **Format**.

3 Click the **Chart Elements** ▼ and then click the chart element you want to format.

Note: You can also directly click the chart element that you want to format.

4 Click **Format Selection**.

A The Format *Element* task pane appears, where *Element* is the name of the element you selected in step **3**.

5 Click ▷ beside the type of formatting you want to apply.

B Excel displays the formatting controls.

6 Change any format settings.

C Excel displays the effect.

D You can click these icons to display more formatting controls (the icons you see vary depending on the element).

E For some elements, you can click **Text Options** to apply text formatting to the element.

7 Click **Close** (✕) to close the task pane.

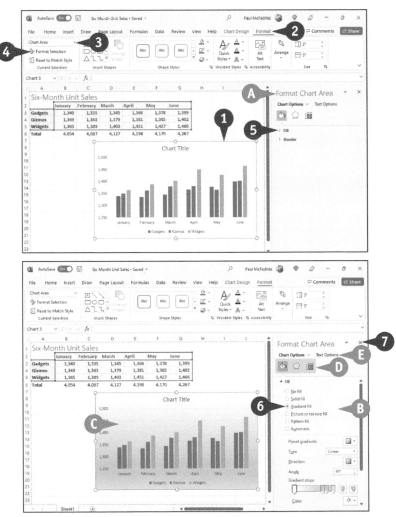

Change the Chart Data

You can work with subsets of your data by filtering the information displayed in your chart. Whenever you change the underlying data visualized by your chart, Excel automatically updates the chart to reflect your changes. But suppose that your chart shows several months of sales data for several products and you want to focus on one product only. There is no need to create a new chart because you can filter your existing chart to show just the data you need. When you are ready, you can quickly redisplay all data in your chart.

Change the Chart Data

1 Click an edge of the chart that you want to change to select it.

2 Click the **Chart Filters** (🔽).

Ⓐ The Filter pane appears.

3 Click a series or category that you want to remove (☑ changes to ☐).

4 Repeat step **3** as necessary to remove additional series or categories.

5 Click **Apply**.

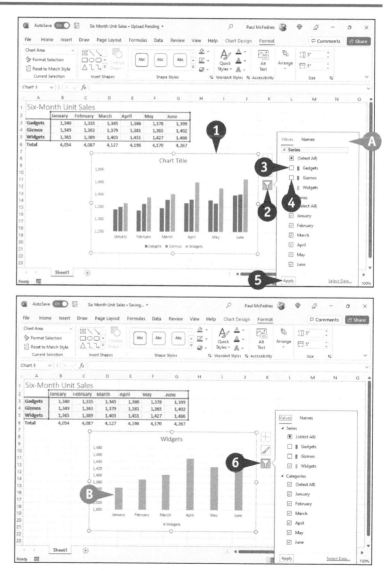

Ⓑ Excel applies the change to your chart.

6 Click the **Chart Filters** button (🔽) again to close the Filter pane.

Using Sparklines to View Data Trends

You can place a micro-chart of data in a single cell in your worksheet. Excel refers to these micro-charts as *sparkline* charts.

You can create three types of sparkline charts: line, column, or win/loss. All three show you, at a glance, trend information for a range of data you select. Excel places a sparkline chart in the cell immediately to the right of the row of cells you use to create the chart. Excel offers several styles that you can apply to your sparklines.

Using Sparklines to View Data Trends

Insert a Sparkline

1. Select the row of cells containing the data you want to include in the sparkline chart.

Note: To avoid having to move the sparkline chart, make sure an empty cell appears to the right of the cells you intend to chart.

2. Click the **Quick Analysis** button (▦).

3. Click **Sparklines**.

4. Click the type of sparkline chart you want to insert.

This example creates a line sparkline chart.

Ⓐ Excel inserts the sparkline chart in the cell to the right of the selected cells.

Ⓑ The Sparkline contextual tab appears.

5. Repeat steps 1 to 4 to add sparklines for the rest of your data.

Ⓒ Alternatively, you can drag the Fill handle down to create a sparkline group. See the upcoming tip for more about sparkline groups.

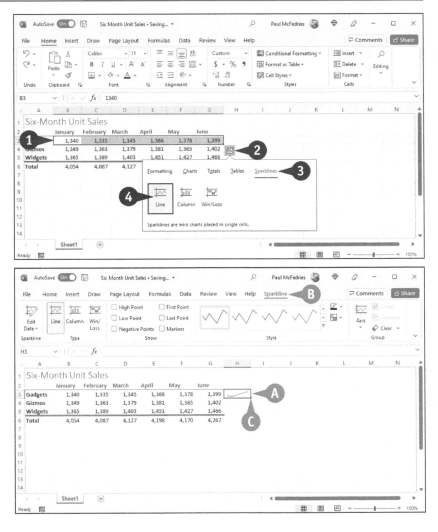

Apply a Sparkline Style

1 Click the cell containing a sparkline that you want to style.

2 Click **Sparkline**.

3 Use the **Style** gallery to select the style you want to apply to the sparkline.

D You can click **More** (▼) to display the full Style gallery.

E Excel applies the style to the sparkline.

Note: To delete a sparkline chart, right-click it and then click **Sparklines**. Click either **Clear Selected Sparklines** or **Clear Selected Sparkline Groups**.

TIPS

Can I create multiple sparklines simultaneously?
Yes. You can select data on multiple rows; Excel creates a sparkline for each row and treats the sparklines as a group. For example, if you change the chart type of one sparkline, Excel changes the chart type for the entire group.

How can I change the chart type of a sparkline?
Click the cell containing the sparkline and then click the **Sparkline** contextual tab. In the Type group, click the sparkline chart type you want to use.

Understanding PivotTables

A PivotTable provides an easy way to summarize information stored in a range, a table, or an external data source. Using a PivotTable helps you make sense of even massive amounts of Excel data in a variety of meaningful ways.

Suppose your worksheet contains sales information by day for products sold during a promotion. The worksheet tracks the date of the sale, the quantity and dollar amount sold, the type of product, which promotion generated the sale, and which type of advertisement made the customer aware of the promotion.

The Native View

Just viewing the worksheet in its native form would not help you analyze any of the information. For example, you could not determine total sales for the month for any individual type of promotion.

Nor could you determine which product sold the most units. Nor could you identify which advertisement generated the most sales.

	A	B	C	D	E	F
1	SUMMER SALES PROMOTION - ORDERS					
2	Date	Product	Quantity	Net $	Promotion	Advertisement
3	6/1/2022	Smartphone case	11	$119.70	1 Free with 10	Social media
4	6/1/2022	HDMI cable	6	$77.82	Extra Discount	Blog network
5	6/1/2022	USB car charger	15	$100.95	Extra Discount	Search
6	6/1/2022	HDMI cable	11	$149.71	1 Free with 10	Blog network
7	6/2/2022	USB car charger	22	$155.40	1 Free with 10	Blog network
8	6/2/2022	USB car charger	3	$20.19	Extra Discount	Search
9	6/2/2022	Earbuds	5	$33.65	Extra Discount	Social media
10	6/2/2022	Smartphone case	22	$239.36	1 Free with 10	Search

PivotTables Make Analysis Easy

You could spend time sorting and filtering the data and setting up a series of formulas that would answer most of your questions, but a PivotTable provides answers much more quickly and easily. Creating a PivotTable takes only a few seconds, does not require any formulas, and displays the information in an attractive format. When you create a PivotTable, Excel automatically displays the PivotTable Fields task pane, which you use to modify the PivotTable.

	A	B	C
3	Row Labels	Sum of Quantity	
4	Earbuds	1439	
5	HDMI cable	1708	
6	Smartphone case	1344	
7	USB car charger	3360	
8	Grand Total	7851	

PivotTable Fields

Choose fields to add to report:

Search

☑ Product
☑ Quantity

Drag fields between areas below:

▼ Filters   ▥ Columns

≡ Rows   Σ Values
Product   Sum of Quantity

☐ Defer Layout Update   Update

The term *pivot* means "to rotate." In the case of a PivotTable, you rotate your data to examine it from a variety of perspectives. You can easily move fields around to view information in many different ways. As a result, a PivotTable is really not static; it changes as you pivot the fields in the table. You can place a PivotTable on the same worksheet that contains the underlying data, or you can place the PivotTable on its own worksheet.

Summarize and Filter PivotTable Information

In a PivotTable, Excel automatically summarizes the data by calculating a sum, but you are not limited to summarizing data that can be added. You can use a PivotTable to count the occurrences of a particular type of data. For example, you can identify the number of people who reside in a certain ZIP code. So, a PivotTable is useful not only to summarize numeric data but also to summarize text data.

You can filter information in a PivotTable. You can also use the data in a PivotTable to create a PivotChart — a chart based on the PivotTable information — that you can use to help you further analyze the data.

Understanding PivotTable Terms

You should be familiar with some terms in order to make working with PivotTables much easier.

An *item* is an element that appears as a row or column header. In the figure, Earbuds, HDMI cable, Smartphone case, and USB car charger are items in the Product field. The Promotion field has two items: 1 Free with 10 and Extra Discount.

Column labels refer to fields that have a column orientation in the PivotTable, each occupying a column. In the figure, Promotion represents a column field.

Grand totals appear below the rows in a PivotTable or to the right of the columns in a PivotTable, and they display totals for all the rows or columns in the PivotTable. You can choose to display grand totals for rows, columns, both, or neither. The PivotTable in the figure shows grand totals for both rows and columns.

Row labels refer to fields that have a row orientation in the PivotTable, each occupying a row. In the figure, Product represents a row field. You can also have nested row fields.

Source data are the data used to create a PivotTable. Source data can reside in a worksheet as a range, a table, or an external database.

Subtotals display subtotal amounts for rows or columns in a PivotTable. The PivotTable in the figure displays row subtotals for each location.

A *report filter* is a field that has a page orientation in the PivotTable. You can display only one item (or all items) in a report filter at one time. In the figure, Advertisement represents a filter field.

The *Values area* refers to an area of the PivotTable field list that displays the cells in the PivotTable that contain the summary data, and the way in which those cells are summarized in the PivotTable.

Create a PivotTable

You can more easily analyze a large amount of data by creating a PivotTable from that data. A PivotTable is a powerful data analysis tool because it automatically groups large amounts of data into smaller, more manageable categories, and it displays summary calculations for each group. You can also manipulate the layout of — or *pivot* — the PivotTable to see different views of your data.

Although you can create a PivotTable from a normal range, for best results, you should convert your range to a table before creating the PivotTable (see Chapter 10).

Create a PivotTable

1 Click inside the range or table of information you want to use to create a PivotTable.

2 Click **Insert**.

3 Click **PivotTable**.

Excel displays the PivotTable from Table or Range dialog box and guesses at the table or range to use to create the PivotTable.

In this example, Excel suggests using the table named Orders to create a PivotTable.

4 If Excel guesses incorrectly, click the **Range selector** button (⬆) to select the correct range or table.

5 Select a location for the PivotTable report (○ changes to ●).

This example places the PivotTable on a new worksheet.

6 Click **OK**.

A Excel displays a PivotTable skeleton.

B The PivotTable Analyze and Design contextual tabs appear on the Ribbon.

C The PivotTable Fields task pane appears on the right side of the window.

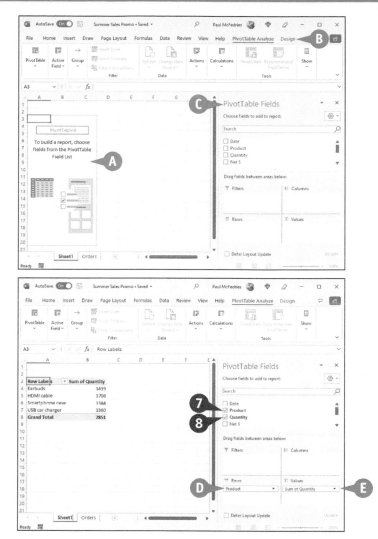

7 Select a field that contains text items (☐ changes to ☑).

D Excel adds the field to the Rows area.

8 Select a field that contains numeric items (☐ changes to ☑).

E Excel adds the field to the Values area.

Note: You can change the information that appears in the PivotTable by moving the fields around in the Areas section of the PivotTable Fields task pane.

TIPS

How do I add a field to the Columns area or to the Filters area of the PivotTable?

When you select the check box for a field that contains text items, Excel automatically adds that field to the Rows area. To add a field that contains text items to the Filters area or the Columns area, drag the field from the top part of the PivotTable Fields task pane and drop it inside either the **Filters** box or the **Columns** box.

How do I remove a field from a PivotTable area?

The easiest way to remove a field from the PivotTable is to click the field's check box in the PivotTable Fields task pane (☑ changes to ☐). Alternatively, drag the field from its area out of the PivotTable Fields task pane.

Create a PivotChart

You can use your PivotTable to create a chart that presents the data graphically. Charted information is often easier to understand than the numbers behind the chart. PivotChart behavior is much like the behavior of other charts in Excel: You choose the type of chart, and you can select a chart layout and a chart style.

If you make changes to the PivotTable data or organization, Excel automatically updates the PivotChart to reflect your changes. And, if you filter your PivotTable, as shown in this section, Excel reflects the filter dynamically in the PivotChart.

Create a PivotChart

Create a PivotChart

1. Click in the PivotTable.

2. Click **PivotTable Analyze**.

3. Click **PivotChart**.

   Excel displays the Insert Chart dialog box.

4. Click a chart type.

5. Click **OK**.

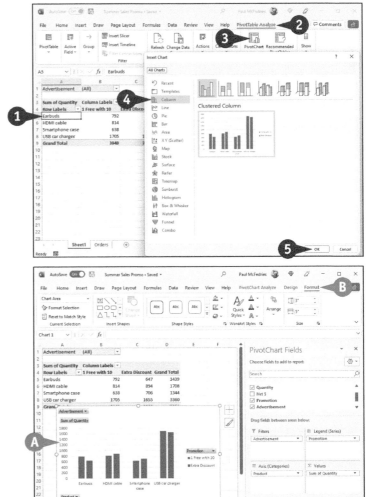

Ⓐ Excel displays a PivotChart.

Ⓑ The PivotChart Analyze, Design, and Format contextual tabs appear on the Ribbon as long as the PivotChart remains selected.

Filter the PivotChart

1 Click any of the buttons shown in the PivotChart.

2 Click **(Select All)** (☑ changes to ☐).

3 Click an item that you want to display (☐ changes to ☑).

4 Repeat step **3** as needed.

5 Click **OK**.

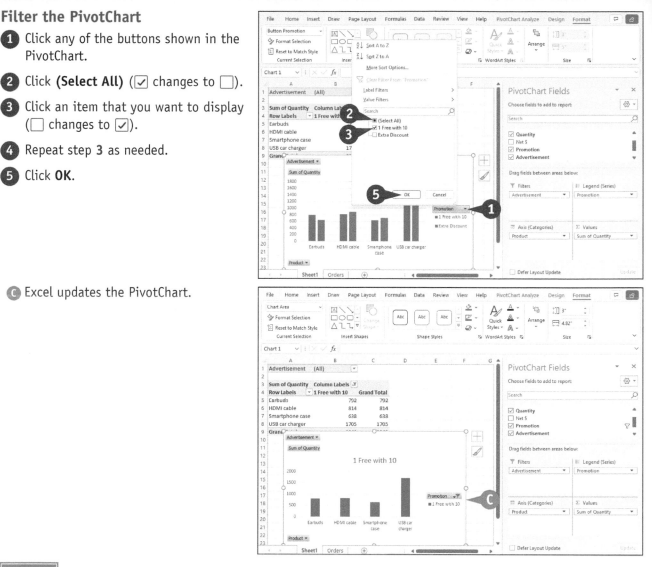

C Excel updates the PivotChart.

What happens if I create a PivotChart and then delete the PivotTable?

Although you must create a PivotChart from a PivotTable, you do not need to retain the PivotTable to retain the PivotChart. If you delete the PivotTable, Excel converts the PivotChart to a regular chart with associated chart tools and converts the chart's series formulas to data stored in arrays.

Is there a way to create a PivotChart that appears in a sheet separate from the PivotTable?

After you create a PivotChart, you can move it. Click the PivotChart to display PivotChart Tools on the Ribbon. Click the **PivotChart Analyze** tab and then click the **Move Chart** button and select **New Sheet**.

Insert a PivotTable Slicer

You can use a PivotTable Slicer to display "slices" of a PivotTable. A slicer is most useful to manipulate PivotTable data using a field that you do not display in the PivotTable.

Suppose your worksheet contains sales information from a promotion, including the date of each sale, the amount sold, the type of product, the promotion type the customer opted for, and the type of advertisement the custom responded to. Suppose that you do not want to display sales dates, but you want to limit the data to a particular date. In that case, use a slicer.

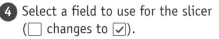

Insert a PivotTable Slicer

1 Click anywhere in the PivotTable.

2 Click **PivotTable Analyze**.

3 Click **Insert Slicer**.

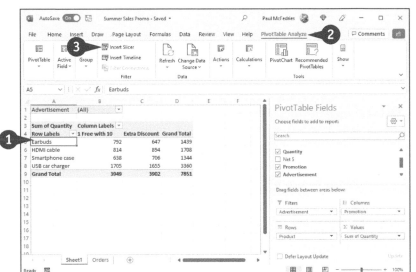

The Insert Slicers dialog box appears.

4 Select a field to use for the slicer
(☐ changes to ☑).

This example selects the Date field.

Note: You can select more than one field to increase your filtering choices.

5 Click **OK**.

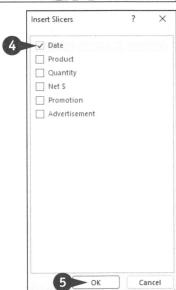

Ⓐ Excel displays a Slicer window containing the unique items in the field you selected in step **4**.

Ⓑ The Slicer contextual tab appears on the Ribbon.

6 Click a field item in the Slicer window.

Ⓒ Excel modifies the PivotTable to display information associated with the choice you made in step **6**. In this example, the PivotTable displays information for June 8, 2022.

You can repeat step **6** to change the information in the PivotTable, effectively displaying different slices of your data.

Ⓓ To select multiple items, click **Multi-select** (⅀≡) and then click each item you want to display.

TIPS

How do I go back to viewing all the data in the PivotTable?

Right-click anywhere on the window showing the choices for the field you selected in step **6**. A contextual menu appears. Click **Remove** to eliminate the Slicer window and redisplay all data in the PivotTable.

Is there a way to see more choices in the Slicer window for the field I selected in step 4?

Yes. Click the **Slicer** tab and, in the Buttons group, click in the **Columns** box. Change the number from 1 to the number of columns you want the Slicer window to display.

PART IV

PowerPoint

PowerPoint is a presentation program that you can use to create slideshows to present ideas to clients, explain a concept or procedure to employees, or teach a class. In this part, you learn how to create slideshows, how to add text, artwork, and special effects to them, and how to rehearse and run a slideshow.

Chapter 13: Creating a Presentation. 202
Chapter 14: Populating Presentation Slides 214
Chapter 15: Assembling and Presenting a Slideshow . . . 232

Create a New Presentation

When you first start PowerPoint, the PowerPoint Start screen appears. From it — or, if PowerPoint is open, from Backstage view — you can choose to create a new blank presentation. Or, you can use a presentation template or theme as the foundation of your presentation.

Templates contain themes that make up the design of the slide. *Themes* are groups of coordinated colors, fonts, and effects such as shadows, reflections, and glows. (See Chapter 14 for more information on themes.) Templates can contain more than just themes, though. For example, they can contain prompts to help you set up the slides in the presentation for a particular subject.

Create a New Presentation

Create a Blank Presentation

1 Start PowerPoint.

The PowerPoint Start screen appears.

2 Click **Blank Presentation**.

A PowerPoint creates a new presentation with one blank slide.

Using a Template

1 With the new presentation from the previous subsection open, click the **File** tab (not shown).

Backstage view appears.

2 Click **New**.

B Potential templates appear here.

C If you are signed into Microsoft 365, you can type a search term and click ▶ or press Enter.

Note: See Chapter 4 for details about signing in to Office 365.

3 Click a template to display a preview of the template design.

4 Click **Create**.

D PowerPoint creates a new presentation with one or two blank slides.

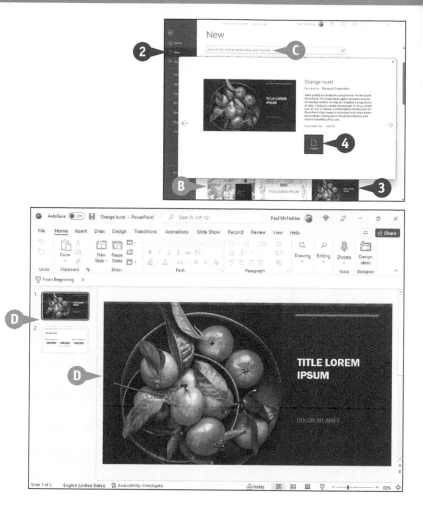

What is the default aspect ratio for PowerPoint slides, and can I change it?

The default aspect ratio is 16:9, but you can change the default aspect ratio for your slides to 4:3 by following these steps. Apply the 4:3 aspect ratio to your slides (see the section "Change the Slide Size," later in this chapter). Click the **Design** tab, and click the **More** button (⤓) in the Themes group. Click **Save Current Theme**. In the Save Current Theme dialog box, type the name of the theme, and then click **Save**. In the Themes Gallery on the Design tab, right-click the saved theme. Click **Set as Default Theme** from the menu that appears.

Create a Photo Album Presentation

You can quickly turn any collection of digital photos on your computer into a slideshow presentation in PowerPoint. For example, you might compile your photos from a recent vacation into a presentation. Alternatively, you might gather your favorite photos of a friend or loved one in a presentation. To liven up the presentation, you can include captions with your photos. You can also vary the layout of slides, including having one (the default), two, three, or more photos per slide. You can then share the presentation with others or e-mail the file to family and friends.

Create a Photo Album Presentation

1 Click the **Insert** tab.

2 Click **Photo Album**.

   The Photo Album dialog box appears.

3 Click **File/Disk**.

   The Insert New Pictures dialog box appears.

4 Navigate to the folder or drive containing the digital pictures that you want to use.

5 Click the pictures that you want to use.

   To use multiple pictures, you can press and hold Ctrl while clicking the pictures.

6 Click **Insert**.

A To change a picture's position within the album, select the picture (☐ changes to ☑) and then click **Move Up** (↑) or **Move Down** (↓).

B To remove a picture, select (☐ changes to ☑) and then click **Remove**.

7 Click **Create**.

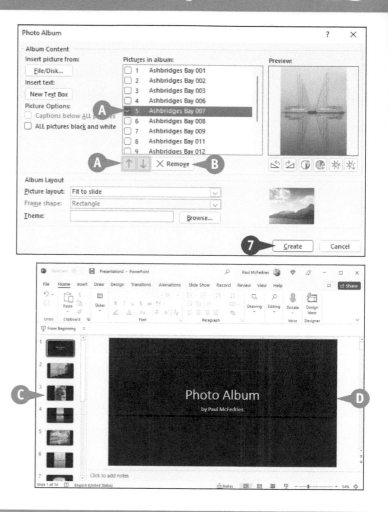

PowerPoint creates the slideshow as a new presentation file.

C Each picture appears on its own slide.

D The first slide in the show is a title slide, containing the title "Photo Album" and your username.

TIP

How do I fit multiple pictures onto a single slide and add captions?

Click the **Insert** tab, and then click ▼ beside **Photo Album** and choose **Edit Photo Album**. In the Edit Photo Album dialog box, click the **Picture layout** ▼ and choose to display as many as four pictures on a slide, with or without title text (A). Select **Captions below ALL pictures** (☐ changes to ☑) (B). If this option is grayed out, choose a different Picture Layout option. Click **Update** (C). You can type your captions after closing the Photo Album dialog box.

Change PowerPoint Views

You can use views in PowerPoint to change how your presentation appears on-screen. By default, PowerPoint displays your presentation in Normal view, with thumbnails of each slide showing the order of slides in your presentation. You can click the **View** tab to see your presentation in an outline format, or you can switch to Slide Sorter view to see all the slides at the same time.

In addition to changing PowerPoint views, you can use the PowerPoint Zoom settings to change the magnification of a slide. You can also change the size of the panes in the PowerPoint window, making them larger or smaller as needed.

Change PowerPoint Views

Using Normal View

1. Click **View**.

2. Click **Normal**.

Ⓐ You can also use these buttons to switch between **Normal** (⊡), **Slide Sorter** (🔡), and **Reading** (📖) views.

Ⓑ Thumbnails of slides appear here.

Ⓒ The currently selected slide appears in the main PowerPoint work area; the selected slide's thumbnail displays an orange border.

Using Outline View

1. Click **View**.

2. Click **Outline View**.

Ⓓ The presentation appears in an outline format.

Ⓔ You can click the outline text to edit it.

Ⓕ You can click a slide icon to view the slide.

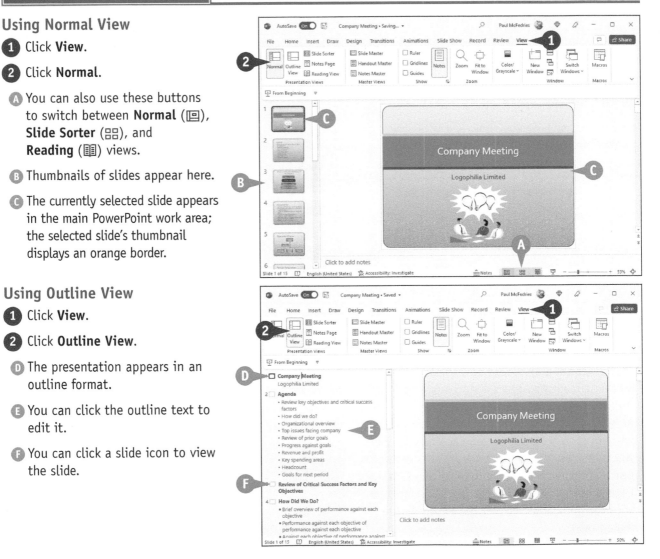

Using Reading View

1 Click 📖 to display the document in Reading view.

PowerPoint fills the screen with the first slide in the presentation.

G To view the next slide, click the slide or click >.

H To view the previous slide, click <.

I To display a menu of reading options, click ▤.

J You can click 🖳 to return to Normal view.

Using Slide Sorter View

1 Click **View**.

2 Click **Slide Sorter**.

K You can also click **Slide Sorter** (🔡).

PowerPoint displays thumbnails of the slides.

L A number appears under each slide representing its position in the presentation.

You can double-click a slide to switch to Normal view and display the slide's content.

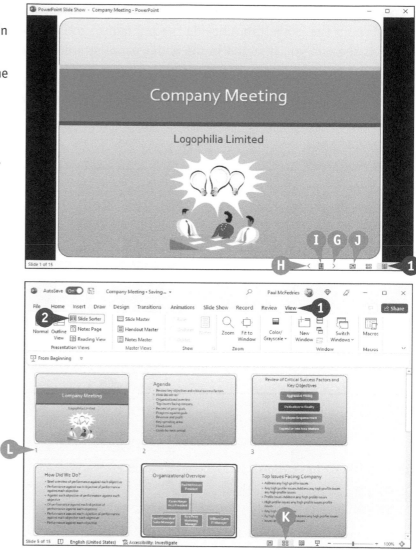

TIPS

How do I zoom my view of a slide?
You can drag the **Zoom** slider, which appears beside the view buttons on the status bar at the bottom of the PowerPoint window. Or, you can click the **View** tab, click the **Zoom** button, and choose the desired magnification in the Zoom dialog box that opens. Click the **Fit to Window** button on the View tab to return slides to the default size for the current view.

Can I resize the PowerPoint pane?
Yes. Position the mouse over the pane's border. When ▷ changes to ⬂, ↕, ⬈, or ↔, click and drag inward or outward to resize the pane.

Insert Slides

PowerPoint makes it easy to add slides to a presentation. To add a slide, you use the New Slide button on the Home tab. Clicking the top half of the New Slide button adds a slide with the same layout as the one you selected in the Slides pane; alternatively, you can click the bottom half of the button and select a different layout.

You can add and remove slides on the Slides tab in Normal view, or you can switch to Slide Sorter view and manage your presentation's slides.

Insert Slides

1 Click the thumbnail of the slide after which you want to insert a new slide.

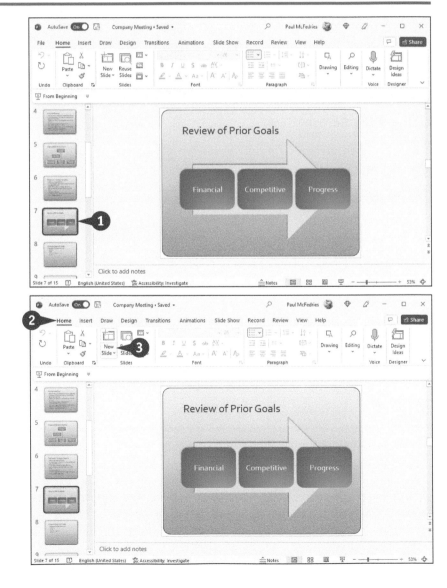

2 Click **Home**.

3 Click the bottom half of the **New Slide** button.

Note: Clicking the top half of the New Slide button adds a slide with the same layout as the one you selected in step **1**.

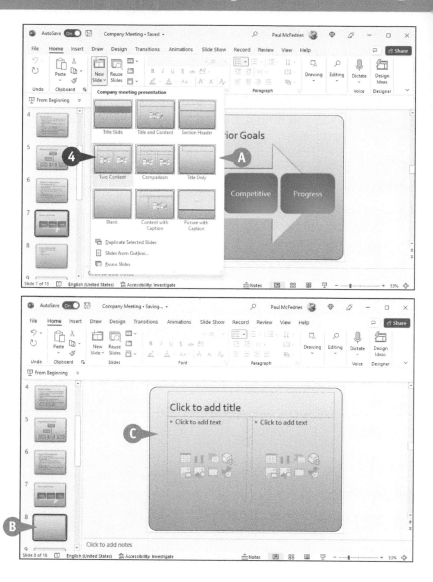

ⓐ A gallery of slide layouts appears.

④ Click a slide layout.

ⓑ PowerPoint adds a new slide after the one you selected in step **1**.

ⓒ The new slide uses the layout you selected in step **4**.

What happens if I click the Slides from Outline command?
You can use this command to create a presentation from an outline you created in another program, such as Microsoft Word. PowerPoint creates one slide for each heading style you applied; if you did not apply heading styles to the outline, PowerPoint creates slides for each paragraph.

Can I duplicate several slides simultaneously?
Yes. Select the slides you want to duplicate; you can press and hold Ctrl as you click each slide. Then, click the bottom of the **New Slide** button and click **Duplicate Selected Slides**. PowerPoint inserts all the duplicate slides after the last slide you selected.

Change the Slide Layout

PowerPoint includes several predesigned slide layouts that you can apply to your slide. For example, you might apply a layout that includes a title with two content sections or a picture with a caption. For best results, you should assign a new layout before adding content to your slides; otherwise, you may need to make a few adjustments to the content's position and size to fit the new layout.

If you find that you do not like a style element, you can make style changes to all slides in your presentation so that you maintain a uniform appearance throughout your presentation.

Change the Slide Layout

1 Click the slide whose layout you want to change in the thumbnail pane.

2 Click **Home**.

3 Click **Layout** (□).

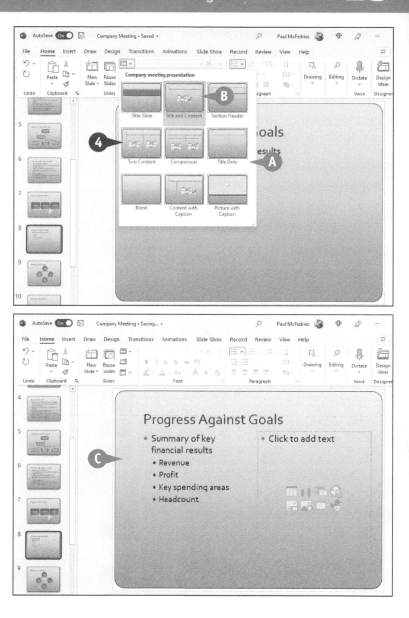

A A gallery of slide layouts appears.

B The currently selected layout is highlighted.

4 Click a layout.

C PowerPoint assigns the layout to the slide.

TIP

How do I make a style change that affects all slides in my presentation?

You can use the Slide Master. Suppose that you do not like the font you selected for your presentation. Using the Slide Master, you can change the font on all slides in one action. Click the **View** tab and then click **Slide Master**. PowerPoint displays the Slide Master tab. Make the changes you want; for example, select a different font for the presentation. When you finish, click the **Close Master View** button to hide the Slide Master tab. Your new font appears on every slide in your presentation.

Change the Slide Size

You can change the size of your presentation's slides. Specifically, you can change the *aspect ratio*, which is the ratio of width to height. The default slide aspect ratio is 16:9.

If you change the size of a slide that contains content, PowerPoint attempts to automatically scale your content; if it cannot, PowerPoint offers two options: Maximize and Ensure Fit. If you apply the Maximize option, your content is displayed full size, but it might not fit on the slide; if you apply the Ensure Fit option, your content fits on the slide, but it might be too small.

Change the Slide Size

1 Open the presentation containing the slides you want to resize.

2 Click **Design**.

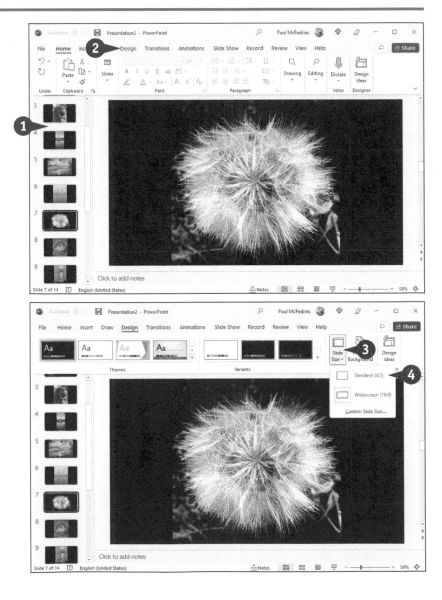

3 Click **Slide Size**.

4 Click the aspect ratio you want to apply.

If PowerPoint cannot scale the presentation content automatically, it displays a message asking how you want to scale your content for the new slide size.

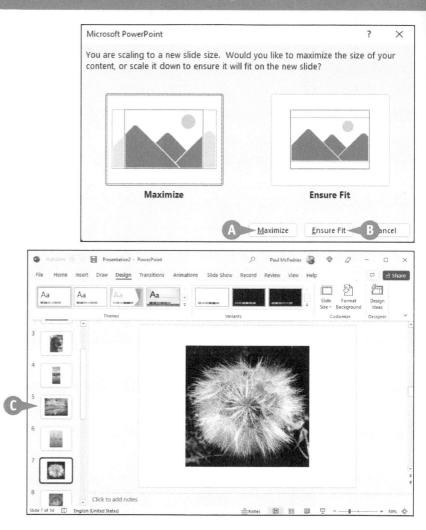

A You can click **Maximize** to increase the size of the slide content when you scale to a larger slide size. Be aware that your content might not fit on the slide.

B You can click **Ensure Fit** to decrease the size of your content when you scale to a smaller slide size. Although the slide content might appear smaller, you can see all content on your slide.

C PowerPoint resizes all the slides in the presentation.

Note: You might need to reapply a theme.

TIP

Can I establish a size for my slides other than 4:3 or 16:9?

Yes. Complete steps **1** to **3** and, from the drop-down menu, click **Custom Slide Size**. In the dialog box that appears, use the **Slides sized for** ⌄ (A) to select a slide size. You can also specify slide width, height, numbering, and orientation. Click **OK** to apply your changes.

Add and Edit Slide Text

All slide layouts except for the blank slide layout come with one or more text boxes in which you can enter text, such as a slide title or bullet points. To help you enter text, each text box contains placeholder text, such as "Click to add title," "Click to add subtitle," or "Click to add text." You can replace the placeholder text with your own text by typing directly in the text box.

After you add your text, you can change its font, size, color, and more, as shown in the next section.

Add and Edit Slide Text

Add Slide Text

1 Click the text box to which you want to add text.

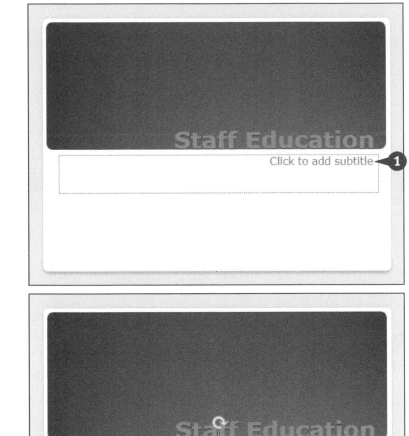

PowerPoint hides the placeholder text and displays an insertion point.

2 Type the text that you want to add.

3 Click anywhere outside the text box to continue working.

Edit Slide Text

1 Click in the text box where you want to edit the contents.

PowerPoint selects the text box and displays an insertion point in the text box.

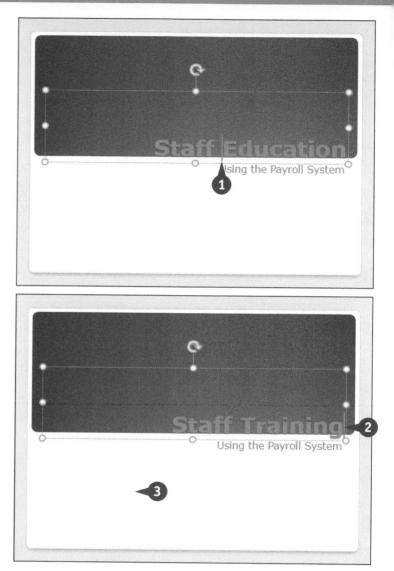

2 Make any changes that you want to the slide text.

You can use the keyboard arrow keys to position the insertion point in the text, or you can click where you want to make a change.

3 When you finish, click anywhere outside the text box to continue working.

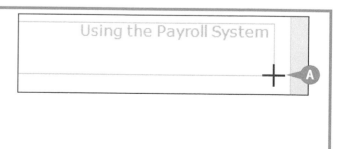

What should I do if my text does not fit in the text box, or fit the way I want?

You can resize the text, as described in the next section, or you can drag one of the handles of the text box to enlarge it, as shown here. When you position the mouse over a handle, the pointer changes to ⬉, ↕, ⬊, or ↔. When you drag, the pointer changes to ╋ (A).

Change the Font, Size, and Color

After you add text to a slide (as described in the previous section, "Add and Edit Slide Text"), you can change the text font, size, color, and style to alter its appearance. For example, you might choose to increase the size of a slide's title text to draw attention to it or change the font of the body text to match the font used in your company logo. Alternatively, you might change the text's color to make it stand out against the background color. You can also apply formatting to the text, such as bold, italics, underlining, shadow, or strikethrough.

Change the Font, Size, and Color

Change the Font

1 Click inside the text box and select the text that you want to edit.

2 Click **Home**.

3 Click the **Font** ▼.

4 Click a font.

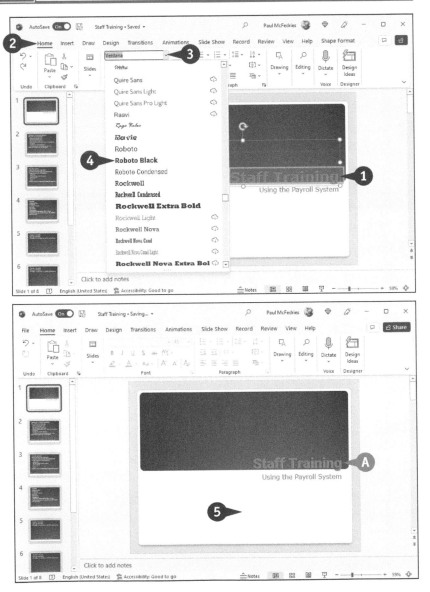

Ⓐ PowerPoint applies the font you chose to the selected text.

5 Click anywhere outside the text box to continue working.

Change the Size

1 Click inside the text box and select the text that you want to edit.

2 Click **Home**.

3 Click the Font Size ▼.

4 Click a size.

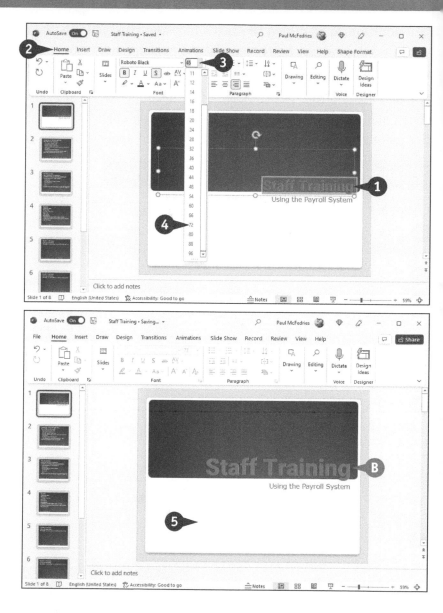

B PowerPoint applies the font size you chose to the selected text.

5 Click anywhere outside the text box to continue working.

Is there a quicker way to change the text size?
Yes. To quickly increase or decrease the font size, you can select the text you want to change and then click the **Increase Font Size** (A˄) or **Decrease Font Size** (A˅) button in the Home tab's Font group as many times as needed until the text is the desired size.

How do I apply text formatting?
Select the text whose format you want to change, and then click the **Bold** button (**B**), the **Italic** button (*I*), the **Underline** button (U̲), the **Text Shadow** button (**S**), or the **Strikethrough** button (a̶b̶).

continued ▶

In addition to changing the text's font and size, you can change its color. You might do so to make the text stand out better against the background, or to coordinate with colors used in other slide elements such as photographs.

You can change the text color in a few different ways. For example, you can select a color from the Font Color button on the Home tab, or you can open the Colors dialog box and select a color from the palette that appears. In addition, you can apply your own custom color to text.

Change the Font, Size, and Color (continued)

Choose a Coordinating Color

1. Click in the text box and select the text that you want to edit.

2. Click **Home**.

3. Click ▼ next to the **Font Color** button (🅰).

C. PowerPoint displays coordinating theme colors designed to go with the current slide design.

4. Click a color.

D. PowerPoint applies the color you chose to the selected text.

5. Click anywhere outside the text box to continue working.

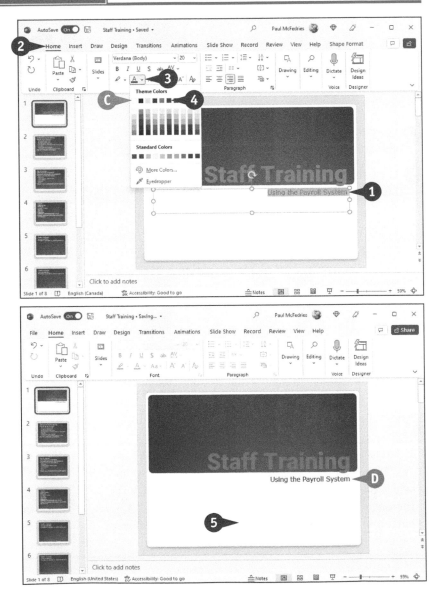

Choose a Color in the Colors Dialog Box

1 Click in the text box and select the text that you want to edit.

2 Click **Home**.

3 Click ▼ next to the **Font Color** button (A).

4 Click **More Colors**.

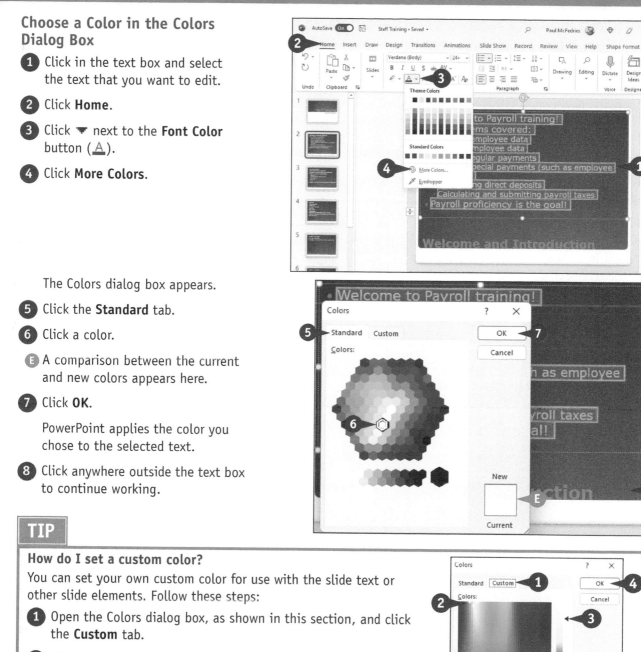

The Colors dialog box appears.

5 Click the **Standard** tab.

6 Click a color.

E A comparison between the current and new colors appears here.

7 Click **OK**.

PowerPoint applies the color you chose to the selected text.

8 Click anywhere outside the text box to continue working.

TIP

How do I set a custom color?

You can set your own custom color for use with the slide text or other slide elements. Follow these steps:

1 Open the Colors dialog box, as shown in this section, and click the **Custom** tab.

2 Click the color that you want to customize.

3 Drag the intensity arrow to adjust the color intensity.

A You can also adjust the color channel settings.

4 Click **OK**.

Apply a Theme

PowerPoint includes a variety of preset designs, called themes. A *theme* is a predesigned set of colors, fonts, backgrounds, and other visual attributes. When you apply a theme to your presentation, you give every slide in your presentation the same look and feel. Alternatively, you can apply a theme to selected slides in your presentation. After you apply the theme, you can use controls in the Design tab to change various aspects of the theme.

Themes are shared among the Office programs; you can use the same theme in your PowerPoint presentations that you have applied to worksheets in Excel or documents in Word.

Apply a Theme

Note: To apply a theme to selected slides, press and hold **Ctrl** as you click each slide thumbnail in Normal view. To apply a theme to all slides, select any slide.

1 Click **Design**.

Ⓐ In the Themes group, you can click ▲ and ▼ to scroll through the palette of themes.

Ⓑ Alternatively, you can click the **More** button (▼) to view all available themes.

2 Click a theme.

Ⓒ PowerPoint applies the theme. Any slides you add will use the same theme.

Ⓓ You can use these controls to select a color variant of the theme.

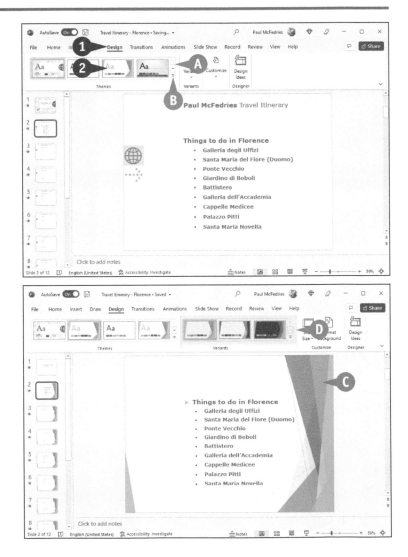

Set Line Spacing

Y ou can change the line spacing in a PowerPoint slide to create more or less space between lines of text. For example, you can increase line spacing from the 1.0 setting to a larger setting to make the text easier to read. If, after increasing the line spacing, your text does not fit in the text box, you can reduce the line spacing or increase the size of the text box, as described in the tip in the section "Add and Edit Slide Text," earlier in this chapter.

Set Line Spacing

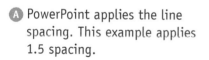

1 Click in the text box and select the text that you want to edit.

2 Click **Home**.

3 Click the **Line Spacing** button ().

4 Click a line spacing amount.

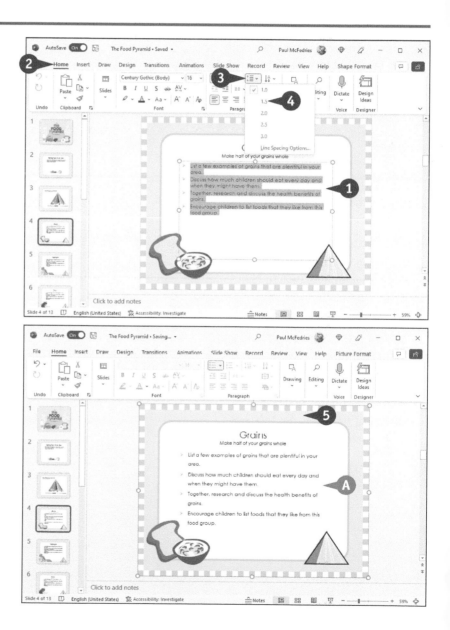

Ⓐ PowerPoint applies the line spacing. This example applies 1.5 spacing.

5 Click anywhere outside the text box to continue working.

Align Text

By default, PowerPoint centers most text in text boxes (bulleted lists are left-aligned). If you want, you can use PowerPoint's alignment commands, located on the Home tab, to change how text is positioned horizontally in a text box. You can choose to center text in a text box (using the Center command), align text to the right side of the text box (using the Right Align command), or justify text and objects so they line up at both the left and right margins of the text box (using the Justify command).

Align Text

1 Click in the text box containing the text that you want to align.

2 Click **Home**.

3 Click an alignment button:

Click the **Align Left** button (≡) to align the text to the left side of the text box.

Click the **Center** button (≡) to align the text in the center of the text box.

Click the **Align Right** button (≡) to align the text to the right side of the text box.

Click the **Justify** button (≡) to justify text between the left and right margins.

Ⓐ PowerPoint applies the formatting. In this example, the text is centered between the left and right margins of the text box.

4 Click anywhere outside the text box to continue working.

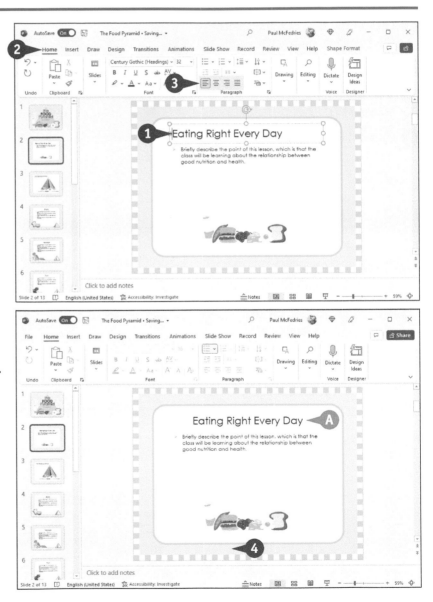

Add a Text Box to a Slide

Typically, you insert slides containing a predefined layout. You can customize the slide layout by adding a *text box*, a receptacle for text in a slide. To add text to a text box, see the section "Add and Edit Slide Text," earlier in this chapter.

When you add a new text box to a slide, you can control the placement and size of the box. (To move and resize text boxes and other slide objects, see the sections "Move a Slide Object" and "Resize a Slide Object," later in this chapter.)

Add a Text Box to a Slide

1. In Normal view, click the slide to which you want to add a text box.

2. Click **Insert**.

3. Click **Text Box**.

   When you move the mouse over the slide, ⇱ changes to ↓.

4. Click at the location where the upper-left corner of the text box should appear, and drag down and to the right (↓ changes to ✛).

Ⓐ As you drag, an outline represents the text box.

5. Release the mouse button to complete drawing the text box.

Ⓑ The insertion point appears in the new text box.

6. Type your text.

7. Click anywhere outside the text box to continue working.

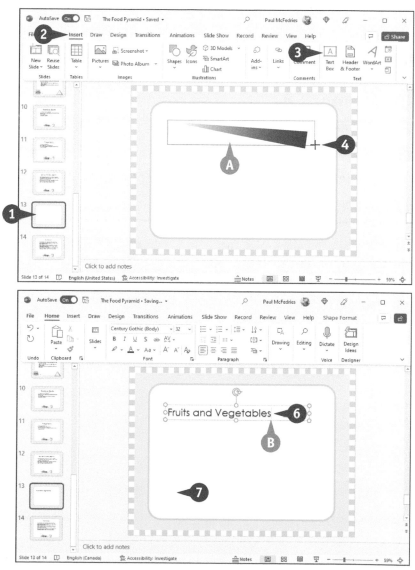

Add a Table to a Slide

You can customize the layout of a slide by adding a table to it. You can add tables to your slides to organize data in an orderly fashion. For example, you might use a table to display a list of products or classes. Tables use a column-and-row format to present information. After you add the table to your slide, you can control the placement and size of the table.

If the table you want to add to the slide already exists in an Excel worksheet, instead of following the steps in this section, you can copy the Excel range or table and then paste it into the slide.

Add a Table to a Slide

1 Click the slide to which you want to add a table.

Note: If an Insert Table icon (⊞) appears in your slide, click it and skip steps **2** to **4**.

2 Click **Insert**.

3 Click **Table**.

4 Click **Insert Table**.

The Insert Table dialog box appears.

5 Type the number of columns and rows that you want to appear in the table.

Note: If you need more rows, just press Tab in the last table cell, and PowerPoint automatically adds a row.

6 Click **OK**.

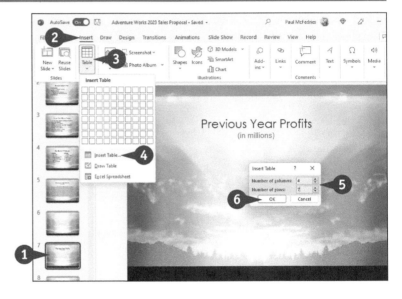

Ⓐ PowerPoint inserts the table into the slide.

Ⓑ PowerPoint displays the Table Design and Layout contextual tabs.

Ⓒ You can change the table's appearance by clicking a style in the Table Styles group.

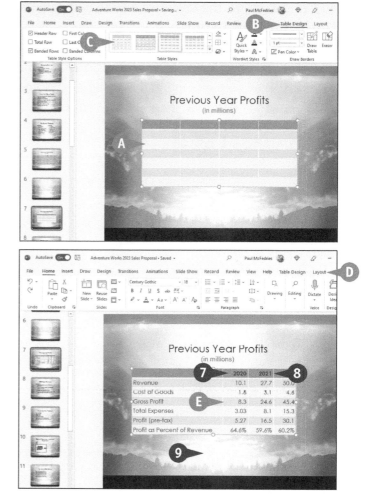

⑦ Click inside the first table cell and type your data.

You can press **Tab** to move to the next table cell.

⑧ Continue typing in each cell to fill the table.

Ⓓ You can use the tools in the Layout tab to merge or split table cells, change alignment, add borders, and more.

Ⓔ You can resize columns or rows by dragging their borders.

⑨ When you finish typing table data, click anywhere outside the table to continue working.

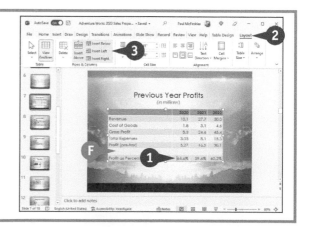

TIP

How do I add a row or column to my table?
To add a row to the bottom of the table, click in the last table cell and press **Tab**. To insert a row in the middle of the table or add a column anywhere in the table, follow these steps:

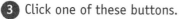

① Click in a cell adjacent to where you want to insert a new row or column.

② Click the **Layout** tab.

③ Click one of these buttons.

Ⓕ PowerPoint inserts a new row or column.

Add a Chart to a Slide

You can customize the layout of a slide by adding a chart to it. You might add a chart to a PowerPoint slide to turn numeric data into a visual element that your audience can quickly interpret and understand. When you add a chart, PowerPoint launches an Excel window, which you use to enter the chart data. After you add a chart to a slide, you can control the placement and size of the chart. (For help moving and resizing charts and other slide objects, see the sections "Move a Slide Object" and "Resize a Slide Object," later in this chapter.)

Add a Chart to a Slide

1 If an **Insert Chart** icon (📊) appears in your slide, click it.

Ⓐ If an Insert Chart icon does not appear in your slide, click **Insert** and then click **Chart**.

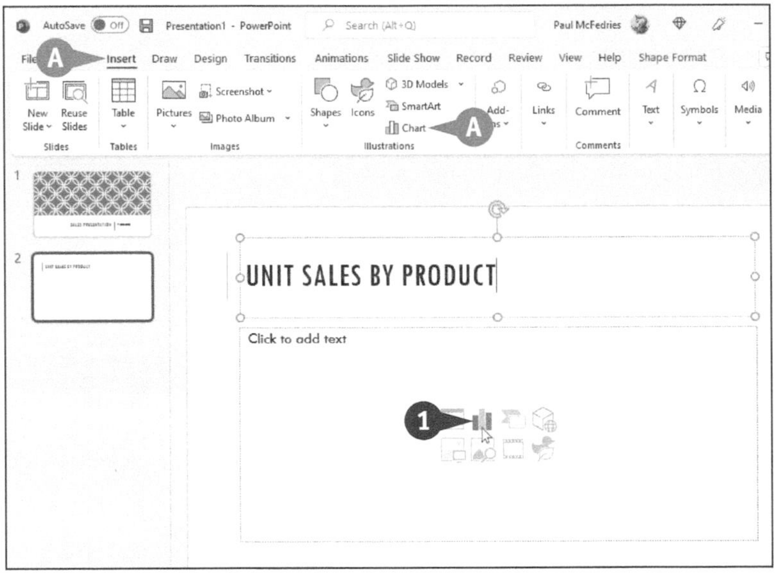

The Insert Chart dialog box appears.

2 Click a chart category.

3 Click a chart type.

Ⓑ A preview of the chart appears here.

4 Click **OK**.

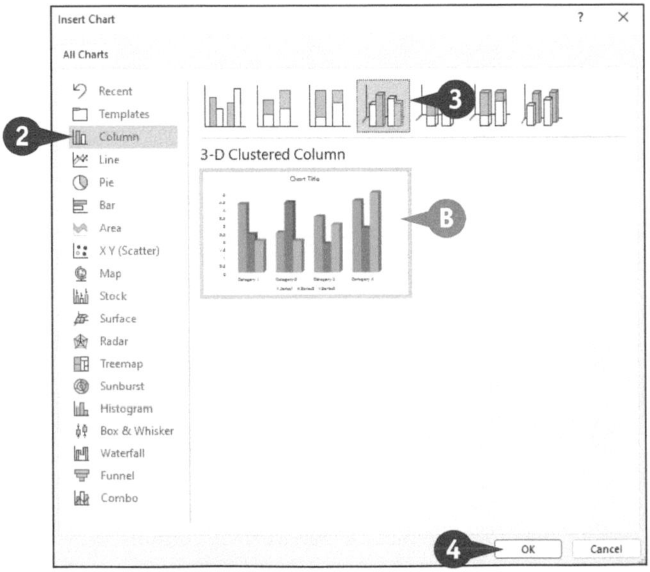

C PowerPoint displays a sample chart on the slide.

D An Excel program window opens.

5 Replace the placeholder data with the chart data that you want to illustrate.

You can press Tab to move from cell to cell.

E PowerPoint updates the chart to reflect the data you enter.

6 Click the **Close** button (✕) to close the Excel window.

F As long as the chart is selected, PowerPoint displays the Chart Design and Format contextual tabs.

7 Click the **Chart Design** tab.

G To edit the chart data, you can click **Edit Data**.

H You can click a **Chart Styles** option to change the chart style.

UNIT SALES BY PRODUCT

TIPS

Can I insert an existing Excel chart into my PowerPoint slide?

Yes. You can use the Copy and Paste commands to copy an Excel chart and insert it into a PowerPoint slide.

How do I make changes to my chart formatting?

When you click a chart in a PowerPoint slide, the Ribbon displays two contextual tabs: **Chart Design**, with options for changing the chart type, layout, data, elements, and style; and **Format**, with tools for changing fill colors and shape styles.

Add a Video Clip to a Slide

You can add video clips to your PowerPoint slides to play during a slideshow presentation. For example, when creating a presentation showcasing the latest company product, you might place a video clip of the department head discussing the new item.

After you add a video to a slide, you can control the placement and size of the video. (For help moving and resizing video clips and other slide objects, see the following sections, "Move a Slide Object" and "Resize a Slide Object.") You can also perform certain edits to the video from within PowerPoint.

Add a Video Clip to a Slide

1 If an **Insert Video** icon
(▣) appears in your slide,
click it.

Ⓐ Alternatively, click **Insert**, click
Media, click **Video**, and then
click **This Device**.

Ⓑ If you do not want to add a video
from your PC, you can click either
Stock Videos or **Online Videos**
instead.

The Insert Video window
appears.

2 Click a folder containing the
video clip.

Select the video.

 Click **Insert**.

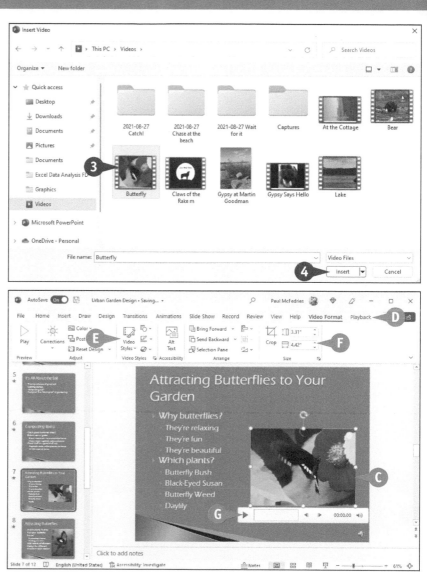

C PowerPoint inserts the clip into the slide.

D PowerPoint displays the Video Format and Playback contextual tabs.

E You can click an option in the Video Styles group to change the appearance of the video.

F You can use the options in the Size group to adjust the size of the clip on the slide.

G You can click the **Play** button (▶) to play the clip.

TIP

What tools appear on the Playback tab?

You can use the settings in the Video Options group to specify options such as when the clip should start playing, whether it should be looped, and how loudly it should play. You can edit your video using the tools in the Editing group; using the **Fade In** and **Fade Out** boxes, you can set up the clip to fade in and fade out. You can also click the **Trim Video** button to open the Trim Video dialog box, where you can change the duration of the video by trimming frames from the beginning or end of the clip.

Move a Slide Object

You can move any element on a slide — a text box, table, chart, picture, video clip, or graphic — to reposition it. These slide elements are often referred to as *objects*. For example, you might move a text box to make room for a video clip or reposition a picture to improve the overall appearance of the slide.

You can move a slide object using the standard Office Cut and Paste buttons. Or you can drag and drop the object, as discussed in this section.

Move a Slide Object

1 Click the slide containing the object that you want to move.

2 Select the slide object by clicking it.

3 Position the ⬚ pointer along any of the object's edges (⬚ changes to ⬚).

4 Drag the object to a new location on the slide. As you drag, ⬚ changes to ⬚.

5 Release the mouse button.

Ⓐ PowerPoint repositions the object.

6 Click anywhere outside the slide object to continue working.

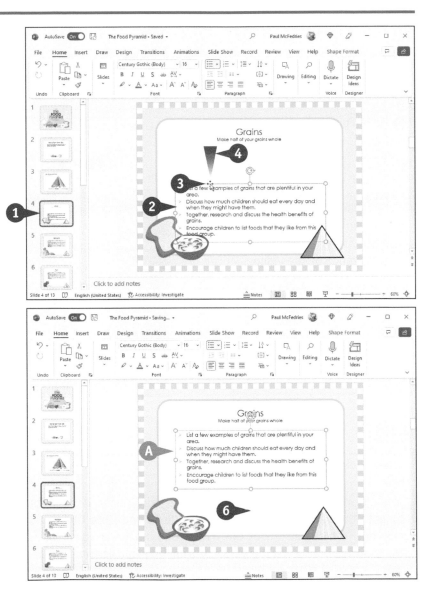

Resize a Slide Object

After you insert a slide object — a text box, table, chart, picture, video clip, or graphic — you may find that you need to make it larger or smaller to achieve the desired effect. For example, you might want to resize a text box to make room for more text or resize a picture object to enlarge the artwork. Fortunately, PowerPoint makes it easy to change the size of a slide object.

Resize a Slide Object

1 Click the slide containing the object that you want to resize.

2 Click the object to select it.

A PowerPoint surrounds the object with handles (○).

3 Position the mouse over a handle (↖ changes to ⬉, ⬍, ⬈, or ↔).

Use a corner handle to resize the object's height and width at the same time.

Use a side handle to resize the object along only the one side.

4 Click and drag the handle inward or outward to resize the slide object (⬉, ⬍, ⬈, or ↔ changes to +).

5 Release the mouse button.

B PowerPoint resizes the object.

6 Click outside the slide object to continue working.

Note: To delete an object that you no longer need, select the object and press Delete.

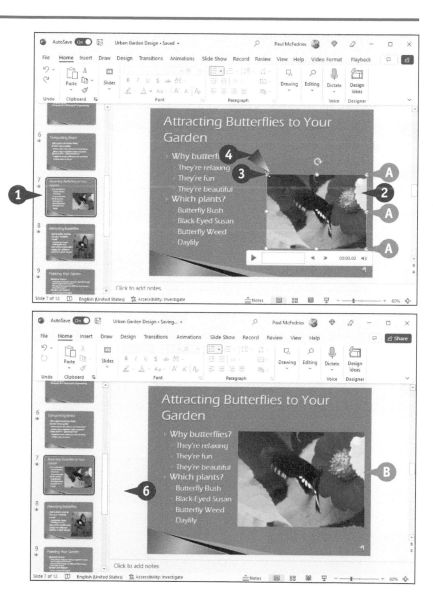

Reorganize Slides

You can change the order of the slides in your presentation. For example, you might want to move a slide to appear later in the presentation or swap the order of two adjacent slides. You can move individual slides or move multiple slides simultaneously.

You can change the slide order in Normal view or Slide Sorter view; choose the view based on the distance from the original position to the new position. If you need to move a slide only a few positions, use Normal view. Slide Sorter view works best when you need to move a slide to a new position several slides away.

Reorganize Slides

Move Slides in Normal View

1 Click 📧 to switch to Normal view.

2 Click to select the slide you want to move.

Note: To move multiple slides, select them by pressing and holding Ctrl as you click each slide.

3 Drag the slide to a new position.

Ⓐ As you drag, ⍌ changes to ⍌.

4 Release the mouse button.

Ⓑ PowerPoint moves the slide.

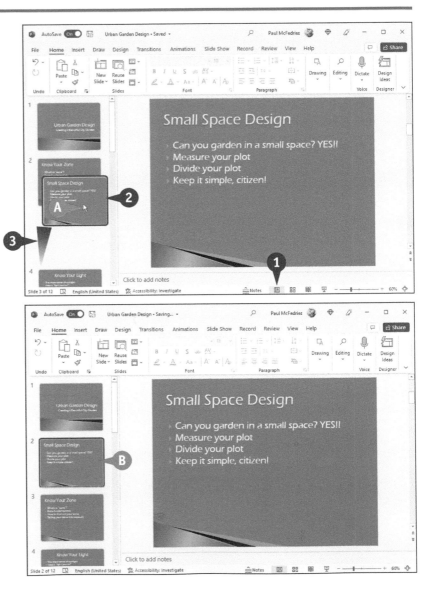

Move Slides in Slide Sorter View

1 Click ⊞ to switch to Slide Sorter view.

2 Click the slide that you want to move to select it.

Note: To move multiple slides, select them by pressing and holding **Ctrl** as you click each slide.

3 Drag the slide to a new location in the presentation.

C As you drag, ⊳ changes to ⊵.

4 Release the mouse button.

D PowerPoint moves the slide.

How do I hide a slide?

Suppose you frequently give the same presentation but your next audience does not require (or time does not permit) the information in one of the presentation slides. In that case, you can hide the slide. Right-click the slide and then click **Hide Slide** from the menu that appears. PowerPoint grays out the slide thumbnail and places a backslash over the slide number. To unhide the slide, repeat these steps.

How do I delete a slide?

To delete a slide, click the slide and then press **Delete**. Alternatively, right-click the slide and then click **Delete Slide** from the menu that appears.

Reuse a Slide

You can reuse a slide from an existing presentation in another presentation. When you are building a presentation, you might find that you need to use a slide that is the same as a slide you created in an earlier presentation. Rather than re-creating that slide from scratch, it is much faster and easier to bring a copy of the existing slide into your new presentation. PowerPoint calls this *reusing* the slide. When you reuse a slide, PowerPoint updates the slide to match the formatting used in the new presentation. You can reuse one or more slides from a presentation.

Reuse a Slide

1. Click the slide that you want to appear before the new slide.

2. Click **Home**.

3. Click **Reuse Slides**.

A. The Reuse Slides pane opens.

4. Click **Browse**.

The Choose Content dialog box opens.

5 Locate and select the presentation containing the slide you want to reuse.

6 Click **Choose Content**.

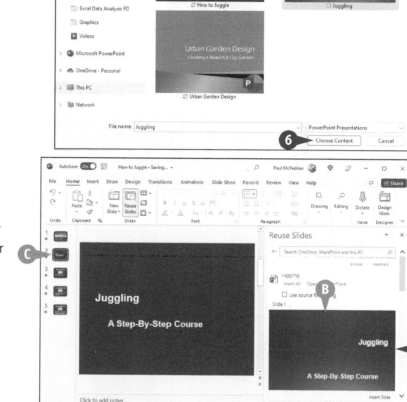

B PowerPoint populates the Reuse Slides pane with slides from the presentation you selected.

7 Click the slide you want to reuse.

C PowerPoint adds the slide to your presentation after the slide you clicked in step **1**.

TIPS

Can I retain the reused slide's original formatting?
Yes. To retain the reused slide's original formatting, select **Use source formatting** (☐ changes to ☑) in the Reuse Slides pane. To change all the slides in the new presentation to match the reused slide, right-click the reused slide in the Reuse Slides pane and choose **Apply Theme to All Slides**.

How do I reuse all the slides in a presentation?
To reuse all the slides in a presentation, click **Insert All** in the Reuse Slides pane. PowerPoint inserts all the slides from the existing presentation into the new presentation.

Organize Slides into Sections

If your presentation has a large number of slides, keeping it organized can be difficult. To more easily manage your slides, you can organize them into sections. For example, you might group all the slides that will be displayed during your introductory speech into a section called "Introduction," place the slides that pertain to your first topic of discussion into a section called "Topic 1," and so on.

Organizing a presentation into sections can also help you move slides around in the presentation. Instead of moving individual slides, you can move sections.

Organize Slides into Sections

Add a Section

① Click the slide that marks the beginning of the section you want to create.

② Click **Home**.

③ Click **Section**.

④ Click **Add Section**.

Ⓐ PowerPoint places a Default Section marker at the beginning of the presentation.

Ⓑ PowerPoint adds an Untitled Section marker before the slide you selected, adding all slides below the marker to the section.

The Rename Section dialog box appears.

⑤ Type a name for the new section.

⑥ Click **Rename**.

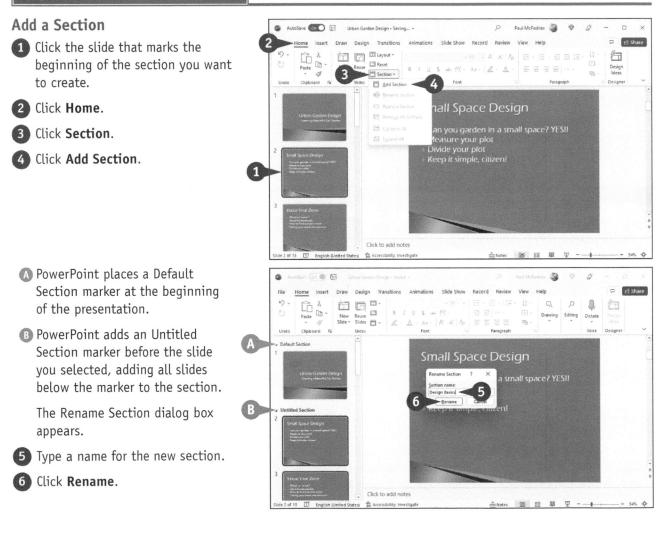

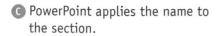

C PowerPoint applies the name to the section.

7 Repeat steps **1** to **6** for each section you want to create.

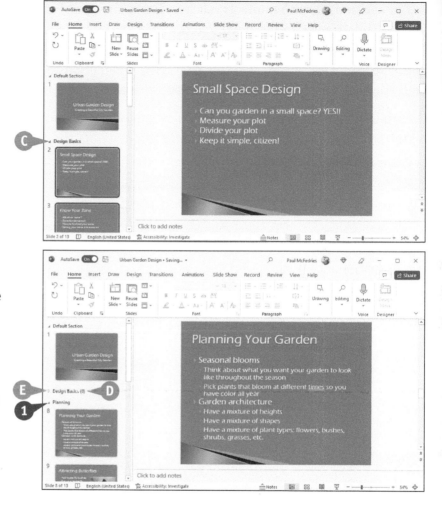

Hide and Display a Section

1 To hide the slides in a section, click the section marker's collapse button (◢).

D PowerPoint collapses the section and identifies the number of slides in the section.

E You can click the section marker's expand button (▷) to redisplay the slides in the section.

TIPS

How do I remove a section marker?
If you decide you no longer want to group a set of slides in a section, you can remove the section marker. To do so, right-click the section marker and click **Remove Section** from the menu that appears. PowerPoint removes the marker.

How can I reorganize the sections in my presentation?
To reorganize the sections in your presentation, right-click a section's marker and click **Move Section Up** or **Move Section Down** as many times as needed. PowerPoint moves the slides in the section accordingly.

Define Slide Transitions

You can add transition effects, such as fades, dissolves, and wipes, to your slides to control how one slide segues to the next. You can control the speed with which the transition appears. You can also specify how PowerPoint advances the slides, either manually using a mouse click or automatically after a time you specify passes. In addition to adding visual transition effects between your slides, you can add sound effects to serve as transitions.

Use good judgment when assigning transitions. Using too many different types of transitions might distract your audience from your presentation.

Define Slide Transitions

1 Click ⊞ to switch to Slide Sorter view.

2 Click the slide to which you want to apply a transition.

3 Click **Transitions**.

A Available transition effects appear in the Transition to This Slide group. You can click ⌃ or ⌄ to scroll through them, or you can click the **More** button (⤓) to view the gallery of transition effects.

4 Click a transition.

B PowerPoint demonstrates the animation as it applies.

C PowerPoint adds an animation indicator (⭐) below the slide's lower-right corner.

D You can click **Preview** to display a preview of the transition effect.

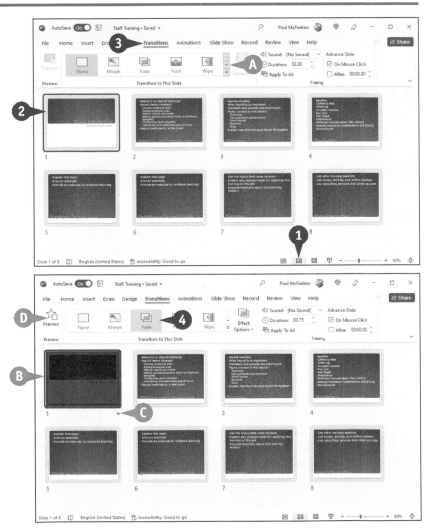

238

⑤ Click the **Duration** ⬍ to specify a speed setting for the transition.

Ⓔ You can click **Apply To All** to apply the same transition to the entire slideshow, and PowerPoint adds the animation indicator below every slide.

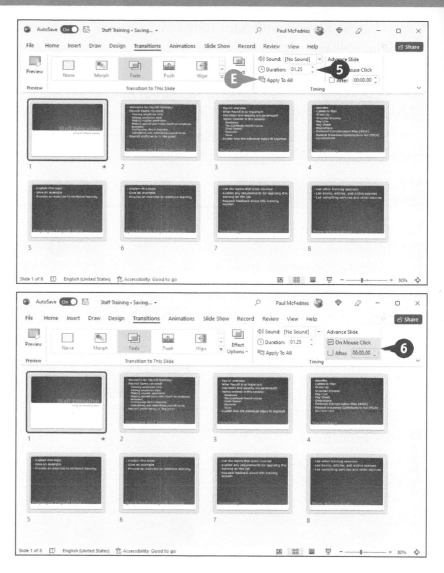

⑥ Under Advance Slide, select an advance option (☐ changes to ☑):

To use a mouse click to move to the next slide, select **On Mouse Click**.

To move to the next slide automatically, select **After** and use ⬍ to specify a duration.

TIPS

How do I remove a transition effect?
To remove all transitions, press Ctrl + A in Slide Sorter view to select all slides; otherwise, select the slide containing the transition that you want to remove. Then click the **Transitions** tab and click the **None** option in the Transition to This Slide group.

How do I assign a sound as a transition effect?
To assign a transition sound, click the **Sound** in the Timing group on the Transitions tab and select a sound. For example, you might assign the Applause sound effect for the first or last slide in a presentation.

Add Animation Effects

Y ou can use PowerPoint's animation effects to add visual interest to your presentation. For example, if you want your audience to notice a company logo on a slide, you might apply an animation effect to that logo.

You can use four different types of animation effects: entrance effects, emphasis effects, exit effects, and motion paths. You can add any of these effects to any slide object. You can also change the direction of your animations. To avoid overwhelming your audience, limit animations to slides in which the effects will make the most impact.

Add Animation Effects

Add an Animation Effect

1 Click 🔲 to display the presentation in Normal view.

2 Click the slide containing the object to which you want to apply an effect.

3 Click the object.

You can assign an animation to any object on a slide, including text boxes, shapes, and pictures.

4 Click **Animations**.

Ⓐ You can click 🔺 and 🔻 to scroll through the available animation effects or click the **More** button (🔽) to view the gallery of animation effects.

5 Click an animation effect.

Ⓑ PowerPoint demonstrates the effect as it applies it and displays a numeric indicator for the effect.

Ⓒ You can click **Preview** to preview the effect.

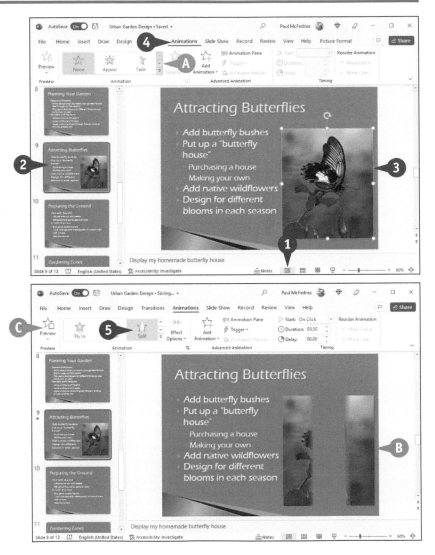

Change an Animation's Direction

1. In Normal view, click the slide element containing the animation you want to edit.

2. Click **Animations**.

3. Click **Effect Options**.

   A list of direction options for the animation appears.

4. Select an option from the list.

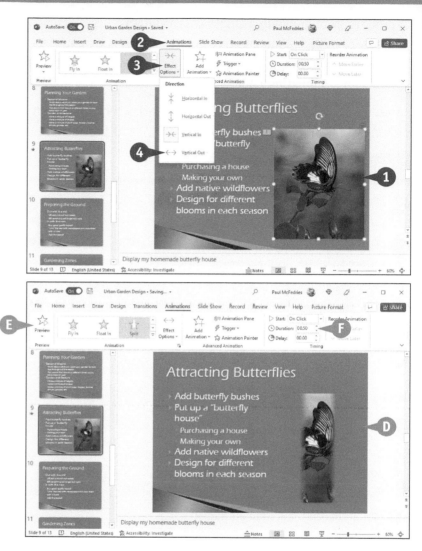

D PowerPoint demonstrates the new direction as it applies the change; the new direction now appears on the Effect Options button.

E You can click **Preview** to preview the effect on the slide.

F You can click the **Duration** 🔄 to specify a speed setting for the animation.

Create a Custom Animation

In addition to applying a single animation effect to any given slide object — a text box, picture, chart, or table — you can create custom effects by applying two or more animations to a slide object. For example, you might opt to have a slide object "fly in" to the slide and then spin. You can use PowerPoint's Animation pane when you create a custom effect to help you review and re-order the effect.

To create a custom animation effect, you use a combination of the technique described in the previous section, "Add Animation Effects," and the technique described in this section.

Create a Custom Animation

1 Click ▣ to display the presentation in Normal view.

2 Click the slide containing the object to which you want to apply an animation.

3 Click the object.

4 Click the **Animations** tab.

5 Apply an animation effect.

Note: See the previous section, "Add Animation Effects," for details.

6 Click **Animation Pane**.

Ⓐ PowerPoint displays the Animation pane.

Ⓑ The animation you applied appears in the pane.

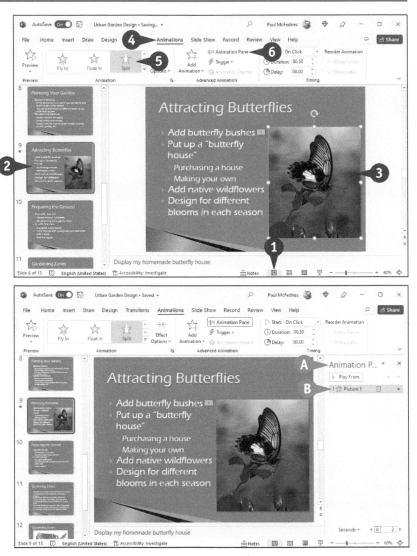

7 To add your next animation, click **Add Animation**.

Note: You add an animation using the **Add Animation** button; if, instead, you choose from the Animation gallery, PowerPoint overwrites the existing animation instead of adding a new one.

8 Click an animation effect.

PowerPoint adds the effect to the Animation pane.

9 Repeat steps **7** and **8** to add more animation effects to the selected object.

C PowerPoint places each effect in the Animation pane in the order you add them.

10 To preview your custom effect, click **Preview**.

D You can also click a starting effect in the Animation pane and then click **Play From**.

11 To change the order in which effects appear, click an effect and then click the **Move Up** button (⬆) or the **Move Down** button (⬇).

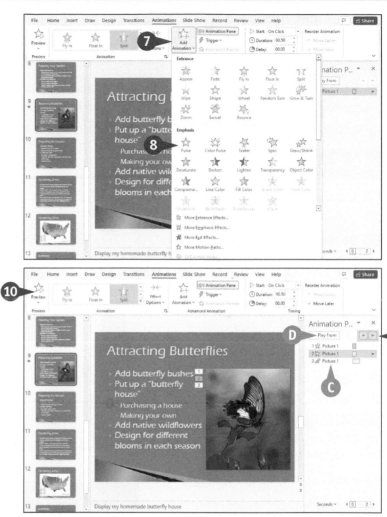

TIPS

How do I remove an animation?
Select the slide element containing the animation effect, click the **Animations** tab, and then click **None** in the Animation gallery. If the animation is a custom animation, click the **Animation Pane** button. Then, in the Animation pane, click the effect that you want to remove, click the ▼ that appears, and click **Remove**.

Can I change the duration of an effect?
Yes. Select the slide element containing the effect, click the **Animation Pane** button, click the effect whose duration you want to change, click the ▼ that appears, click **Timing**, and use the settings in the dialog box that opens to change the effect's duration.

Record Narration

Most presentations benefit from narration. You can speak as you present, or you can use PowerPoint's Record Narration feature to record a narration track to go along with the show. That way, you do not need to be present for your audience to receive the full impact of your presentation.

To record narration for a presentation, your computer must be equipped with a microphone. When you finish recording, an audio icon appears at the bottom of each slide for which you have recorded narration. When you save the presentation, PowerPoint saves the recorded narration along with the presentation file.

Record Narration

1 Click the slide where you want your narration to begin.

2 Click **Record**.

3 Click **From Current Slide**.

4 Click **Record** (⏺) to start the slideshow.

5 Speak into the computer's microphone.

A Click ▶ to move to the next slide in the show and continue recording.

B Click **Pause** (⏸) to pause the recording. To continue recording, click **Record** (⏺).

6 When you finish, click **Record** (⏺).

7 Click **Close** (✕).

An audio indicator appears in the lower-right corner on each slide for which you record narration. You can click the indicator to hear that slide's narration.

Note: You do not need to record all narration at one time. If you end the show and later want to complete the narration, select the first slide that needs narration. Then, click the **Record** tab and then click **From Current Slide**.

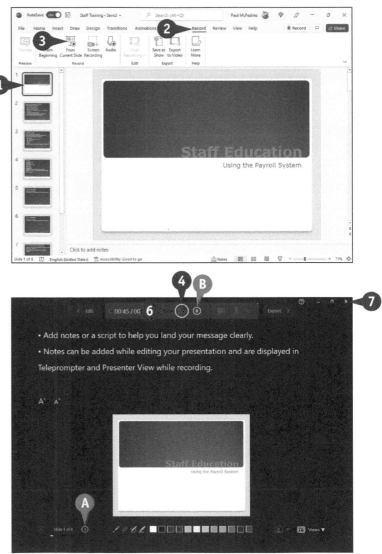

Insert a Background Song

You can insert a song that plays repeatedly in the background during your presentation. Playing a background song can be most effective in setting a mood for your presentation with no narration. PowerPoint can play AIFF Audio (.aif), AU Audio (.au), MIDI (.mid or .midi), MP3 (.mp3), Advanced Audio Coding - MPEG-4 (.m4a, .mp4), Windows Audio (.wav), and Windows Media Audio (.wma) files, among others.

You can download music from the Internet for your presentation, but you must first download it to your computer's hard drive.

Insert a Background Song

1 Click the first slide in your presentation.

2 Click **Insert**.

3 Click **Audio**.

4 Click **Audio on My PC**.

The Insert Audio dialog box appears.

5 Navigate to and select the audio file you want to add to your presentation.

6 Click **Insert**.

A An audio indicator and playback tools appear on the slide.

B The Audio Format and Playback contextual tabs appear on the Ribbon.

7 Click **Playback**.

8 Click **Play in Background**.

When you run your slideshow (see the section "Run a Slideshow," later in this chapter, for details), the song loops in the background from the first slide until the show ends.

C If you prefer that the background song play only once, click **Loop until Stopped** (☑ changes to ☐).

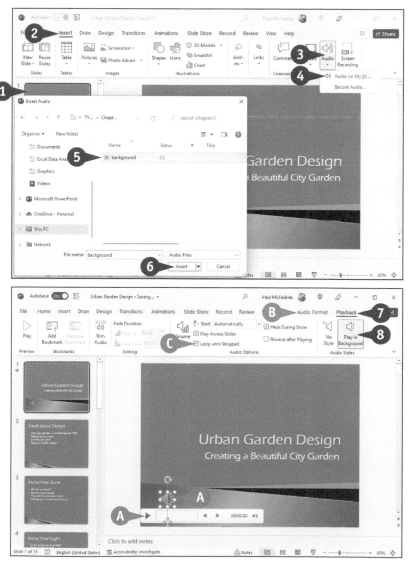

Create Speaker Notes

You can create speaker notes for your presentation. Speaker notes, also called notes pages, are notations that you add to a slide and that you can print out and use to help you give a presentation. You can also use speaker notes as handouts for your presentation. When creating notes pages, PowerPoint includes any note text that you add, as well as a small picture of the actual slide. You can add speaker notes in the Notes pane or on the Notes page.

You can print your speaker notes along with their associated slides. For details, see the tip at the end of this section.

Create Speaker Notes

Using the Notes Pane

1 Click 🖳 to switch to Normal view.

2 Click a slide to which you want to add notes.

3 Click **Notes** in the status bar to display the Notes pane.

Note: The Notes button acts as a toggle; each click displays or hides the Notes pane.

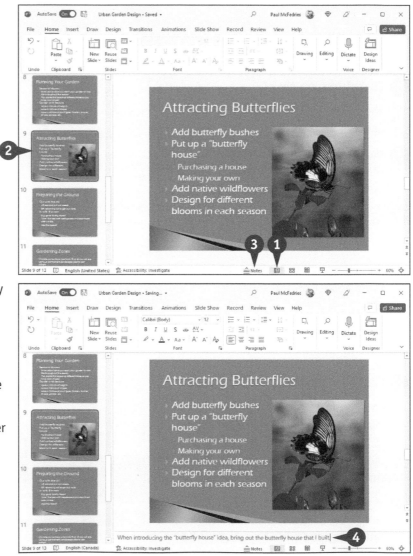

4 Click in the Notes pane and type any notes about the current slide that you want to include.

Note: You can enlarge the Notes pane. Position the mouse (⇖) over the line separating the Notes pane from the slide (⇖ changes to ⇕) and drag up.

You can repeat steps **2** to **4** for other slides to which you want to add notes.

Using the Notes Page

1 Click a slide to which you want to add notes.

2 Click **View**.

3 Click **Notes Page**.

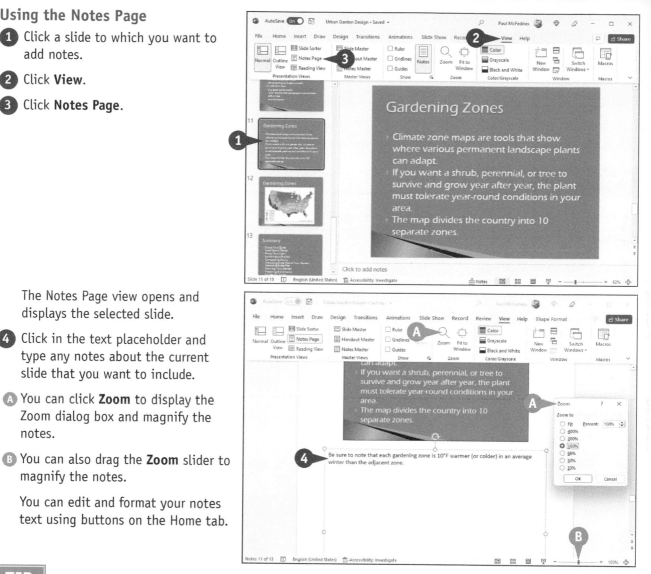

The Notes Page view opens and displays the selected slide.

4 Click in the text placeholder and type any notes about the current slide that you want to include.

A You can click **Zoom** to display the Zoom dialog box and magnify the notes.

B You can also drag the **Zoom** slider to magnify the notes.

You can edit and format your notes text using buttons on the Home tab.

How do I print my notes with my slides?
Follow these steps: Click the **File** tab, and then click **Print**. Click to select your printer. In the Settings section, click ▼ for the second setting (A) and click **Notes Pages** (B). Click **Print**.

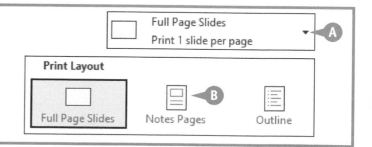

Rehearse a Slideshow

You can determine exactly how long PowerPoint displays each slide during a presentation using PowerPoint's Rehearse Timings feature. When you use Rehearse Timings, PowerPoint switches to Slide Show view, displaying your slides in order; you control when PowerPoint advances to the next slide in the show.

When recording how long PowerPoint displays each slide, you should rehearse what you want to say during each slide as well as allow the audience time to read the entire content of each slide. After you record the timings, PowerPoint saves them for use when you present the slideshow to your audience.

Rehearse a Slideshow

1 Click ▦ to switch to Slide Sorter view.

2 Click **Slide Show**.

3 Click **Rehearse Timings**.

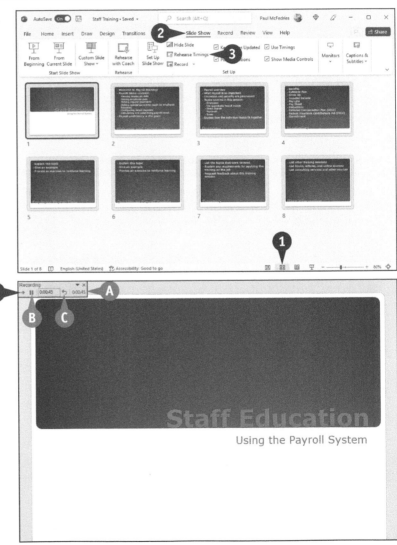

PowerPoint switches to Slide Show view and displays the first slide.

Ⓐ PowerPoint displays the Recording toolbar and starts a timer.

4 Rehearse what you want to say.

Ⓑ Click ‖ to pause the timer. To restart the timer, click **Resume Recording** in the window that appears.

Ⓒ To cancel the timer on a slide and start timing that slide again, click ↩.

5 When you finish timing the first slide, click → to proceed to the next slide.

PowerPoint displays the next slide.

6 Repeat steps **4** and **5** for each slide in your presentation.

When the slideshow finishes, a dialog box appears and displays the total time for the slideshow. PowerPoint asks if you want to keep the new slide timings.

7 Click **Yes**.

D PowerPoint saves the timings and displays them below each slide.

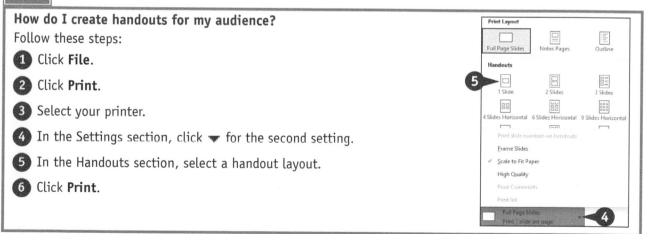

TIP

How do I create handouts for my audience?
Follow these steps:

1 Click **File**.

2 Click **Print**.

3 Select your printer.

4 In the Settings section, click ▼ for the second setting.

5 In the Handouts section, select a handout layout.

6 Click **Print**.

Run a Slideshow

You can run a presentation using PowerPoint's Slide Show view, which displays full-screen images of your slides. Slides advance in order, but you can, if necessary, view thumbnails of all your slides so that you can display a particular slide out of order.

To enrich the experience for your audience, you can use PowerPoint's pointer options to draw directly on the screen using the mouse (⌐). You can choose from several pen tools and colors, and you can present your slideshow using a single monitor or two monitors.

Run a Slideshow

Run a Presentation

1 Click **Slide Show**.

2 Click **From Beginning**.

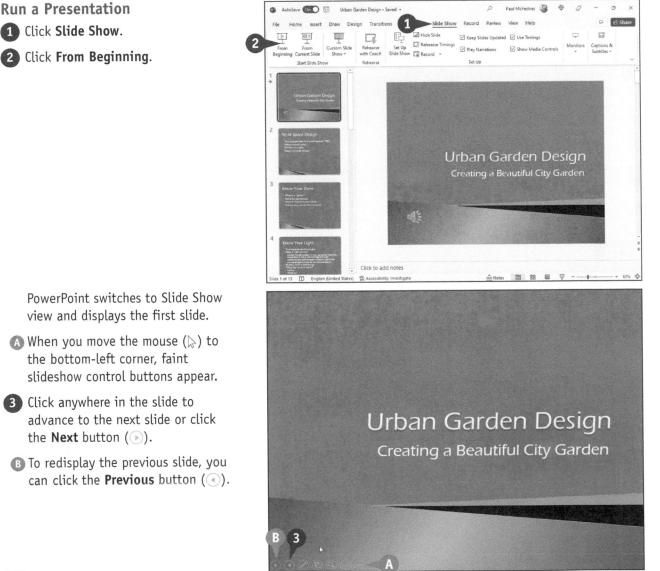

PowerPoint switches to Slide Show view and displays the first slide.

Ⓐ When you move the mouse (⌐) to the bottom-left corner, faint slideshow control buttons appear.

3 Click anywhere in the slide to advance to the next slide or click the **Next** button (⊙).

Ⓑ To redisplay the previous slide, you can click the **Previous** button (⊙).

Work with Thumbnails

1 Click the **See All Slides** button
(⊞) (not shown).

C PowerPoint displays thumbnails of
all slides in your presentation.

2 Click any slide to display it in
Slide Show view.

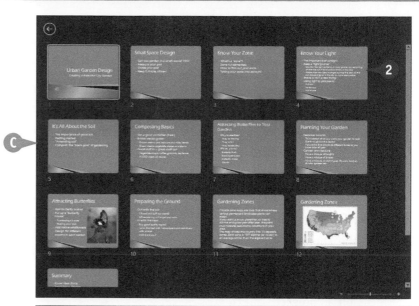

Point Out Slide Information

1 Click the **Pen and Laser Pointer
Tools** button (✎).

2 Select a tool.

D When you move the mouse
(⇱) over the slide, the mouse
appears as the tool you selected.

Note: To redisplay the mouse (⇱), repeat
steps **1** and **2**, selecting the same tool.

To erase all marks, click the
Pen and Laser Pointer Tools
button (✎) and then click
Erase All Ink on Slide.

Planning Your Garden

▸ Seasonal blooms

   Think about what you want your garden to look
like throughout the season

   Pick plants that bloom at different times so you
have color all year

▸ Garden architecture

   Have a mixture of heights

   Have a mixture of shapes

   a mixture of plant types: flowers, bushes,
s, grasses, etc

2 Laser Pointer
✎ Pen
✎ Highlighter
◻ Eraser
▭ Erase All Ink on Slide

TIPS

**Can I change the color of the ink I use for pen
and laser pointer tools?**

Yes. Follow the steps in the subsection "Point Out
Slide Information" once to select a pointing tool
and once again to select the tool's color. The order
in which you make these selections does not matter.

Can I hide a slide while I talk?

Yes. You can do this by changing the screen color
to black or white. Click the **Menu** button (⋯),
click **Screen**, and then click **Black Screen** or **White
Screen**. To redisplay the slide, click anywhere
on-screen.

continued ▶

In addition to using pen and laser pointer tools, you can call the audience's attention to objects by zooming in on them. This approach can be particularly useful if you display a slide for a lengthy time; zooming in can recapture your audience's attention.

Many people like to work in PowerPoint's Presenter view, which displays your notes as you present, but your audience sees only your slides. If you present on two monitors, PowerPoint automatically uses Presenter view to display notes and slides on separate monitors. Using only one monitor, you can still set up your presentation to use Presenter view.

Run a Slideshow (continued)

Zoom an Object

1 Click the **Zoom** button () (not shown).

E PowerPoint grays the slide background and displays a lighted square that you can use to focus on an object.

2 Slide ⊕ over the object you want to enlarge and click.

F PowerPoint zooms in on the object.

To redisplay the original size of the slide, press Esc.

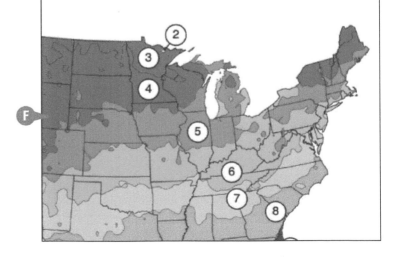

Using Presenter View

1 Click the **Menu** button (⋯).

2 Click **Show Presenter View**.

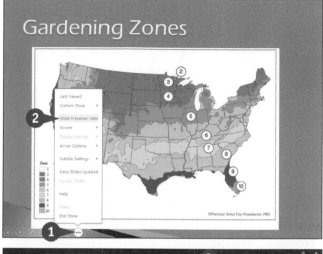

PowerPoint displays your presentation in Presenter view while your audience continues to see Slide Show view.

G The tools to control your presentation appear here.

H You can use these buttons (A˄ and A˅) to increase or decrease the font size of your notes.

I You can click these arrows (◁ and ▷) to display the previous or next slide.

Note: When you display your last slide, the next slide area displays "End of slide show."

3 Press Esc or click **End Slide Show** to end your slideshow.

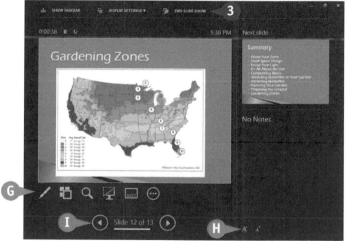

TIP

Can I display the Windows taskbar so that I can switch to another program if necessary?

Yes. When working with a single monitor, click the **Menu** button (⋯) (A), click **Screen**, and then click **Show Taskbar** (B). From Presenter view, you can click **Show Taskbar** at the top of the screen.

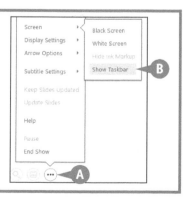

PART V

Access

Access is a robust database program that you can use to store and manage large quantities of data related to anything from a home inventory to a giant warehouse of products. Access organizes your information into tables, speeds up data entry with forms, and performs powerful analysis using filters and queries. In this part, you learn how to build and maintain a database file, add tables, create forms, and analyze your data using filters, sorting, and queries.

Chapter 16: Database Basics 256

Chapter 17: Adding, Finding, and Querying Data 276

Understanding Database Basics

Access is a popular database program that you can use to catalog and manage large amounts of data. You can use Access to manage anything from a simple table of data to large, multifaceted collections of information. For example, you might use Access to maintain a list of your clients or a catalog of products you sell.

If you are new to Access, you should take a moment and familiarize yourself with the basic terms associated with the program, such as *database*, *table*, *record*, *field*, *form*, *report*, and *query*. This section contains definitions of all these key terms.

Databases

Simply defined, a *database* is a collection of related information. You may not be aware, but you use databases every day. Common databases include the list of movies and TV shows offered by a streaming media service or a sports league's schedule of upcoming games. A company database might include a list for each aspect of the business, including product categories, customers, employees, orders, products, shippers, and suppliers.

All Access Objects

Tables
- Categories
- Customers
- Employees
- Orders
- Products
- Shippers
- Suppliers

Tables

The heart of any Access database is a table. A *table* is a list of information organized into columns and rows. In the example of a company database, the employees table might list the first name, last name, job title, address, phone number, and

Employees			
ID ▾	First Name ▾	Last Name ▾	Title ▾
1	Nancy	Davolio	Sales Representative
2	Andrew	Fuller	Vice President, Sales
3	Janet	Leverling	Sales Representative
4	Margaret	Peacock	Sales Representative
5	Steven	Buchanan	Sales Manager

e-mail address of each person who works for the company. You can have numerous tables in your Access database. For example, you might have one table listing customer information and another table listing your company's products.

Records and Fields

ID ▾	First Name ▾	Last Name ▾	Title ▾	Address ▾
1	Nancy	Davolio	Sales Representative	507 - 20th Ave. E.

Every entry that you make in an Access table is called a *record*. Records always appear as rows in a database table. Every record consists of *fields*, which are the separate pieces of information that make up each record. Each field of a record appears in a separate column. For example, in a company employee table, each record (row) might include fields (columns) for first name, last name, title, address, city, postal code, phone number, and e-mail address. Field names appear at the top of each column.

Forms

You can enter your database records directly into an Access table, or you can simplify the process by using a *form*. Access forms present your table fields in an easy-to-read, fill-in-the-blank format. Forms enable you to enter records one at a time. Forms are a great way to ensure consistent data entry, particularly if other users are adding information to your database table.

Nancy Davolio

Company Info   Personal Info

Employee ID:	1
First Name:	Nancy
Last Name:	Davolio
Title:	Sales Representative
Reports To:	Fuller, Andrew
Hire Date:	01-May-2002
Extension:	5467

Reports and Queries

You can use the *report* feature to summarize data in your tables and generate printouts of pertinent information, such as your top ten salespeople and your top-selling products. You can use *queries* to sort and filter your data. For example, you can choose to view only a few of your table fields and filter them to match certain criteria.

Employee Report

Steven Buchanan
Sales Manager
14 Garrett Hill
London UK
(71) 555-4848

Laura Callahan
Inside Sales Coordinator
4726 - 11th Ave. N.E.
Seattle USA
(206) 555-1189

Plan a Database

The first step to building an Access database is deciding what sort of data you want it to contain. What sorts of actions do you want to perform on your data? How do you want to organize it? How many tables of data do you need? What types of fields do you need for your records? What sort of reports and queries do you hope to create? Consider sketching out on paper how you want to group the information into tables and how the tables will relate to each other. Planning your database in advance can save you time when you build the database file.

Create a Database Based on a Template

Y ou can build web apps — a kind of database designed with Access and published online — or desktop databases based on any of the predefined Access templates. For example, you can create databases to track contact lists, assets, and task management. You can also search Office.com to find new, featured templates. This book focuses on building desktop databases.

When you create a new database using a template, the database includes prebuilt tables and forms, which you populate with your own data. You control the structure of your database by modifying or eliminating preset tables and fields and adding database content such as tables, forms, and reports.

Create a Database Based on a Template

1 Start Access.

2 Click **New**.

Note: You can also create a new database from within Access; click the **File** tab and then click **New**.

Ⓐ On the New screen, templates appear.

Ⓑ You can search for additional templates online by typing keywords here.

Note: To get Microsoft's Northwind sample database, type **Northwind** in the search field and press Enter.

3 Click a template.

A window appears, displaying the template information.

Ⓒ To view the previous or next template, click these arrows (← and →).

4 Type a new name in the **File Name** field.

5 To change the folder in which you store the database file, click the **Open file** button (🗁).

Note: If you are satisfied with the folder Access suggests, skip to step **8**.

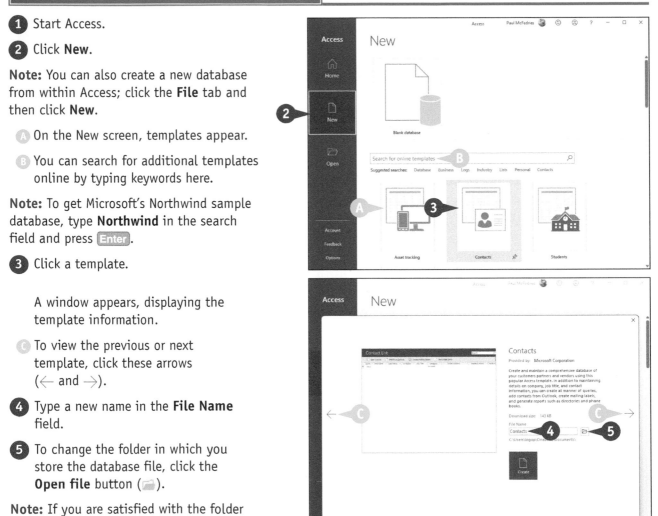

The File New Database dialog box appears.

6 Locate and select the folder in which you want to store the database file.

7 Click **OK**.

8 Click **Create**.

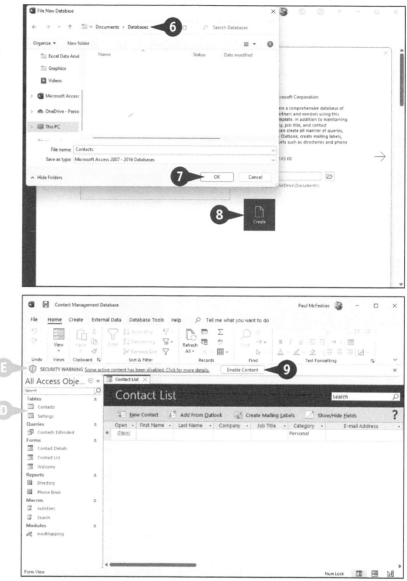

D Access downloads the template and creates a new blank database, ready for data.

E A security warning appears.

9 To hide the warning and enable the macros in this template, click **Enable Content**.

TIP

How do I know what fields to keep in or remove from my table?
To determine the fields you need in your database, decide the kinds of information you want to track in your database and the types of reports and queries you want to generate to view your data. For best results, use the suggested fields; you can always remove or hide fields that you do not use at a later time. (For help removing or hiding fields from a table, see the sections "Delete a Field from a Table" and "Hide a Field in a Table," later in this chapter.)

Create a Blank Database

If you determine that none of the predesigned database templates suits your purposes, you can create a new blank database and then decide on the tables, forms, and other objects your database will include. Creating a blank database is the way to go if you find that the predesigned templates that Access offers are too complicated for your needs. Creating a database from scratch is also the better choice when you know exactly what data you want to store and have a good idea of what tables, forms, and reports you will need.

Create a Blank Database

1 Start Access.

Note: You can also create a new blank database from within Access; click the **File** tab and then click **New**.

2 Click **Blank database**.

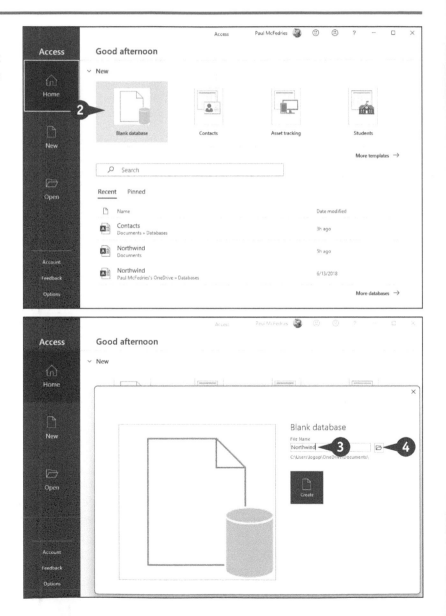

A window appears, displaying the template information.

3 Type a new name in the **File Name** field.

4 To change the folder in which you store the database file, click the **Open file** button (📁).

Note: If you are satisfied with the folder Access suggests, skip to step **7**.

The File New Database dialog box appears.

5 Locate and select the folder in which you want to store the database file.

6 Click **OK**.

7 Click **Create**.

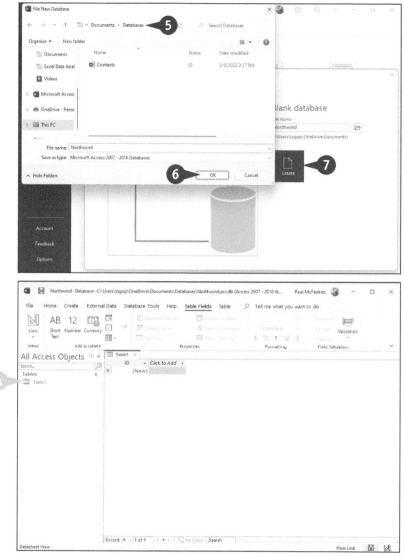

Ⓐ Access creates a new blank database and creates a new table named Table1, ready for data.

TIPS

What is the pane on the left?
This is the Navigation pane, which you can use to open various database objects. Click the **Shutter Bar Open/Close** button (≪) to collapse the pane; click the button again (≫) to expand the pane.

How do I open an existing database?
Click the **File** tab, click **Open**, click **Recent**, and then click the database in the Recent Databases list that appears. If the database is not listed in the Recent Databases list, click **This PC** or your OneDrive to look for the database. You can also click **Browse** to display an Open dialog box, locate and select the database file, and click **Open**.

Create a New Table

Access databases store all data in tables. A *table* is a list of information organized into columns and rows. A table might list the names, addresses, phone numbers, company names, titles, and e-mail addresses of your clients. Each row in a table is considered a *record*. You use columns to hold *fields*, which are the individual units of information contained within a record.

If you need to add a table to a database, you can easily do so. All table objects that you create appear listed in the Navigation pane; double-click a table object to open it.

Create a New Table

1 With your database open in Access, click the **Create** tab.

2 Click **Table**.

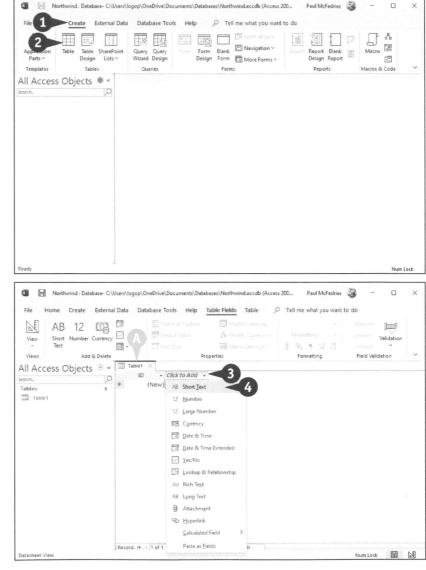

Ⓐ Access creates a new table and displays it in Datasheet view.

Note: See the next section, "Change Table Views," to learn more about Datasheet view.

3 Click the **Click to Add** link at the top of the field column.

4 Click the type of field you want to add.

In this example, a Short Text field is added.

5 Type a name for the field and press Enter.

6 Repeat steps **3** to **5** to create more fields for the table.

7 When you are finished adding fields, close the table by clicking the **Close** button (✕).

Access prompts you to save the table changes.

8 Click **Yes**.

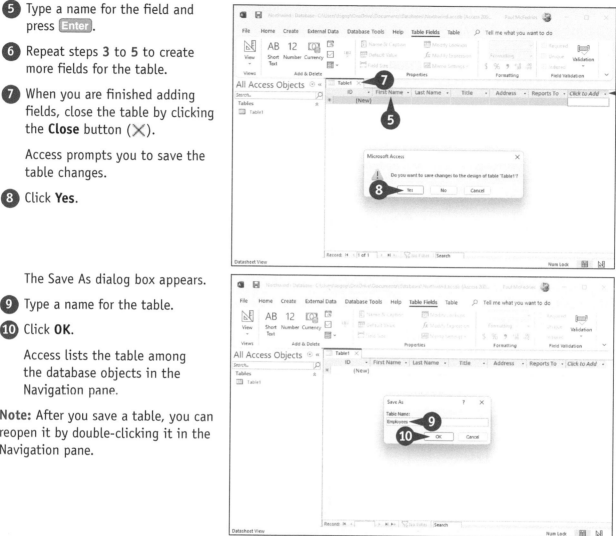

The Save As dialog box appears.

9 Type a name for the table.

10 Click **OK**.

Access lists the table among the database objects in the Navigation pane.

Note: After you save a table, you can reopen it by double-clicking it in the Navigation pane.

Can I rename table fields?

Yes. To do so, just double-click the field label and type a new name. When you finish, press Enter.

How do I remove a table that I no longer want?

Before attempting to remove a table, ensure that it does not contain any important data that you need, because deleting a table also deletes the data in the table. To delete the table, select it in the Navigation pane and press Delete. Access asks you to confirm the deletion before permanently removing the table, along with any data that it contains.

Change Table Views

Y ou can view your table data using two different view modes: Datasheet view and Design view. In Datasheet view, the table appears as an ordinary grid of intersecting columns and rows where you can enter data. In Design view, you can view the underlying structure of your fields and their properties and modify the design of the table.

In either view, you can add fields by typing new field names in the final (blank) column or change the field names. In Design view, you can also change the type of data allowed within a field, such as text or number data.

Change Table Views

Switch to Design View

1 Open any table by double-clicking it in the Navigation pane.

Access displays the table in the default Datasheet view.

2 Click **Home**.

3 Click the bottom half of the **View** button.

4 Click **Design View**.

Note: You can quickly switch from Datasheet view to Design view by clicking the top half of the **View** button.

Ⓐ Access displays the table in Design view.

Ⓑ The bottom of the view displays the properties of the field you select in the top of the view.

Ⓒ Access displays the Table Design contextual tab.

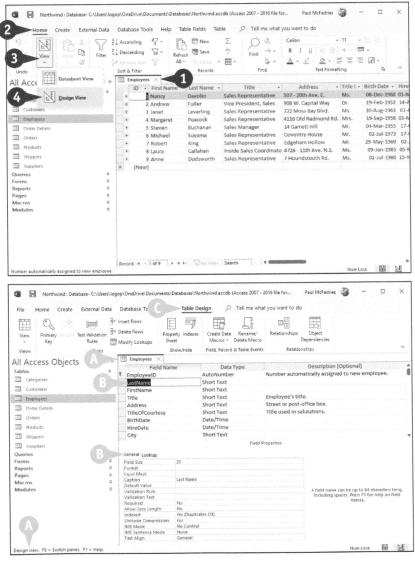

Switch to Datasheet View

1 Click **Home**.

2 Click the bottom half of the **View** button.

3 Click **Datasheet View**.

Note: You can quickly switch from Design view to Datasheet view by clicking the top half of the **View** button.

D Access displays the default Datasheet view of the table.

Do all Access objects have the same views?
No. All Access objects have a Design view, but other available views depend on the object you select in the Navigation pane. For example, in addition to a Design view, reports have a Report view, a Print Preview, and a Layout view, and forms have a Form view and a Layout view.

What is the purpose of the Field Properties area in Design view?
The Field Properties area enables you to change the design of the field, specifying how many characters the field can contain, whether fields can be left blank, and other properties.

Add a Field to a Table

Y ou can add fields to your table to include more information in your records. For example, you may need to add a separate field to an Employees table for e-mail addresses. Or you may need to add a field to a table that contains a catalog of products to track each product's availability.

After you add a field, you can name it whatever you want. To name a field, double-click the field label in Datasheet view, type a new name, and press Enter. Alternatively, you can change the field name in Design view.

Add a Field to a Table

1. Double-click to open the table to which you want to add a field in Datasheet view.

2. Click the column heading to the left of where you want to insert a new field.

Note: Access adds the column for the new field to the right of the column you select.

3. Click **Table Fields**.

4. In the Add & Delete group, click the button for the type of field you want to add.

   In this example, a Short Text field is added.

Ⓐ Access adds the new field to the right of the column you selected in step **2**.

5. Type a name for the new field and press Enter.

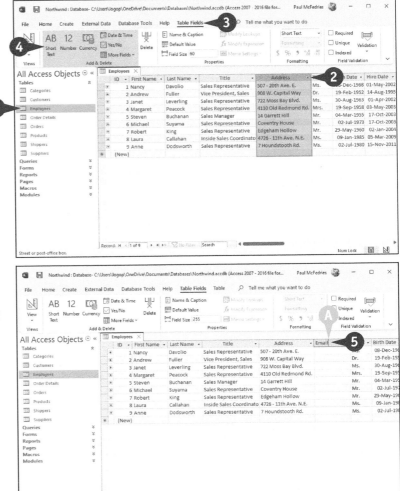

Delete a Field from a Table

You can delete a field that you no longer need in a table. For example, if your employee contact information database contains a Pager Number field, you might opt to delete that field.

When you remove a field, Access permanently removes any data contained within the field for every record in the table. If you do not want to delete the information in the field, you might choose to hide the field. For information, see the next section, "Hide a Field in a Table."

Delete a Field from a Table

1 Double-click to open the table that you want to edit in Datasheet view.

2 Click the column header for the field you want to remove.

A Access selects the entire column.

3 Click **Table Fields**.

4 Click **Delete**.

Access prompts you to confirm the deletion.

5 Click **Yes**.

Note: You might also see a message warning you that deleting the field will also delete an index; click **Yes**.

B Access removes the field and any record content for the field from the table.

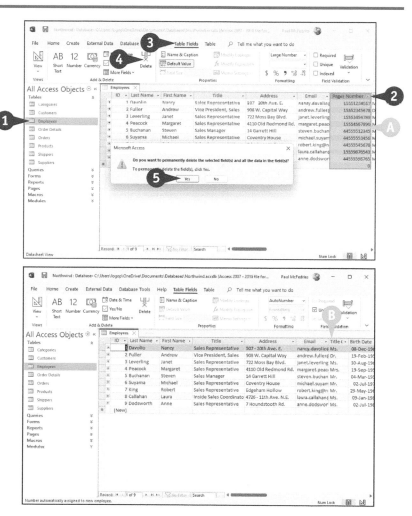

Hide a Field in a Table

Yerou can hide a table field that you do not want to view regularly but that you do not want to delete from the table. For example, a table containing a catalog of products might include a field indicating the name of the supplier from which your company obtains the product — information that you might need to view only occasionally. You also might hide a field to prevent another user on your computer from seeing the field. Whatever the reason, you can hide the field. When you are ready to view the field again, you can unhide it.

Hide a Field in a Table

1 Double-click the table that you want to edit to open it in Datasheet view.

2 Right-click the column heading of the field you want to hide.

3 Click **Hide Fields**.

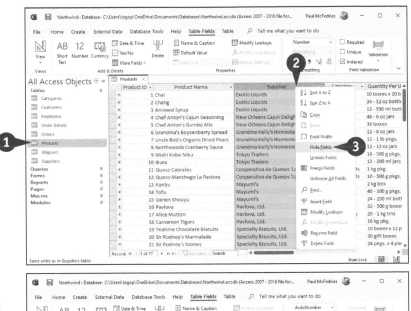

A Access hides the field.

Note: To view the field again, right-click any column heading and click **Unhide Fields**. In the Unhide Columns dialog box that appears, select the column that you want to display again (☐ changes to ☑) and click **Close**. Access displays the field in the table.

Move a Field in a Table

You can change the order of fields in a table. Moving fields is particularly useful if you built your database from a predesigned template, because you may find that the order in which fields appear in the table does not suit your needs.

It is important to understand that moving a field changes its position in Datasheet view but does not change the order of the fields in the table design. If you create a form after re-ordering fields, the form fields appear in their original position.

Move a Field in a Table

1 Double-click the table that you want to edit to open it in Datasheet view.

2 Click the column heading of the field you want to move.

A Access selects the entire column.

3 Drag the column to a new position in the table (⊠ changes to ⊠).

B A bold vertical line marks the new location of the column as you drag.

4 Release the mouse button.

C Access moves the field to the new location.

Create a Form

Although you can enter data into your database by typing it directly into an Access table, you can simplify data entry, especially if someone else will be entering the data, by creating a form based on your table. Forms present your table fields in an easy-to-read, fill-in-the-blank format. When you create a form based on a table, Access inserts fields into the form for each field in the table.

Using forms is a great way to help ensure accurate data entry, particularly if other users are adding information to your database.

Create a Form

1 Double-click the table that you want to edit to open it in Datasheet view.

2 Click **Create**.

3 Click **Form**.

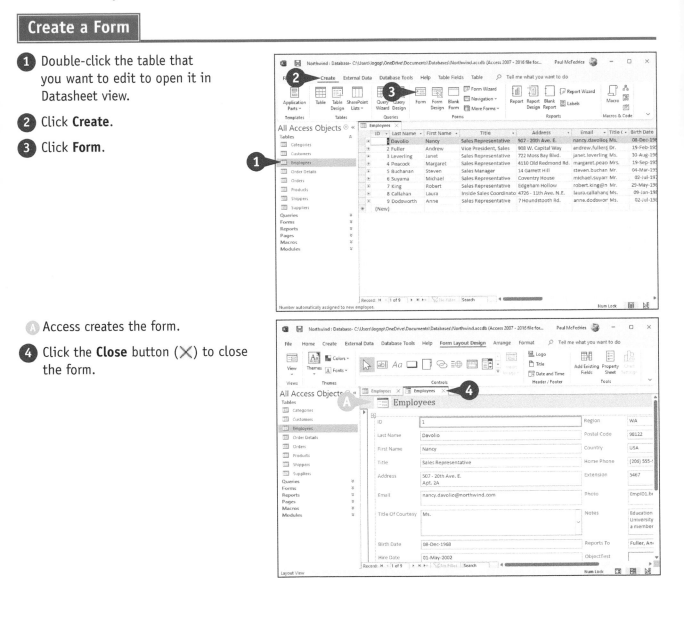

Ⓐ Access creates the form.

4 Click the **Close** button (✕) to close the form.

Access prompts you to save your changes.

5 Click **Yes**.

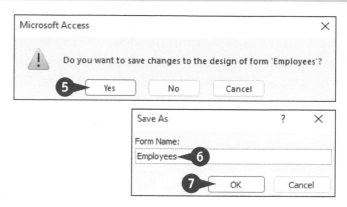

The Save As dialog box appears.

6 Type a name for the form.

7 Click **OK**.

Access lists the form among the database objects in the Navigation pane.

Note: After you save a form, you can reopen it by double-clicking it in the Navigation pane.

TIPS

How do I delete a form that I no longer need?

To delete a form, click it in the Navigation pane, and then press Delete or click the **Delete** button on the Home tab. Access asks you to confirm the deletion; click **Yes**.

Can I create a blank form?

Yes. Click the **Blank Form** button on the Create tab to open a blank form. A field list appears, containing all the fields from all the tables in the database. To add a field to the form, drag it from the list onto the form. You can populate the form with as many fields as you need.

Change Form Views

Υου can view your form using three form views: Form view, Design view, and Layout view. Form view is the default; in this view, you can enter data. In Design view, each form object appears as a separate, editable element. For example, in Design view, you can edit both the box that contains the data and the label that identifies the data. In Layout view, you can rearrange the form controls and adjust their sizes directly on the form. Access makes it easy to switch from Form view to Design view to Layout view and back.

Change Form Views

Switch to Design View

1. Double-click the form that you want to edit to open it in Form view.

2. Click **Home**.

3. Click the bottom half of the **View** button.

4. Click **Design View**.

Ⓐ Access displays the form in Design view.

Switch to Layout View

1. Click **Home**.

2. Click the bottom half of the **View** button.

3. Click **Layout View**.

Ⓑ Access displays the form in Layout view.

Ⓒ To return to Form view, you can click the bottom half of the **View** button and then click **Form View**.

Move a Field in a Form

You can move a field to another location on your form. For example, you might move a field to accommodate the order in which data is entered in the form. To easily move both a field label and the field contents, select both at the same time.

Although you can move a field in either Design view or Layout view, you might find it easier to make changes to your form in Layout view.

Move a Field in a Form

1 Double-click the form that you want to edit to open it in Form view.

2 Switch to Layout view (see the previous section "Change Form Views" for details).

3 Click the label of the field that you want to move (⬚ changes to 🕂).

4 Press and hold **Ctrl** as you click the contents of the field.

5 Click and drag the field label and contents to the new location on the form.

Ⓐ This symbol (a pink line) identifies the proposed position of the field label and contents.

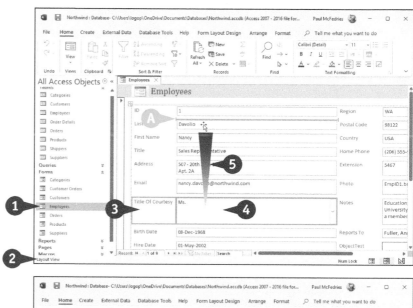

Ⓑ When you release the mouse button, Access repositions the field.

6 Click anywhere outside the field label and contents to deselect them.

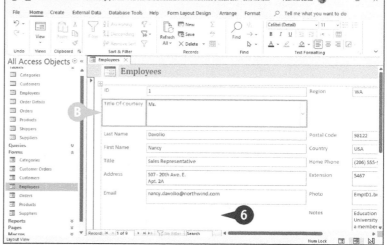

Delete a Field in a Form

You can delete a field that you no longer need in a form. When you remove a field, you need to remove both the data box and the field label. Although you can delete a field in Design view or in Layout view, you might find it easier to do this in Layout view.

Note that removing a form field does not remove the field from the table upon which the form is originally based or any of the data within that field; it only removes the field from the form.

Delete a Field in a Form

1 Double-click the form that you want to edit to open it in Form view.

2 Switch to Layout view (see the section "Change Form Views," earlier in this chapter, for details).

3 Click the label of the field that you want to delete (⊳ changes to ⬚).

4 Press and hold Ctrl as you click the contents of the field.

5 Click **Home**.

6 Click **Delete**.

Note: You can also delete the selected items by pressing Delete.

Ⓐ Access removes the field and label from the form.

Format Form Fields

To change the look of a form, you can apply formatting to fields in the form. You might format a form field to draw attention to it in order to make it easier to locate that field for data-entry purposes. Or, you might opt to change the font of all field labels, make them larger, and change their color to make them stand out on the form for those who enter data.

You can apply the same types of formatting to form fields that you apply to words in Word documents, PowerPoint presentations, Outlook messages, and Excel cells.

Format Form Fields

1 Double-click the form that you want to edit to open it in Form view.

2 Switch to Layout view (see the section "Change Form Views," earlier in this chapter, for details).

3 Click to select the field whose text you want to format.

Ⓐ To select multiple fields, you can press and hold Ctrl as you click additional fields.

4 Click the **Format** tab.

5 Use these tools to format the fields:

Click the **Font** ▼ and choose a font.

Click the **Font Size** ▼ and choose a font size.

Click to the right of the **Font Color** button (A) and choose a color for text.

Click to the right of the **Background Color** button (✎) and choose a background color.

Ⓑ Access formats the text in the selected fields.

6 Click anywhere outside the selected fields to deselect them.

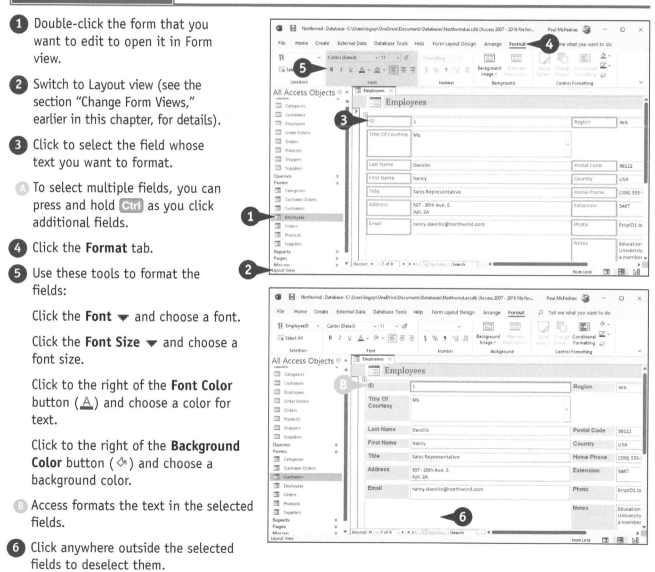

Add Records to a Table

You build a database by adding records to each table in the database. You add records to a table in Datasheet view, and each new record that you add appears at the end of the table. As your table grows longer, you can use the navigation keys on your keyboard to navigate it. You can press `Tab` to move from cell to cell, or you can press the keyboard arrow keys. To move backward to a previous cell, press `Shift`+`Tab`.

After you enter a record in a database table, you can edit it if necessary. You edit records in a table in Datasheet view.

Add Records to a Table

1 In the Navigation pane, double-click the table to which you want to add a record.

(A) Access opens the table, placing the cell pointer in the first cell of the first row.

(B) By default, the first field in each table is a unique ID number for the record. Access sets this value automatically as you create a record.

2 Click in the second cell of the first empty row.

3 Type the desired data in the selected cell.

4 Press `Tab`.

(C) Access fills in the ID number to add the new record.

5 Repeat steps **3** and **4** until you have filled the entire row.

6 Press `Enter` or press `Tab` to move to the next row or record.

D The new record appears here.

E Access moves the cell pointer to the first cell in the next row.

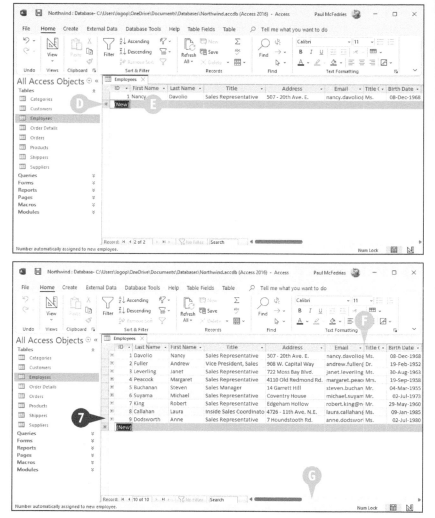

7 Repeat steps **3** to **6** to add more records to the table.

Access adds your records.

F You can resize a column by dragging the column border left or right.

G You can use the scroll bar to view different parts of the table.

What is a primary key?

A *primary key* uniquely identifies each record in a table. For many tables, the primary key is the ID field by default. The ID field, which Access creates automatically, stores a unique number for each record entered into the database. If you want, however, you can designate another field (or even multiple fields) as a primary key. To do so, switch the table to Design view, select the field that you want to set as the primary key, and click the **Primary key** button on the Design tab.

Add a Record Using a Form

You can use forms to quickly add a record to an Access table. A form presents your record fields in an easy-to-read format. When you use a form to add a record, the form presents each field in your table as a labeled box that you can use to enter data.

For fields that take only a limited set of values, you can configure those values to appear in a convenient drop-down list. (See the second tip for more information.) For help locating a particular record in the form window to edit it, see the next section, "Navigate Records Using a Form."

Add a Record Using a Form

① In the Navigation pane, double-click the form to which you want to add a record.

Ⓐ Access opens the form.

② Click **Home**.

③ Click **New** in the Records group.

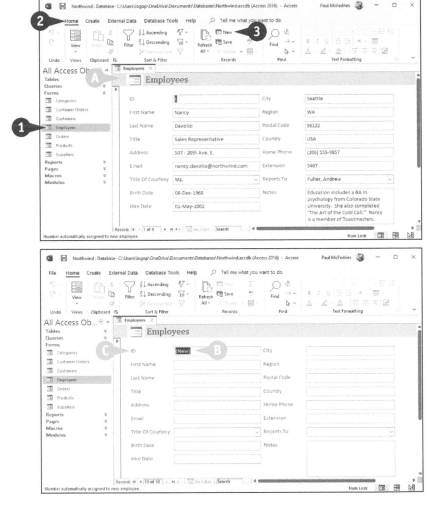

Ⓑ Access displays a blank form, placing the insertion point in the first field.

Ⓒ By default, the first field in the table associated with this form is a unique ID number for the record. Access sets this value automatically.

④ Press **Tab**.

Ⓓ Access assigns an ID number and moves the insertion point to the next field in the form.

⑤ Type the desired data in the selected field.

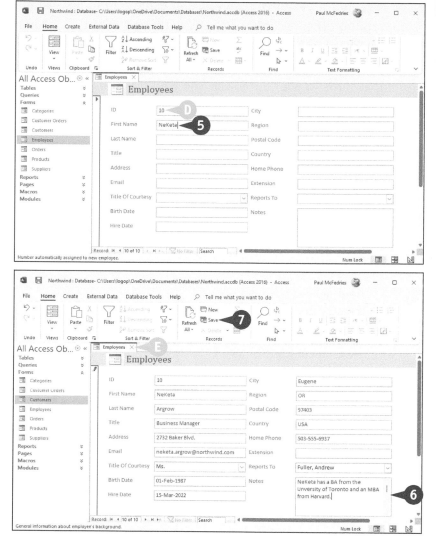

⑥ Repeat steps **4** and **5** until you have filled the entire form.

⑦ Click **Save** or press Enter and press Tab.

Access saves the record and displays another blank form, ready for data.

Ⓔ To close the form window, you can click the **Close** button (✕).

TIPS

Are there other ways to insert a new record?

Yes. You can click the **New (Blank) Record** button (⯈⁕) on the form window's Navigation bar, located along the bottom of the form.

How do set up a form field as a drop-down list?

Open the table in Design view. Right-click the form field that you want to use as a list box. In the menu that appears, click **Change To** and then click **Combo Box**. Click the **Form Design** tab, and then click **Property Sheet**. In the Property Sheet task pane that appears, click the **Data** tab. Click the **Row Source Type** ⌄ and then click **Value List**. Use the **Row Source** property to type each value you want to appear in the list, separated by semicolons. Save the form and switch back to Form view.

Navigate Records Using a Form

Y ou may find it easier to read a record using a form instead of reading it from a large table containing other records. Similarly, editing a record in a form may be easier than editing a record in a table. You can locate records you want to view or edit using the Navigation bar that appears along the bottom of the form window. The Navigation bar contains buttons for locating and viewing different records in your database. The Navigation bar also contains a Search box for locating a specific record. (You learn how to search for a record in a form in the next section.)

Navigate Records Using a Form

1 In the Navigation pane, double-click the form whose records you want to navigate.

A Access displays the form.

B The Current Record box indicates which record you are viewing.

2 Click the **Previous Record** button (◀) or **Next Record** button (▶) to move back or forward by one record.

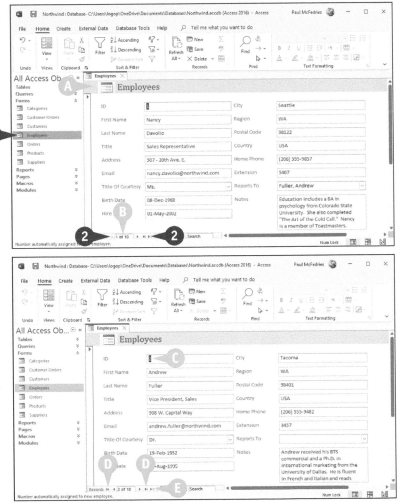

C Access displays the previous or next record in the database.

D You can click the **First Record** button (|◀) or **Last Record** button (▶|) to navigate to the first or last record in the table.

E You can click the **New (Blank) Record** button (▶*) to start a new, blank record.

Search for a Record Using a Form

You may find it easier to read and edit records in a form than in a large table containing other records. As described in the previous section, you can navigate records by using the various buttons in the Navigation bar. However, that method can become time-consuming if the table associated with the form contains many records. This section describes how to search for specific text in a record — an easier approach to finding a record while using a form. You search using the form Navigation bar's Search box.

Search for a Record Using a Form

1 In the Navigation pane, double-click the form containing the record you want to find.

A Access displays the form.

2 Click in the **Search** box.

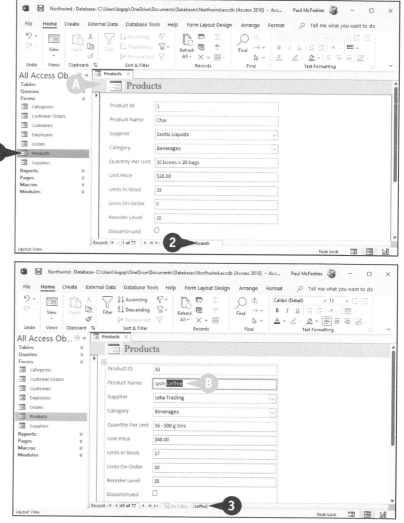

3 Type a keyword that relates to the record you want to find.

B As you type, Access displays the first record containing any field that matches your search.

4 After you finish typing your keyword, press Enter to display the next match, if any.

Delete a Record from a Table

You can remove a record from your database if it holds data that you no longer need. Removing old records can reduce the overall file size of your database and make it easier to manage. When you delete a record, all the data within its fields is permanently removed.

You can remove a record from a database by deleting it from a table or by deleting it from a form. This section shows you how to delete a record from a table. (For help deleting a record from a form, see the next section, "Delete a Record Using a Form.")

Delete a Record from a Table

1 In the Navigation pane, double-click the table that contains the record you want to delete.

A Access opens the table.

2 Position your mouse over the gray box to the left of the record that you want to delete (⌖ changes to ➡) and click.

B Access selects the record.

3 Click **Home**.

4 Click **Delete**.

Note: You can also right-click the record, and then click **Delete Record**.

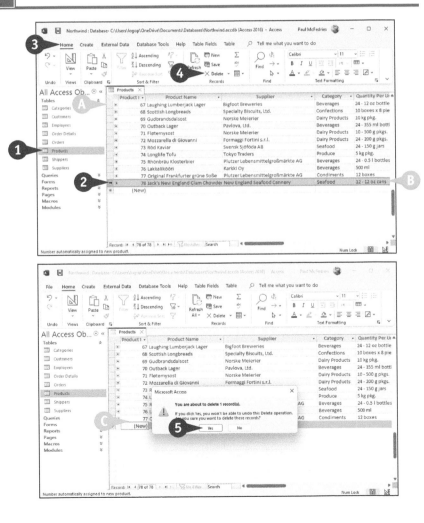

Access asks you to confirm the deletion.

5 Click **Yes**.

C Access permanently removes the row containing the record from the table.

Delete a Record Using a Form

In addition to removing records directly from a table, as described in the previous section, you can remove records that you no longer need by using a form. Removing old records can reduce the overall file size of your database and make it easier to manage. When you delete a record, whether from a table or a form, Access permanently removes all the data within its fields.

The first step is to locate the record you want to delete; refer to the sections "Navigate Records Using a Form" and "Search for a Record Using a Form," earlier in this chapter, for help locating the record.

Delete a Record Using a Form

1 In the Navigation pane, double-click the form containing the record you want to delete.

Ⓐ Access displays the form.

2 Navigate to the record you want to delete.

3 Click this strip to select the entire record.

4 Click **Home**.

5 Click ▼ beside the **Delete** button.

6 Click **Delete Record**.

Access asks you to confirm the deletion.

7 Click **Yes**.

Access permanently removes the record.

Sort Records

Sorting enables you to arrange your database records in a logical order to match any criteria that you specify. By default, Access sorts records in ID order. However, you may want to sort the records alphabetically or based on the ZIP or postal code. You can sort in ascending order or descending order.

You can sort records in a table, or you can use a form to sort records. Sorting records in a table has no effect on the order in which records appear in an associated form; similarly, sorting in a form has no effect on the records in an associated table.

Sort Records

Sort a Table

1 In the Navigation pane, double-click the table you want to sort.

2 Position your mouse over the column heading for the field by which you want to sort (⇩ changes to ⬇) and click to select the column.

3 Click **Home**.

4 Click a sort button:

Click **Ascending** to sort the records in ascending order.

Click **Descending** to sort the records in descending order.

Access sorts the table records based on the field you choose.

Ⓐ In this example, Access sorts the records alphabetically by company name in ascending order.

5 Click ✕ to close the table.

6 In the dialog box that appears, you can click **Yes** to make the sort permanent or **No** to leave the original order intact.

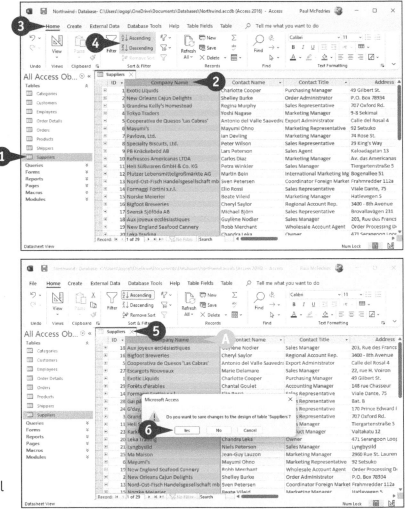

Sort Using a Form

1 In the Navigation pane, double-click the form you want to use to sort records.

2 Click in the field by which you want to sort.

3 Click the **Home** tab.

4 Click a sort button:

Click **Ascending** to sort the records in ascending order.

Click **Descending** to sort the records in descending order.

Access sorts the table records based on the field you chose.

B In this example, Access sorts the records alphabetically by company name in ascending order.

C You can use the navigation buttons (◀, ▶, ◀, and ▶) to navigate through the sorted records.

How are empty records sorted?

If you sort using a field for which some records are missing data, those records are included in the sort; they appear first in an ascending sort or last in a descending sort.

How do I remove a sort order?

With the sorted table or form open, click **Home** and then click the **Remove Sort** button in the Sort & Filter group. This returns the table to its original sort order. You can also use this technique to remove a sort from a query or report. (Queries and reports are covered later in this chapter.)

Filter Records

You can use an Access filter to view only specific records that meet criteria you set. For example, you may want to view all clients buying a particular product, anyone in a contacts database who has a birthday in June, or all products within a particular category. You can also filter by exclusion — that is, filter out records that do not contain the search criteria that you specify.

You can apply a simple filter on one field in your database using the Selection tool, or you can filter several fields using the Filter by Form command.

Filter Records

Apply a Simple Filter

1. In the Navigation pane, double-click the table or form you want to use to filter records.

2. Navigate to the record that contains the field value you want to use as a filter; then click that field.

   This example uses the Condiments value in the Category field as the filter.

3. Click **Home**.

4. Click **Selection**.

5. Click a criterion.

   Ⓐ Access filters the records.

   Ⓑ In this example, Access finds 12 records matching the filter criterion.

   Ⓒ You can use the navigation buttons (◀, ▶, ◀|, and |▶) to view the filtered records.

   Ⓓ To remove the filter, you can click **Toggle Filter**.

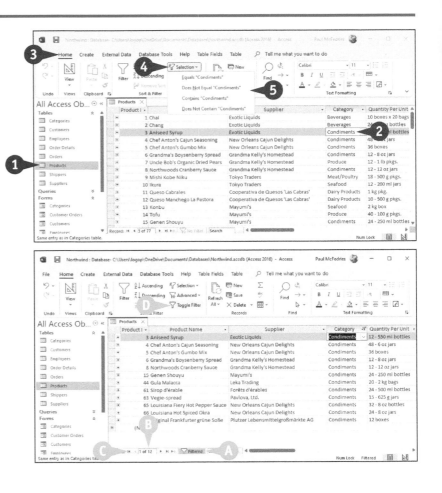

Filter by Form

1 In the Navigation pane, double-click the table or form you want to use to sort records.

2 Click **Home**.

3 Click **Advanced**.

4 Click **Filter By Form**.

E A blank table or form appears.

5 Click in the field that contains the value you want to use as a filter.

6 Click the ⌄ that appears and choose a criterion.

7 Repeat steps **5** and **6** to add more criteria to the filter using other fields (not shown).

F You can set OR criteria using the tab at the bottom of the form.

8 Click **Toggle Filter** to filter the records.

To remove the filter, you can click **Toggle Filter** again. Then, click **Advanced** and click **Clear All Filters**.

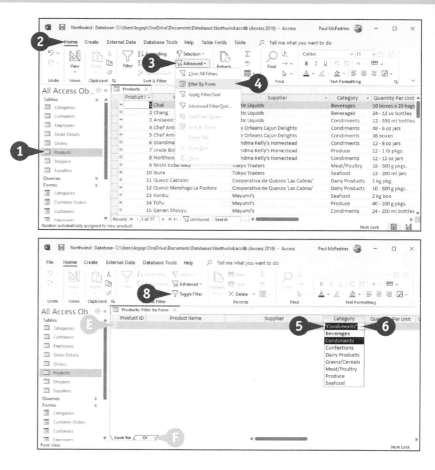

How do I filter by exclusion?

Click in the field that you want to filter in the form, click the **Selection** button on the Home tab, and then click an exclusion option, such as **Does Not equal** "*Value*".

What are OR criteria?

Setting OR criteria enables you to display records that match one set of criteria or another. For example, you might set up your filter to display only those records with the value 46989 or 46555 in the ZIP field. After you set a criterion, Access adds an OR tab. If you set an OR criterion using that tab, Access adds another OR tab, and so on.

Perform a Simple Query

You can use a query to extract information that you want to view in a database. A query defines a subset of your data based on one or more criteria. For example, in a table of products, you could create a query that shows only those records where the Units In Stock field is less than 25 and the Units On Order field is 0.

You can use the Query Wizard to help you select the fields you want to include in the analysis. There are several types of query wizards. This section covers using the Simple Query Wizard.

Perform a Simple Query

Create a Query

1 In the Navigation pane, double-click the table for which you want to create a simple query.

2 Click **Create**.

3 Click **Query Wizard**.

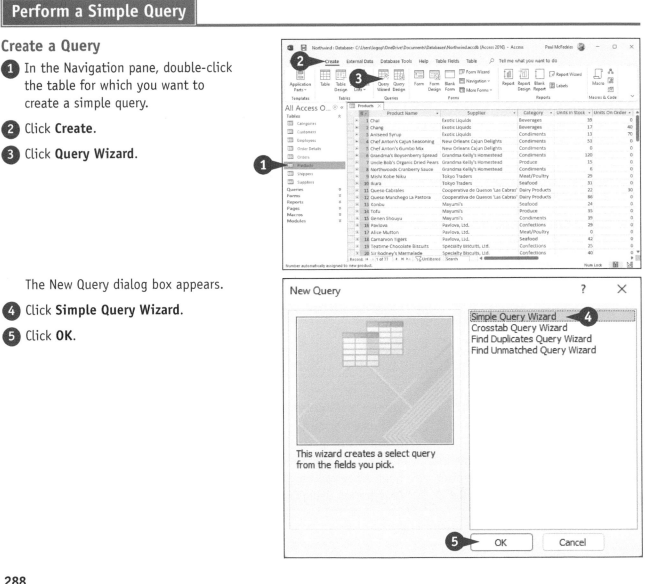

The New Query dialog box appears.

4 Click **Simple Query Wizard**.

5 Click **OK**.

The Simple Query Wizard opens.

6 Click the **Tables/Queries** ⌄ and choose the table containing the fields on which you want to base the query.

7 In the Available Fields list, click a field that you want to include in the query.

8 Click the **Add** button (>).

Ⓐ The field appears in the Selected Fields list.

9 Repeat steps **7** and **8** to add more fields to your query.

You can repeat step **6** to choose another table from which to add fields.

Note: When using fields from two or more tables, the tables must have a relationship. See the tip for more information.

10 Click **Next**.

The Simple Query Wizard asks if you want a detail or summary query.

11 Leave the **Detail** option selected and click **Next** (not shown).

TIP

What is a table relationship?

A table relationship enables you to combine related information for analysis. For example, you might define a relationship between one table containing customer contact information and another table containing customer orders. With that table relationship defined, you can then perform a query to, for example, identify the addresses of all customers who have ordered the same product. To access tools for defining table relationships, click the **Database Tools** tab on the Ribbon and then click **Relationships**. If you created your database from a template, then certain table relationships are predefined.

continued ▶

During the process of creating a new query, the Query Wizard asks you to give the query a unique name so that you can open and use the query later. All queries that you create appear in the Navigation pane; you can double-click a query in the Navigation pane to perform it again.

If, after creating and performing a query, you determine that you need to add more criteria to it, you can easily do so. For example, you may realize that the query needs to include an additional table from your database or additional criteria to expand or limit the scope of the query.

Perform a Simple Query (continued)

12 Type a name for the query.

13 Select **Open the query to view information** (○ changes to ●).

14 Click **Finish**.

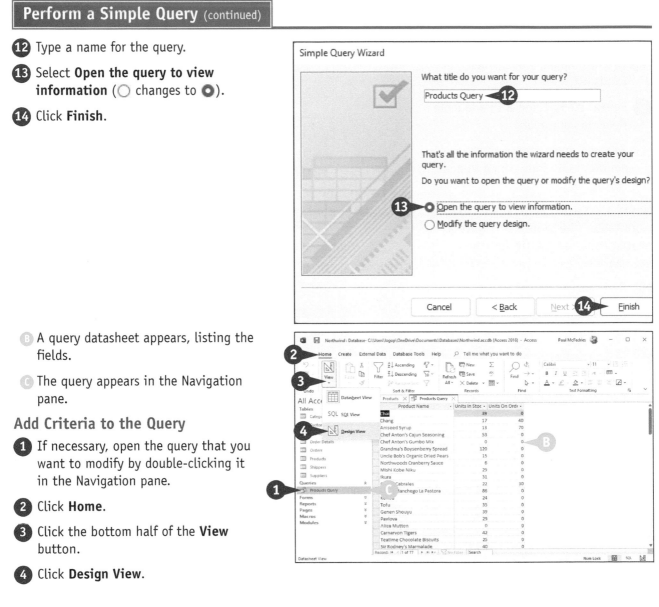

Ⓑ A query datasheet appears, listing the fields.

Ⓒ The query appears in the Navigation pane.

Add Criteria to the Query

1 If necessary, open the query that you want to modify by double-clicking it in the Navigation pane.

2 Click **Home**.

3 Click the bottom half of the **View** button.

4 Click **Design View**.

Ⓓ Access displays the Query Design contextual tab.

5 Click in the **Criteria** box for the field you want to use as a criterion and type the data that you want to view.

The example criteria match records where the UnitsInStock field is less than 25 and the UnitsOnOrder field is 0.

Note: When you add two or more criteria in the same row, Access only matches records that satisfy all the criteria.

6 Click the bottom half of the **View** button.

7 Click **Datasheet View**.

Ⓔ The table now shows only the records matching the criteria.

TIPS

How do I add another table to my query?
Switch to Design view, click the **Query Design** tab on the Ribbon, and then click **Add Tables** to display the Add Tables task pane. Click the **Tables** tab and then double-click the table you want to add to the query.

What kinds of criteria can I add to my queries?
The simplest criterion is to type a value in a field's Criteria field. Access matches all records where the field equals the value you typed. For numeric fields, you can use operators such as less than (<), less than or equal to (<=), greater than (>), greater than or equal to (>=), and not equal to (<>).

Create a Report

You can use Access to create a report based on one or more database tables. You can create a simple report, which contains all the fields in a single table, or a custom report, which can contain data from multiple tables in a database. Note that to use fields from two or more tables, the tables must have a relationship. Refer to the tip "What is a table relationship?" in the previous section, "Perform a Simple Query."

To create a custom report, you can use the Report Wizard; it guides you through the steps to turn database data into an easy-to-read report.

Create a Report

Create a Simple Report

1 In the Navigation pane, double-click the table for which you want to create a simple report.

2 Click the **Create** tab.

3 Click **Report**.

Ⓐ Access creates a simple report based on the table you selected in step **1** and displays it in Layout view.

4 Click ✕ to close the report.

Access prompts you to save the report.

5 Click **Yes**.

6 In the dialog box that appears, supply a report name and click **OK** (not shown).

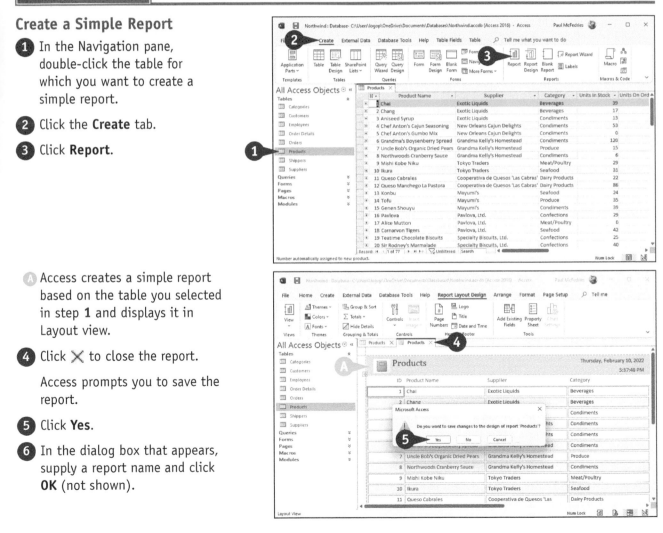

Ⓑ The report appears in the Navigation pane.

Create a Custom Report

① Double-click the table for which you want to create a simple report.

② Click the **Create** tab.

③ Click **Report Wizard**.

The Report Wizard opens.

④ Click the **Tables/Queries** ∨ and choose the table containing the fields on which you want to base the report.

⑤ In the Available Fields list, click a field that you want to include in the report.

⑥ Click the **Add** button (>).

Ⓒ The field appears in the Selected Fields list.

⑦ Repeat steps **5** and **6** to add more fields to your report (not shown).

⑧ Click **Next**.

⑨ Optionally, click the field you want to use to group the data.

⑩ Click the **Add** button (>).

Ⓓ A preview of the grouping appears here.

⑪ Click **Next**.

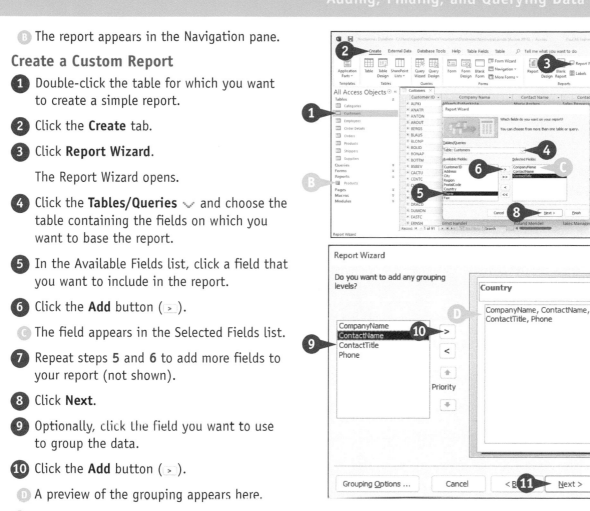

TIPS

How do I choose fields from different tables in a custom report?
Repeat step **4** in the subsection "Create a Custom Report" for each additional table that contains fields you want to include.

How do I remove a field from a custom report?
If you have not yet completed the wizard, you can remove a field from the report by clicking the **Back** button until you reach the wizard's first screen. Then click the field you want to remove in the Selected Fields list and click the **Remove** button (<) to remove the field. To remove all the fields, click the **Remove All** button (<<).

continued ▶

A s you walk through the steps for building a report, the Report Wizard asks you to specify a sort order. You can sort records by up to four fields, in ascending or descending order. The wizard also prompts you to select a layout for the report. Options include Stepped, Block, and Outline, in either portrait or landscape mode.

Note that you can change other design aspects of the report by opening it in Design view. And, after you create the report, you can print it. For more information, see the tips at the end of this section.

Create a Report (continued)

12 To sort your data, click the first ∨ and click the field by which you want to sort.

You can add more sort fields as needed.

Note: Fields are sorted in ascending order by default. Click the **Ascending** button to toggle to descending order.

13 Click **Next**.

14 Select a layout option (○ changes to ◉)

E You can set the page orientation for a report here (○ changes to ◉).

15 Click **Next**.

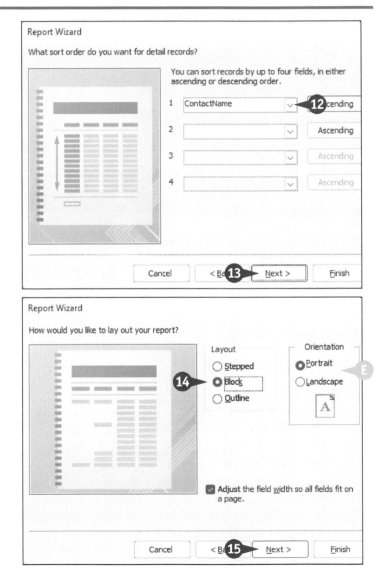

16 Type a name for the report.

17 Select **Preview the report**
(○ changes to ◉).

18 Click **Finish**.

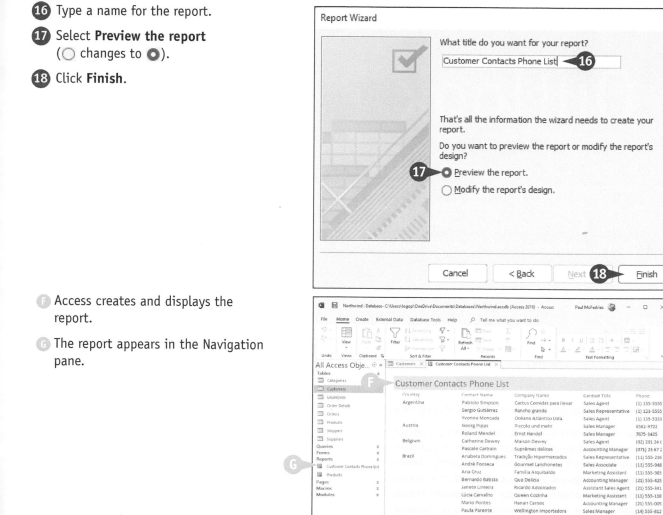

F Access creates and displays the report.

G The report appears in the Navigation pane.

How do I print a report?
Click **Home**, click the lower half of the **View** button, and then click **Print Preview**. In the Print Preview tab, set your print options and then click the **Print** button. Click **Close Print Preview**. Alternatively, click the **File** button and click **Print** to open the Print dialog box, where you can select various printing options.

How can I customize a report in Access?
You can customize a report using Design view. You can change the formatting of fields, move fields around, and more. You can even apply conditional formatting to the report by clicking the **Conditional Formatting** button on the Format tab.

PART VI

Outlook

Outlook is an email program and a personal information manager for the computer desktop. You can use Outlook to send and receive email messages, schedule calendar appointments, keep track of contacts, organize lists of things to do, and more. In this part, you learn how to put Outlook to work for you using each of its major components to manage everyday tasks.

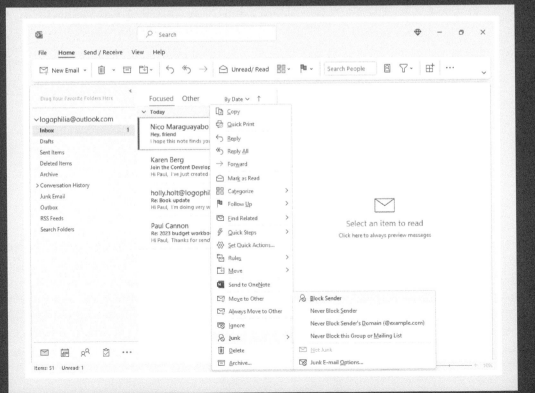

Chapter 18: Organizing with Outlook 298

Chapter 19: Emailing with Outlook 312

Navigate in Outlook

Outlook functions as a personal organizer, with Mail, Calendar, People, Tasks, and Notes components. You switch between these components using the Navigation bar.

The Outlook Mail component appears by default when you open Outlook, and it enables you to send and receive e-mail messages. The Outlook Calendar component enables you to keep track of appointments. The Outlook People component enables you to maintain a database of your contacts and include those contacts in e-mail messages you send and appointments you schedule. The Outlook Tasks component enables you to keep a to-do list.

Navigate in Outlook

1 Start Outlook.

Note: When Outlook opens, the Mail component (✉) appears by default. You can read more about using the Mail component in Chapter 19.

2 Click **Calendar** (📅) in the Navigation bar.

Note: As you hover the mouse (⟍) over Calendar (📅), Outlook displays a preview of upcoming appointments.

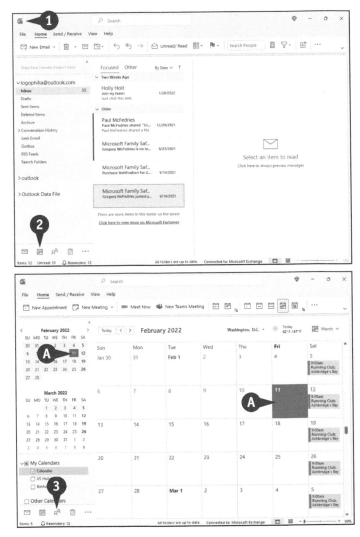

Outlook displays the Month view of the Calendar component.

Ⓐ Today's date appears selected in the main calendar and in the navigational calendars.

3 Click **People** (👥) in the Navigation bar.

Note: As you hover the mouse (⟍) over People (👥), Outlook displays a Search box so you can easily find a contact.

Note: In earlier versions of Outlook, People was called Contacts, and the two terms are often used interchangeably.

Outlook displays the People component.

4 Click **Tasks** (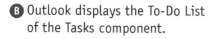) in the Navigation bar.

Note: As you hover the mouse (🔩) over Tasks (🗹), Outlook displays a preview of upcoming tasks.

B Outlook displays the To-Do List of the Tasks component.

How do I change which component opens by default when I start Outlook?

To start with a different Mail folder or another component, such as Calendar (📅), click the **File** tab, and click **Options** to display the Outlook Options dialog box. On the left, click **Advanced**. In the Outlook Start and Exit section, click the **Browse** button to display the Select Folder dialog box. Click the component or Mail folder that you want to set as the default component (A). Click **OK** twice to close both dialog boxes.

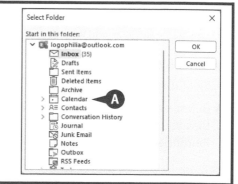

Schedule an Appointment

You can use Outlook's Calendar component to keep track of your schedule. When adding new appointments to the Calendar, you fill out appointment details, such as the name of the person with whom you are meeting, the location and date, and the start and end times. You can also enter notes about the appointment, as well as set up Outlook to remind you of the appointment in advance.

If your appointment occurs regularly, such as a weekly department meeting, you can set it as a recurring appointment. Outlook adds recurring appointments to each day, week, or month as you require.

Schedule an Appointment

1 Click **Calendar** (▦) in the Navigation bar.

2 Click the date for which you want to set an appointment.

Ⓐ You can click these arrows (‹ and ›) to navigate to a different month.

Ⓑ You can click these buttons to select a different calendar view, such as a daily or weekly view.

3 Click **New Appointment** to display the Appointment window.

4 Type a name for the appointment.

Ⓒ You can type the appointment location here.

5 Click the **Start time** ▼ and set a start time.

6 Click the **End time** ▼ and set the end time.

Ⓓ You can type notes about the appointment here.

Ⓔ Outlook automatically sets a reminder that you can change by clicking the **Reminder** ▼.

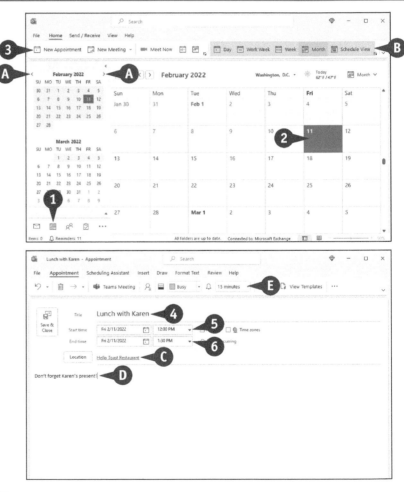

7 If your appointment occurs regularly, click **Make Recurring**. Otherwise, skip to step **10**.

The Appointment Recurrence dialog box appears.

8 Select the recurrence pattern.

F In the Range of Recurrence section, you can limit the appointments if they continue only for a specified time.

9 Click **OK**.

G Outlook marks the appointment as a recurring appointment.

10 Click **Save & Close**.

Outlook displays the appointment in the Calendar. To view the appointment details or make changes, double-click the appointment. To delete an appointment, right-click it and click **Delete**.

Note: If other people have access to your calendar, you can mark a personal event as private by right-clicking the event and then clicking **Private**.

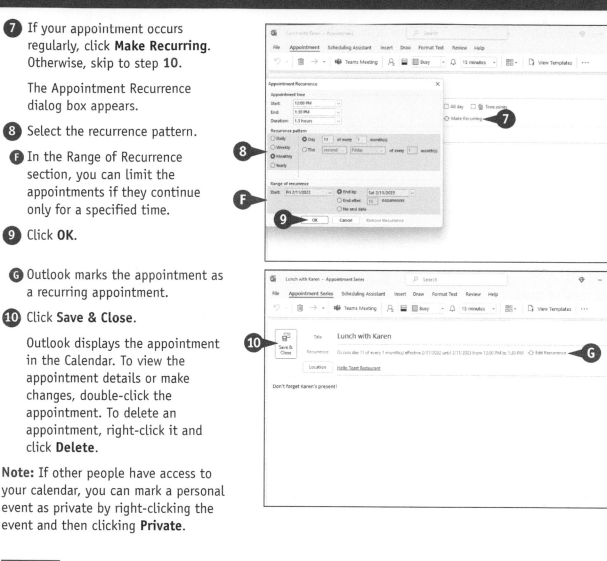

TIPS

How do I set up an event that has no set time?
If you are scheduling an event such as a birthday, anniversary, or sales meeting that has no start or end time, then you need to set up an all-day event instead of a regular event. Follow steps **1** to **4** to create and title a new event. Click **All day** (☐ changes to ☑). Set the event's start and end dates, and then continue with steps **7** to **10**.

Why do certain dates on the navigation calendars appear in bold?
Dates that appear in bold indicate that you have appointments scheduled on those days.

Create a New Contact

You can use Outlook's People component to maintain a list of contact information. You can track information such as your contacts' home and business addresses; e-mail addresses; instant message addresses; company information; home, work, fax, and mobile phone numbers; and social media updates. You can also enter notes about a contact.

By default, Outlook displays contact information using the People view; you can edit contact information and interact with your contacts from the People view. You can also switch to other views such as the Business Card or List view.

Create a New Contact

Create a Contact

1 Click **People** (⌾) in the Navigation bar.

2 Click **New Contact**.

Outlook opens a Contact window.

3 Fill in the contact's information.

You can press **Tab** to move from field to field.

Ⓐ You can click **More commands** (⋯) and then click **Details** to fill in additional information about the contact.

4 Click **Save & Close**.

Ⓑ Outlook saves the information and displays the contact in the People component.

Ⓒ On the **View** tab, you can click **Change View** to see and switch to the available views.

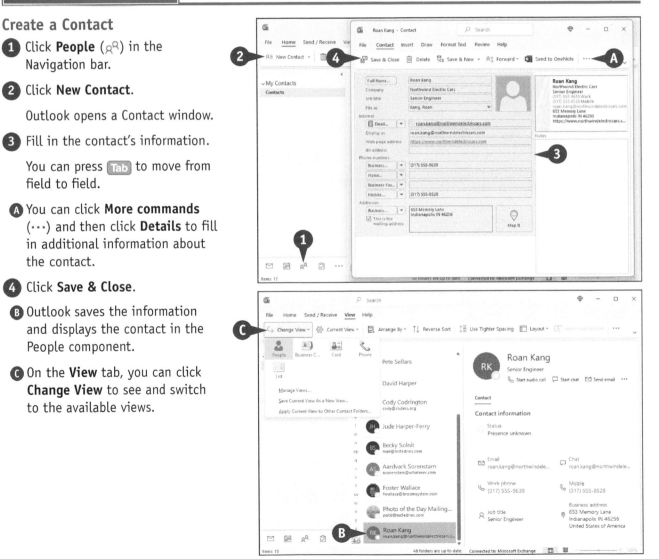

302

Work with the People Card

1 Click a contact.

D To find the contact, you can click here and type part of the contact's name.

E Information about the contact appears here.

F You can click these links to call the contact or send an e-mail to the contact.

2 To edit using the People card, click **More commands** (···) and then click **Edit Contact**.

Outlook displays People card fields in an editable format.

3 Make any changes.

4 Click **Save & Close**.

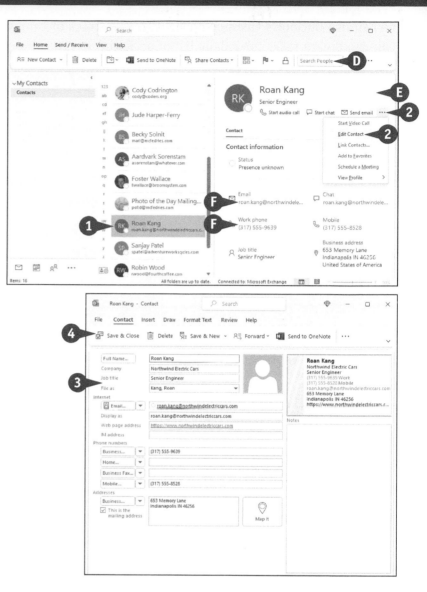

Is there an easy way to set up an appointment or e-mail one of my contacts if I am using Business Card view?
Yes. Right-click the contact and click **Create**. Click **Email** or **Meeting** (A). If you click **Email**, Outlook opens a Message window containing the contact's e-mail address in the To field; see Chapter 19 for details on completing the message. If you click **Meeting**, a Meeting window appears, where you can enter appointment details and e-mail a meeting request to the contact.

Create a New Task

You can use Outlook's Tasks component to keep track of things that you need to do; for example, you can create tasks for a daily list of activities or project steps that you need to complete. You can assign a due date to each task, prioritize and categorize tasks, and set a reminder date and time. You can set up a recurring task and even assign tasks to other people.

When you finish a task, you can mark it as complete. Depending on the current view, completed tasks may appear with a strikethrough on the Tasks list or they may not appear at all.

Create a New Task

① Click **Tasks** (⬛) in the Navigation bar to open the Tasks component.

② Click **New Task**.

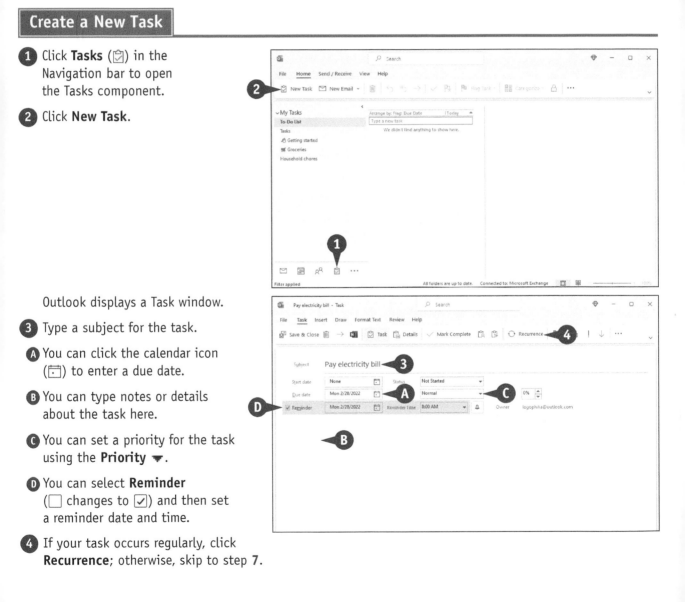

Outlook displays a Task window.

③ Type a subject for the task.

Ⓐ You can click the calendar icon (🗓) to enter a due date.

Ⓑ You can type notes or details about the task here.

Ⓒ You can set a priority for the task using the **Priority** ▼.

Ⓓ You can select **Reminder** (☐ changes to ☑) and then set a reminder date and time.

④ If your task occurs regularly, click **Recurrence**; otherwise, skip to step **7**.

The Task Recurrence dialog box appears.

⑤ Select the recurrence pattern.

Ⓔ In the Range of Recurrence section, you can limit the tasks if they continue only for a specified time.

⑥ Click **OK**.

⑦ Click **Save & Close**.

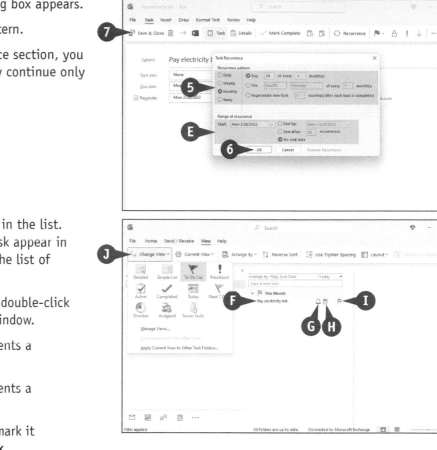

Ⓕ Outlook displays the task in the list. Details of the selected task appear in the pane to the right of the list of tasks.

Note: To edit a task, you can double-click the task to reopen the Task window.

Ⓖ This indicator (🔔) represents a reminder.

Ⓗ This indicator (🔄) represents a recurring task.

Ⓘ You can click a task and mark it complete by clicking **Mark Complete** (🏳).

Ⓙ On the **View** tab, you can click **Change View** and choose a different view of tasks.

TIP

What happens if I click Tasks on the left side of the Tasks component?

You see an alternative view of the items in the To-Do List. From the To-Do List view (shown throughout this section), you see only outstanding tasks you have not yet completed. From the Tasks view, you see all your tasks; the ones you have completed (A) appear with a strikethrough line and a check mark to indicate they are complete.

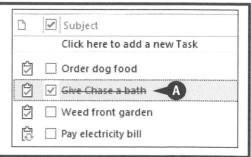

Add a Note

Outlook includes a Notes component, which you can use to create notes for yourself. Much like an electronic version of yellow sticky notes, Outlook's Notes component enables you to quickly and easily jot down your ideas and thoughts. You can attach Outlook Notes to other items in Outlook, as well as drag them from the Outlook window onto the Windows desktop for easy viewing.

Add a Note

1 Click **More** (···) to display a pop-up menu.

2 Click **Notes** to open the Notes component.

3 Click **New Note**.

Ⓐ Outlook displays a yellow note.

4 Type your note text.

5 When you finish, click the note's **Close** button (✕).

Ⓑ Outlook adds the note.

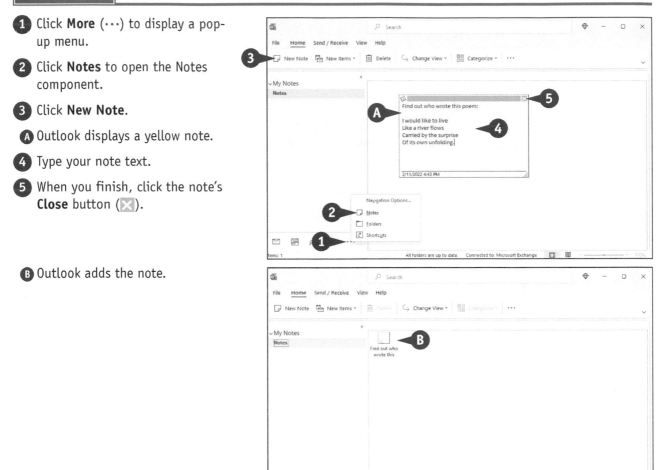

To view the note again or to make changes, you can double-click it.

C To change your view of notes, you can click **Change View**.

This example displays the Notes List view.

TIP

How do I delete a note that I no longer want?

Click the note in the Notes list and then press Delete. To delete multiple notes at the same time, press and hold Ctrl while clicking the notes. Once you delete a note, Outlook places it in the Deleted Items folder. If you accidentally delete a note, you can click the **Undo** button (↺) immediately after you delete the note. If you discover later that you need the note, follow these steps:

1 Click the **More** button (···).

2 Click **Folders**.

3 Click **Deleted Items**.

4 Find the note and drag it to the Notes folder.

Customize the Navigation Bar

You can control the appearance of the Navigation bar, displaying fewer items or more items to suit your needs. For example, suppose that you use the Notes component regularly. You can save mouse clicks if you display the Notes component as part of the Navigation bar.

In addition to determining which components appear on the Navigation bar, you can control the order in which they appear. You can also control the size of the Navigation bar by choosing to display buttons that represent each component instead of displaying the component name.

Customize the Navigation Bar

1 From any Outlook component, click **More** (···).

A A pop-up menu appears.

2 Click **Navigation Options**.

The Navigation Options dialog box appears.

③ Click ⬍ to specify the number of items you want visible on the Navigation bar.

④ To reorder the Navigation bar entries, click an item and then click **Move Up** or **Move Down**.

Ⓑ You can click **Reset** if you want to return the Navigation bar to its original state.

⑤ Click **OK**.

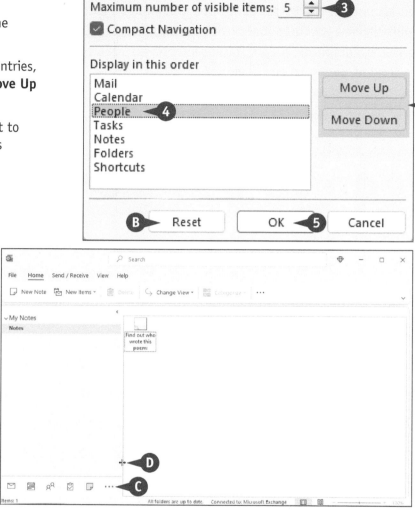

Navigation Options ✕

Maximum number of visible items: 5 ⬍ ③

☑ Compact Navigation

Display in this order

Mail
Calendar
People ④
Tasks
Notes
Folders
Shortcuts

Move Up ④

Move Down

Ⓑ Reset   OK ⑤   Cancel

Ⓒ The Navigation bar appears with your changes.

Ⓓ You might need to widen the left pane in Outlook to see all the Navigation buttons. Slide the mouse over the pane divider (⬉ changes to ↔) and drag the pane divider to the right.

Can I display labels rather than icons in the Navigation bar?

Mail Calendar People Tasks Notes ⋯ Ⓐ

Yes. Complete steps **1** and **2** to display the Navigation Options dialog box shown earlier in this section. Then, select **Compact Navigation** (☑ changes to ☐). Click **OK**, and labels for each Outlook module replace the buttons on the Navigation bar (A).

Peek at Appointments and Tasks

From any Outlook component, you can take a peek at today's appointments and at your task list. You do not need to select the Calendar component or the Tasks component to view appointments or tasks.

If you also unpin the Folder pane, which is pinned by default, you hide the leftmost pane in each component view and give more real estate to each component. When you hide the Folder pane, you can peek at appointments and tasks, and you also can pin the peeked view so that it remains visible for as long as you need to see it.

Peek at Appointments and Tasks

1 To hide the Folder pane, click the **Minimize the Folder Pane** button ( ).

A Outlook hides the Folder pane and instead displays the Expand Folder Pane button ( ).

B Outlook docks the Navigation bar buttons on the left side of the screen.

2 To peek at your appointments, hover the mouse ( ) over Calendar ( ) on the Navigation bar.

C Outlook displays a small window that enables you to "peek" at your calendar.

3 To peek at your tasks, hover the mouse ( ) over Tasks ( ).

D Outlook displays a list of your tasks.

E You can click here and type a name to add a new task.

Note: When you press Enter to add the task, Outlook adds the task to your list as a task for today. See the section "Create a New Task," earlier in this chapter, for details on editing the task.

4 To pin a peek view so that it is permanently visible, click the **Dock the Peek** button (⬚).

F Outlook pins the tasks or appointments to the right side of the current component's window.

Note: The pinned peek view appears only in the component you were viewing when you pinned it.

G You can click the **Close** button (✕) to unpin the peek view.

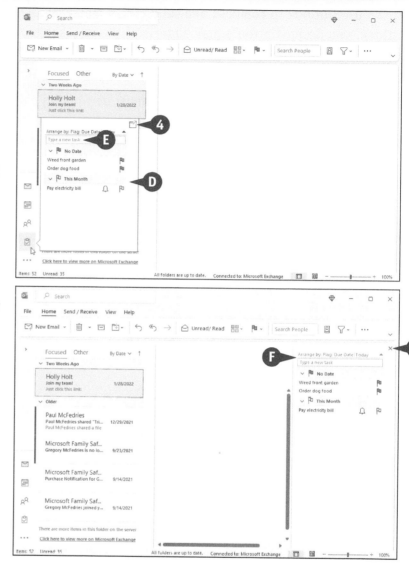

Compose and Send a Message

You can use Outlook to compose and send e-mail messages. When you compose a message in Outlook, you designate the e-mail address of the message recipient (or recipients) and type your message text. You also give the message a subject title to identify the content of the message for recipients.

You can compose a message offline, but you must be working online to send it. If you do not have time to finish composing your message during your current work session, you can save the message as a draft and come back later to finish it.

Compose and Send a Message

1 In the Navigation bar, click **Mail** (✉) to display the Mail component.

2 Click **Home**.

3 Click **New Email**.

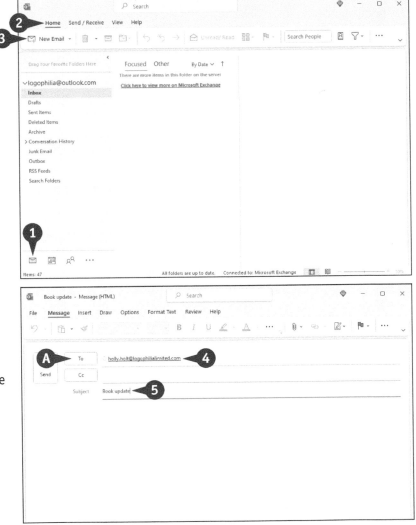

Outlook opens an untitled message window.

4 Type the recipient's e-mail address.

A If the e-mail address is already in your Address Book, you can click the **To** button and select the recipient's name.

If you enter more than one e-mail address, you must separate each address with a semicolon (;) and a space.

5 Type a subject for the message.

6 Type the message text.

B You can use the formatting buttons to change the appearance of your message text.

C To set a priority level for the message, you can click **More commands** (···) and then click **High Importance** or **Low Importance**.

Note: By default, the message priority level is Normal.

7 Click **Send**.

Outlook places the message in your Outbox.

Note: You might need to press F9 or click the **Send/Receive** tab and click **Send All** or **Send/Receive All Folders** to send the message.

8 Click the **Sent Items** folder.

D The message you sent appears in the list; Outlook stores a copy of all messages you send in the Sent Items folder.

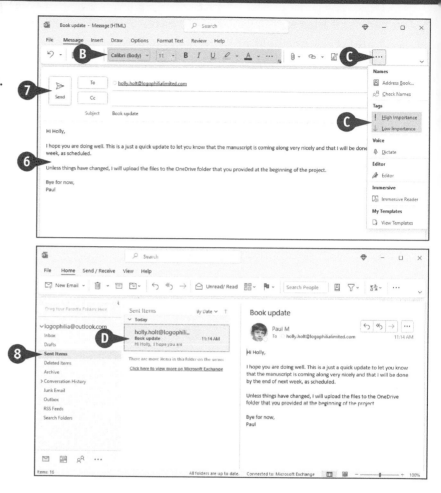

TIPS

How do I save a message as a draft?
Click the message window's **Close** button (✖) and click **Yes** when prompted to save the message. Outlook saves the message in the Drafts folder. When you are ready to continue composing your message, click the **Drafts** folder and double-click the saved message to open it.

How do I send a copy of my message to someone?
To copy the message to another recipient, either type the recipient's e-mail address directly in the Cc field or click the **Cc** button to select the address from your contacts. To add the Bcc (blind courtesy copy) field, click **Options**, click **More** (···), and then click **Bcc**.

Send a File Attachment

You can send files stored on your computer to other e-mail recipients. For example, you might send an Excel worksheet or Word document to a work colleague or send a digital photo of your child's birthday to a relative. Assuming that the recipient's computer has the necessary software installed, that person can open and view the file on their own system.

Note that some e-mail systems are not set up to handle large file attachments (say, 10MB or more). If you are sending a large attachment, check with the recipient to see if their system can handle it.

Send a File Attachment

1 Create a new e-mail message as described in the previous section, "Compose and Send a Message."

2 Click **Message**.

3 Click **Attach File** (🔗).

The Recent Items list appears, showing attachments you have sent recently.

4 Click the file you want to send.

Ⓐ If the file does not appear in the Recent Items list, click **Browse This PC**, navigate to the folder containing the file, and select it.

If you see a dialog box asking how you want to attach the file, click **Attach as copy**.

Ⓑ Outlook adds the file attachment to the message, displaying the filename and file size.

5 Click **Send**.

Outlook sends the e-mail message and attachment.

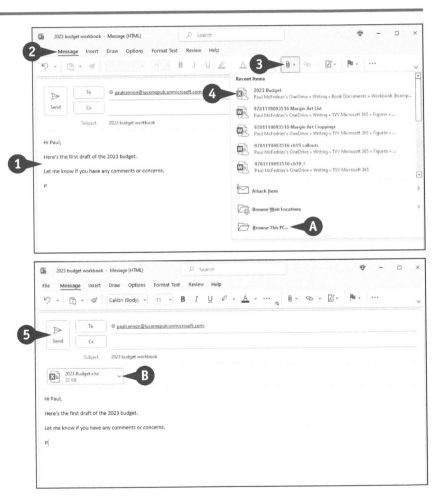

Read an Incoming Message

You can use Outlook's Mail feature to retrieve new e-mail messages that others have sent you and view them on-screen. You can view a message in a separate message window or in the Reading pane, as described in this section. By default, the Reading pane appears beside the list of messages, but you can place it below the message list.

Note that you must be connected to the Internet to receive e-mail messages.

Read an Incoming Message

① Click **Mail** (✉).

② Click **Send/Receive**.

③ Click **Send/Receive All Folders**.

Outlook retrieves new e-mail messages.

④ If the Inbox is not selected, click the **Inbox** folder.

Ⓐ Messages appear in the Message list pane, with a preview.

Ⓑ Messages you have not opened display a vertical bar.

⑤ Click a message.

Ⓒ The contents of the message appear in the Reading pane.

Note: You can double-click a message to open it in a message window.

Ⓓ Messages containing attachments display a paper clip (📎).

Note: To open an attachment, open the message, click the attachment's ⌄, and then click **Open**. Alternatively, click **Save As** to save the attachment. Never open a file unless you trust the sender.

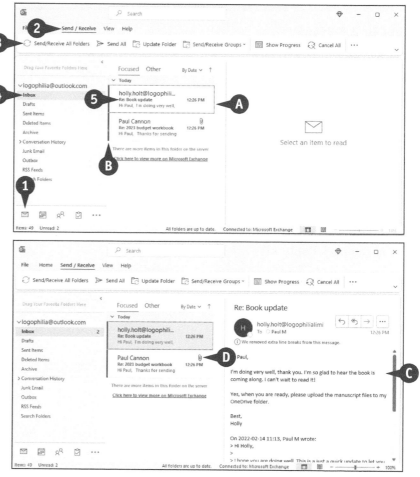

Reply to or Forward a Message

You can reply to an e-mail message by sending a return message to the original sender. For example, if you receive an e-mail message containing a question, you can reply to that e-mail with your answer. When you reply to an e-mail, the original sender's name is added to the To field in the message.

You can also forward the message to another recipient. For example, you might forward a message that you receive from one co-worker to another co-worker who will find its contents useful. Note that you must be connected to the Internet in order to send replies or forward e-mail messages.

Reply to or Forward a Message

Reply to a Message

1 Click **Mail** (✉).

2 In the Message list pane, click the message to which you want to reply.

3 In the Reading pane, click **Reply** (↩) to reply to the original sender.

Ⓐ To reply to the sender as well as to everyone else who received the original message, you can click **Reply All** (↩).

Ⓑ The original sender's address appears in the To field.

Ⓒ You can click **Pop Out** to open your reply in its own message window.

4 Type your reply.

Ⓓ If you change your mind and do not want to reply to the message, you can click **Discard**.

5 Click **Send**.

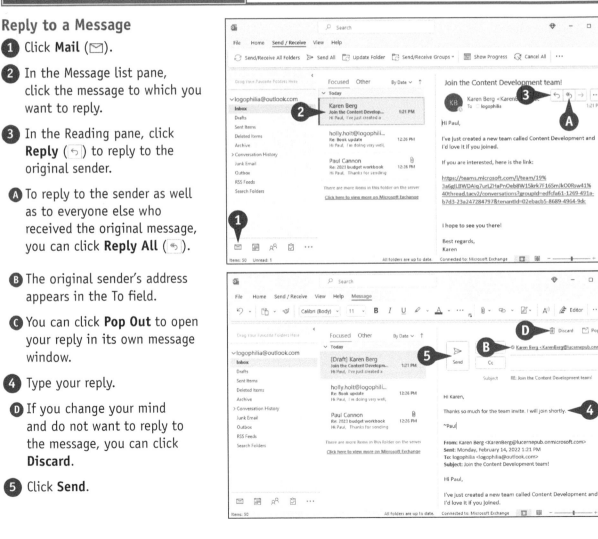

316

E Outlook places the e-mail message in the Outbox.

F Outlook sends the message at its next automatically scheduled send/receive action; to send the message, click **Send/Receive All Folders** on the Send/Receive tab.

Forward a Message

1 Click **Mail** (✉).

2 In the Message list pane, click the message you want to forward.

3 In the Reading pane, click **Forward** (→).

4 Type the recipient's e-mail address in the **To** field.

G You can click **Pop Out** to open your message in its own window.

5 Perform steps **4** and **5** in the previous subsection, "Reply to a Message."

TIP

How do I look up an e-mail address when forwarding a message?

Perform steps **1** to **3** in the subsection "Forward a Message." Click the **To** button to display a list of your contacts. Type a few letters to identify the contact. Outlook highlights the first contact that matches what you typed. If necessary, use the arrow keys to highlight the correct contact. Press **Enter** to display the contact in the To field. Click **OK** and Outlook places the contact name in the To field of your message.

Add a Sender to Your Outlook Contacts

Suppose you receive an e-mail message from someone with whom you expect to correspond regularly, but you do not have a record for that individual in Outlook contacts. You can easily add the contact information of the sender of any message you receive to your Outlook contacts, directly from the message. If you want to send a new message to that person later, you can click the **To** button in the Message window and choose their name from the Select Names: Contacts dialog box.

Add a Sender to Your Outlook Contacts

① Click **Mail** (✉).

② In the Message list pane, click the message from the sender you want to add as a contact.

③ In the Reading pane, right-click the sender's name.

④ Click **Add to Outlook Contacts**.

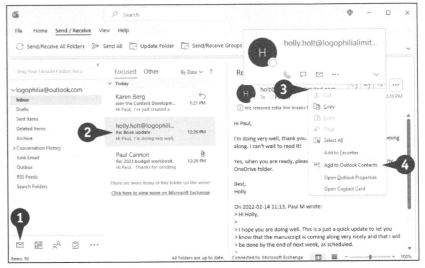

Ⓐ A window opens with the sender's e-mail address already filled in.

⑤ Type a name for the contact.

⑥ Fill in the rest of the contact's information, as needed.

⑦ Click **Save & Close**.

Outlook saves the contact information.

Delete a Message

As you receive e-mail messages, you can eliminate clutter and keep things manageable if you delete messages you no longer need from your Inbox and other Outlook folders.

Note that when you delete a message from your Inbox or any other Outlook folder, Outlook does not remove it from your system. Rather, it moves it to the Deleted Items folder. To permanently remove deleted messages from your system, thereby maximizing your computer's storage capacity, you should empty the Deleted Items folder regularly.

Delete a Message

1 Click **Mail** (✉).

2 In the Message list pane, click the message you want to delete.

3 Move the mouse (🔓) over the message you clicked in step **2**.

The Delete icon (🗑) appears.

4 Click the **Delete** icon (🗑) in the Message list pane.

Ⓐ Alternatively, click **Delete** on the Home tab or press `Delete`.

Outlook deletes the message from the Inbox and the Message list pane and adds it to the Deleted Items folder.

Ⓑ You can click the **Deleted Items** folder to view the message that you deleted.

Ⓒ To empty the Deleted Items folder, right-click it and click **Empty Folder**.

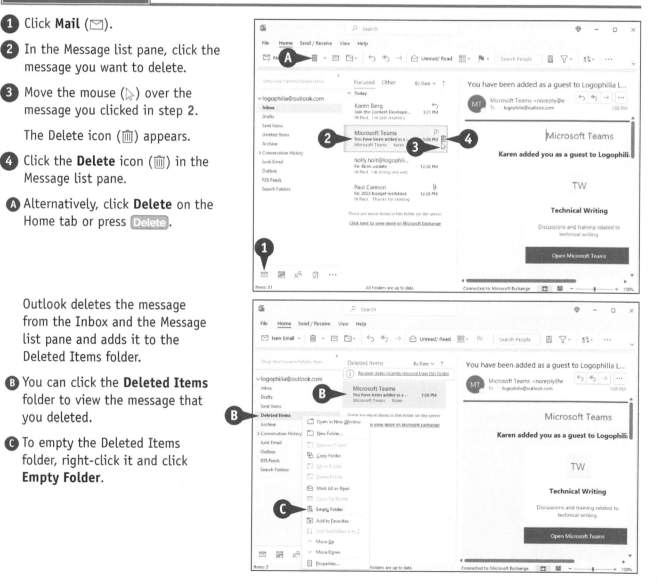

Screen Junk E-Mail

Junk e-mail, also called *spam*, is overly abundant on the Internet and often finds its way into your Inbox. You can safeguard against wasting time viewing unsolicited messages by setting up Outlook's Junk Email feature. This feature enables you to make sure that Outlook bypasses e-mail from specific web domains and instead deposits those messages into the Outlook Junk Email folder.

Note that Outlook might erroneously place e-mail that is *not* spam in the Junk Email folder. For this reason, you should periodically scan the contents of this folder to ensure that it does not contain any legitimate messages you want to read.

Screen Junk E-Mail

View Junk E-Mail Options

1. Click **Mail** (✉).
2. Click **Home**.
3. Click **More** (⋯).
4. Click **Junk**.
5. Click **Junk E-mail Options**.

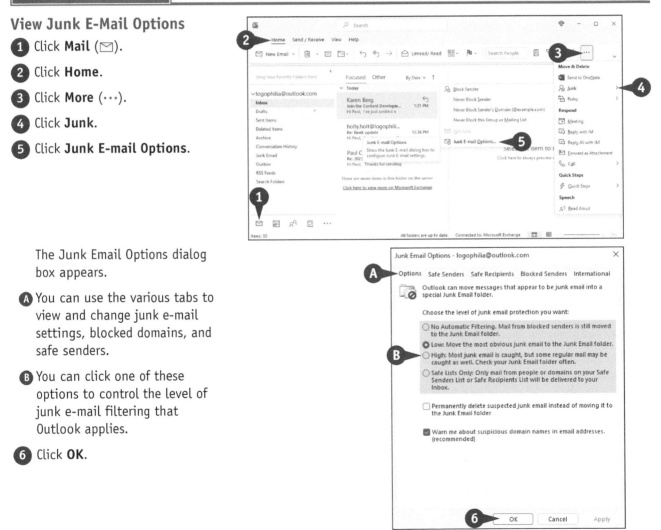

The Junk Email Options dialog box appears.

Ⓐ You can use the various tabs to view and change junk e-mail settings, blocked domains, and safe senders.

Ⓑ You can click one of these options to control the level of junk e-mail filtering that Outlook applies.

6. Click **OK**.

Designate a Message as Junk

1. Click **Mail** (✉).

2. Right-click the message in the Message list pane.

3. Click **Junk**.

4. Click **Block Sender**.

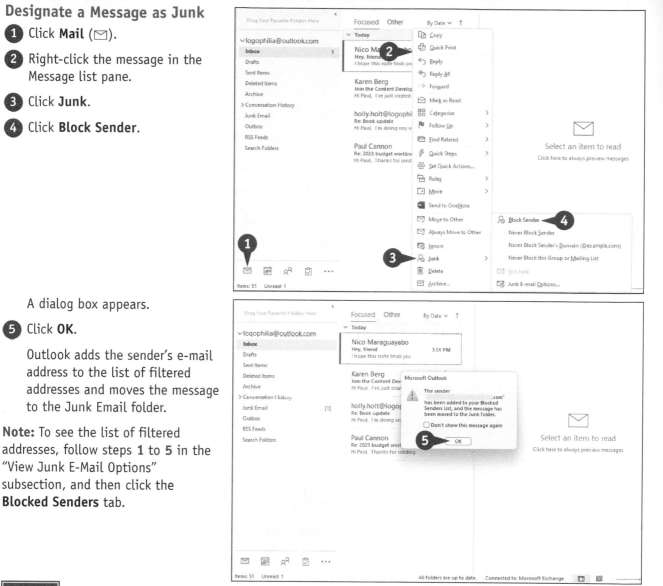

A dialog box appears.

5. Click **OK**.

Outlook adds the sender's e-mail address to the list of filtered addresses and moves the message to the Junk Email folder.

Note: To see the list of filtered addresses, follow steps **1** to **5** in the "View Junk E-Mail Options" subsection, and then click the **Blocked Senders** tab.

TIPS

How can I restore a junk e-mail to my safe list?
Right-click the message in the Junk Email folder and, from the menu that appears, click **Junk** and then click **Not Junk**. Outlook alerts you that it will move the message back to its original location and gives you the option of removing the sender from the filter list; click **OK**.

Does Outlook empty the Junk Email folder?
No. To empty the folder, right-click it and click the **Empty Folder** button. Outlook permanently removes all items in the Junk Email folder.

Create a Message Rule

You can use rules to determine what Outlook does when you receive a message that meets a specific set of conditions. For example, you might create a rule that ensures that any message from a certain sender is placed directly into a folder of your choosing as soon as Outlook downloads the message. Alternatively, you might set up Outlook to play a certain sound when you receive a message that meets the criteria you set.

You can set rules that are quite simple, as outlined in this section, or rules that are very complex — involving various criteria, exceptions to the rule, and so on.

Create a Message Rule

1. Click **Mail** (✉).

2. Click the message on which you want to base a rule.

3. Click **Home**.

4. Click **More** (···).

5. Click **Rules**.

6. Click **Create Rule**.

   The Create Rule dialog box appears.

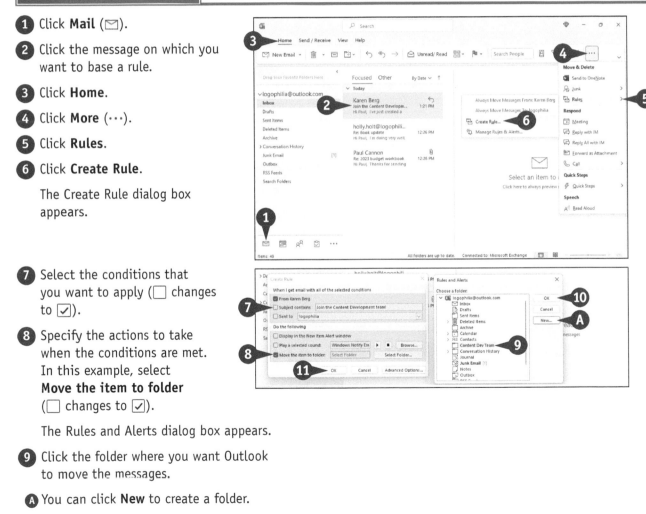

7. Select the conditions that you want to apply (☐ changes to ☑).

8. Specify the actions to take when the conditions are met. In this example, select **Move the item to folder** (☐ changes to ☑).

   The Rules and Alerts dialog box appears.

9. Click the folder where you want Outlook to move the messages.

   Ⓐ You can click **New** to create a folder.

10. Click **OK**.

11. Click **OK**.

Outlook prompts you to run the rule now.

12 Select the check box (☐ changes to ☑).

13 Click **OK**.

Success

The rule "Karen Berg" has been created.

12 ☑ Run this rule now on messages already in the current folder

13 OK

B Outlook runs the rule; in this example, Outlook moves any existing messages to the folder you specified.

The next time you receive a message matching the criteria you set, Outlook runs the rule.

Search

File Home Send / Receive View Help

New Email ⌄

Drag Your Favorite Folders Here

Content Dev Team   By Date ⌄ ↑

⌄ Today

⌄logophilia@outlook.com
Inbox
Drafts
Sent Items
> Deleted Items
Archive
Content Dev Team ◄ **B**
> Conversation History
Junk Email   [1]
Outbox
RSS Feeds
Search Folders

Karen Berg   ↩ **B**
Join the Content Developm... 1:21 PM
Hi Paul, I've just created a

TIPS

How do I add more criteria to a message rule?
Perform steps **1** to **6**. Then, click the **Advanced Options** button to display the Rules Wizard, which includes several sets of criteria that you can specify, such as exceptions to the rule, actions, and even a dialog box for naming the rule.

How do I remove a rule?
Click the **Home** tab, click **More** (···), click **Rules**, and then click **Manage Rules & Alerts**. In the Rules and Alerts dialog box that appears, click the rule you want to remove and click the **Delete** button.

Index

A

absolute cell references, applying in Excel, 172–173

Access. *See* Microsoft Access

adding
- animation effects in PowerPoint, 240–241
- borders
  - to cells in Excel, 138–139
  - in Word, 86–87
- captions in PowerPoint, 205
- chart elements in Excel, 187
- charts to slides in PowerPoint, 226–227
- columns to tables in PowerPoint, 225
- commands to Quick Access Toolbar, 14–15
- comments in Word, 120
- criteria to queries in Access, 290–291
- effects, 35
- fields
  - to PivotTables, 195
  - to tables in Access, 266
- fill color in Excel, 139
- footers in Word, 94–95
- headers in Word, 94–95
- notes in Outlook, 306–307
- page number fields in Word, 95
- picture borders, 35
- records in Access, 276–279
- rows
  - to tables in PowerPoint, 225
  - to tables in Word, 91
- sections to slides in PowerPoint, 236–237
- senders to contacts in Outlook, 318
- shading
  - to cells in Excel, 138–139
  - to text in Word, 87
- slide text in PowerPoint, 214–215
- special characters in Word, 61
- tables
  - to queries in Access, 291
  - to slides in PowerPoint, 224–225
- text boxes to slides in PowerPoint, 223

Touch/Mouse mode to Quick Access Toolbar, 16

vertical lines between columns in Word, 89

video clips to slides in PowerPoint, 228–229

worksheets in Excel, 152

adjusting
- animation direction in PowerPoint, 241
- aspect ratio in PowerPoint, 203
- background color in Word, 85
- cell alignment in Excel, 132–133
- chart data in Excel, 189
- chart layout in Excel, 186
- chart style in Excel, 185
- chart type in Excel, 184
- color
  - about, 34
  - of ink in pen/laser pointer tools, 251
  - of pages in Word, 99
  - of text in Word, 64
- color schemes, 8–9
- column width in Word, 101
- default font/size in Word, 65
- duration of effects in PowerPoint, 243
- font
  - in Excel, 134–135
  - in PowerPoint, 216–217
  - in Word, 62
- font size
  - in Excel, 134–135
  - in PowerPoint, 217
- form views in Access, 272
- number formats in Excel, 136
- orientation of data in Excel, 133
- page setup options in Excel, 154–155
- slide layout in PowerPoint, 210–211
- slide size in PowerPoint, 212–213
- table views in Access, 264–265
- text size in Word, 63
- views
  - in PowerPoint, 206–207
  - in Word, 54–55

aligning text, 66, 222
Alt Text, 29
analyzing data, in Excel, 164–165
animations (PowerPoint), 240–243
app window, 6
applying
    absolute cell reference sin Excel, 172–173
    artistic effects, 35
    cell styles in Excel, 140
    conditional formatting in Excel, 142–143
    data bars in Excel, 143
    relative cell references in Excel, 172–173
    Sparkline styles in Excel, 191
    styles
        to graphics, 35
        to tables in Word, 92
        in Word, 79
    text formatting
        in PowerPoint, 217
        in Word, 63
    themes
        in Excel, 141
        in PowerPoint, 220
        in Word, 84
appointments (Outlook), 300–301, 310–311
apps
    exiting, 4–5
    online, 44–45, 46
    starting, 4–5
    using with a touch screen, 16–17
arguments (Excel), 174
artistic effects, applying, 35
aspect ratio, for PowerPoint slides, 203
assigning
    range names in Excel, 148–149
    sounds as transition effects in PowerPoint, 239
    themes in Word, 84–85
AutoCorrect, customizing in Word,
  108–109
AutoFill, using in Excel, 128–129
AutoSum, using in Excel, 178–179

B
backgrounds
    changing color in Word, 85
    inserting songs in PowerPoint, 245
    removing from images, 35
    troubleshooting, 9
Backstage view, 7
Bcc, 313
borders, adding in Word, 86–87
bulleted lists, creating in Word, 75
Business Card view (Outlook), 303
buttons, removing from Quick Access Toolbar, 15

C
captions, adding in PowerPoint, 205
Cc, 313
cells
    adding
        borders in Excel, 138–139
        shading in Excel, 138–139
    adjusting alignment in Excel, 132–133
    clearing in Excel, 150–151
    entering data in Excel, 124–125
    indenting data in Excel, 133
    ranges of, in Excel, 168
    referencing in Excel, 168, 171
    selecting
        in Access, 27
        in Excel, 27, 126–127
    table, 91
    totaling in Excel with AutoSum, 178–179
centering data across columns in Excel, 131
charts
    adding
        elements in Excel, 187
        to slides in PowerPoint, 226–227
    adjusting
        data in Excel, 189
        layout in Excel, 186
        style in Excel, 185
        type in Excel, 184

charts *(continued)*
    as an analysis choice in Excel, 165
    creating in Excel, 180–181
    deleting in Excel, 182
    formatting
        elements in Excel, 188
        in PowerPoint, 227
    moving in Excel, 182
    resizing in Excel, 182
checking spelling and grammar in Word, 106–107
Clear Contents (Excel), 151
Clear Formats (Excel), 151
clearing
    cells in Excel, 150–151
    formatting in Word, 77
    searches, 11
cloud, 36–37
color
    adjusting
        about, 34
        color schemes, 8–9
        for pages in Word, 99
        for text in Word, 64
    background, 85
    of ink in pen/laser tools, 251
columns
    adding to tables in PowerPoint, 225
    adjusting width in Word, 101
    centering across, in Excel, 131
    creating in Word, 88–89
    deleting in Excel, 151
    freezing titles on-screen in Excel, 147
    inserting in Excel, 145
    labels for, in PivotTables, 193
    resizing in Excel, 146
    selecting in Excel, 127
combining reviewers' changes in Word, 118–119
commands, 12, 14–15
comments (Word), 101, 120–121
composing messages in Outlook, 312–313

compressing pictures, 29
conditional formatting, applying in Excel, 142–143
contacts, creating in Outlook, 302–303
copying
    absolute references in Excel, 173
    animation effects in PowerPoint, 241
    cell formatting in Excel, 135
    formatting in Word, 76
    relative references in Excel, 172
    slides in PowerPoint, 209
    worksheets in Excel, 156
corner handles, 33
correcting images, 34
creating
    blank databases in Access, 260–261
    charts in Excel, 180–181
    column breaks in Word, 89
    columns in Word, 88–89
    contacts in Outlook, 302–303
    custom animations in PowerPoint, 242–243
    custom borders in Word, 87
    custom lists in Excel, 129
    databases based on templates in Access, 258–259
    files, 18–19
    folders in OneDrive, 49
    forms in Access, 270–271
    formulas in Excel, 170–171
    handouts in PowerPoint, 249
    lists in Word, 74–75
    message rules in Outlook, 322–323
    photo album presentations in PowerPoint, 204–205
    PivotCharts, 196–197
    PivotTables in Excel, 194–195
    presentations in PowerPoint, 202–203
    Quick Parts in Word, 58–59
    Quick Styles in Word, 78
    reports in Access, 292–295
    rules for conditional formatting in Excel, 143
    shortcuts to apps, 5
    speaker notes in PowerPoint, 246–247

tables
    in Access, 262–263
    in Excel, 160–161
tasks in Outlook, 304–305
templates for Word, 81
Creative Commons, 31
cropping pictures, 34
custom lists, creating in Excel, 129
customizing
    AutoCorrect in Word, 108–109
    Navigation bar in Outlook, 308–309
    Quick Access Toolbar, 14–15
    reports in Access, 295
    styles in Word, 79

D

data
    analyzing in Excel, 164–165
    finding and replacing in Excel, 158–159
    formatting with styles in Excel, 140–141
    selecting, 26–27
    viewing trends in Excel using Sparklines, 190–191
data bars, applying in Excel, 143
databases
    about, 256–257
    creating based on templates in Access, 258–259
    creating blanks in Access, 260–261
    opening in Access, 261
    planning, 257
Datasheet view (Access), 265
decimals, increasing/decreasing in Excel, 137
decreasing decimals in Excel, 137
defining slide transitions in PowerPoint, 238–239
definitions, displaying in Word, 111
deleting
    animations in PowerPoint, 243
    backgrounds from images, 35
    buttons from Quick Access Toolbar, 15
    charts in Excel, 182

columns in Excel, 151
comments in Word, 121
conditional formatting in Excel, 143
fields
    in Access, 267, 274, 293
    from PivotTables, 195
footers in Word, 95
forms in Access, 271
headers in Word, 95
message rules in Outlook, 323
messages in Outlook, 319
notes
    in Excel, 167
    in Outlook, 307
Quick Parts in Word, 59
records in Access, 282, 283
rows in Excel, 151
section markers in PowerPoint, 237
slides in PowerPoint, 233
sort order in Access, 285
styles in Word, 79
tab stops in Word, 70
tables
    in Access, 263
    in Word, 91
transition effects in PowerPoint, 239
worksheets in Excel, 157
Design view (Access), 264, 272
desktop apps, opening documents in, from OneDrive, 46–47
dialog boxes, launching, 13
Dictionary (Word), 111
displaying
    calculations in tatus bar in Excel, 179
    definitions in Word, 111
    labels in Outlook, 309
    Quick Access Toolbar, 14
    sections in PowerPoint, 237
    synonyms in Word, 111
    Windows taskbar, 253

documents
    about, 37
    navigating in Word, 104–105
    opening
        about, 37, 44
        in desktop apps from OneDrive, 46–47
    passwords for shared, 51
    saving in Word, 119
    sharing
        about, 37
        from Microsoft 365, 40–41
        using OneDrive, 50–51
        via email, 50
        via links, 51
    tracking changes in Word, 114–115
    translating in Word, 113
    uploading to OneDrive, 48–49
drawing outlines, 35
drop-down lists, 279

E

editing
    formulas in Excel, 171
    functions in Excel, 177
    slide text in PowerPoint, 215
    text in Word, 57
Editing mode, 45
Editor (Word), correcting errors via, 106–107
effects, adding, 35
email, sharing documents via, 50
endnotes, inserting in Word, 97
entering cell data in Excel, 124–125
Excel. *See* Microsoft Excel
exclusion, filtering by, in Access, 287
exiting apps, 4–5

F

Field Properties area (Access), 265
fields (Access)
    about, 256
    adding to tables, 266

deleting
    in forms, 274
    from reports, 293
    from tables, 267
    hiding in tables, 268
    moving
        in forms, 273
        in tables, 269
files
    creating, 18–19
    opening, 22–23
    printing, 24–25
    saving, 20–21
    sending attachments in Outlook, 314
    types, 21
fill color, adding in Excel, 139
filtering
    PivotCharts, 197
    PivotTable information, 193
    records in Access, 286–287
    tables in Excel, 162–163
finding and replacing
    data in Excel, 158–159
    text in Word, 102–103
flipping graphics, 34
Folder pane (Outlook), 311
folders (OneDrive), 47, 49
font/font size, adjusting
    default in Word, 65
    in Excel, 134–135
    in PowerPoint, 216–217
    in Word, 62
Font dialog box (Word), 65
footers, adding in Word, 94–95
footnotes, inserting in Word, 96–97
form fields, formatting in Access, 275
form views, adjusting in Access, 272
formatting
    as an analysis choice in Excel, 165
    chart elements in Excel, 188

charts in PowerPoint, 227

clearing in Word, 77

copying in Word, 76

data with styles in Excel, 140–141

form fields in Access, 275

with styles in Word, 78–79

forms (Access)

about, 257

adding records using, 278–279

creating, 270–271

deleting

about, 271

fields in, 274

records using, 283

filtering by, 287

moving fields in, 273

navigating records using, 280

searching for records using, 281

sorting using, 285

Formula Bar, typing data into in Excel, 125

formulas (Excel), 168–171

forwarding messages in Outlook, 317

freezing column/row titles on-screen in Excel, 147

functions (Excel), 174–177

G

galleries, choosing items from, 13

grammar, checking in Word, 106–107

grand totals, in PivotTables, 193

graphic objects

applying styles to, 35

flipping, 34

modification techniques for, 34–35

moving, 33

resizing, 32–33

rotating, 34

zooming in PowerPoint, 252

H

handouts, creating in PowerPoint, 249

headers, adding in Word, 94–95

headings, navigating documents using, 104–105

hiding

fields in tables in Access, 268

sections in PowerPoint, 237

slides in PowerPoint, 233, 251

highlighting text in Word, 100

I

images

adding borders, 35

compressing, 29

correcting, 34

cropping, 34

inserting from PCs, 28–29

online, 30–31

removing backgrounds from, 35

zooming in Word, 55

increasing decimals in Excel, 137

indenting

cell data in Excel, 133

text in Word, 68–69

Insert mode (Word), 57

Insert Options button (Excel), 145

inserting

background songs in PowerPoint, 245

columns in Excel, 145

comments in Word, 101

endnotes in Word, 97

footnotes in Word, 96–97

functions in Excel, 176–177

notes in Excel, 166–167

online pictures, 30–31

online videos in Word, 82–83

page breaks in Excel, 155

pictures from PCs, 28–29

PivotTable Slicers, 198–199

Quick Parts in Word, 58–59

rows in Excel, 144–145

slides in PowerPoint, 208–209

Sparklines in Excel, 190

symbols in Word, 60–61

inserting *(continued)*

    table rows/columns in Word, 93

    tables in Word, 90–91

J

junk e-mail, screening in Outlook, 320–321

Junk Email folder (Outlook), 321

K

keyboard shortcuts, 27, 127

L

labels, displaying in Outlook, 309

Layout tools (Word), setting margins using, 72

Layout view (Access), 272

layout views, switching in Word, 55

leader tabs (Word), 70

line spacing, setting, 67, 221

links, sharing documents via, 51

lists, creating in Word, 74–75

locking tracked changes in Word, 116–117

M

margins, setting in Word, 72–73

mathematical operators, in Excel, 169

menus, running commands from, 12

message rules (Outlook), 322–323

messages (Outlook)

    composing, 312–313

    deleting, 319

    forwarding, 317

    reading incoming, 315

    replying to, 316–317

    saving as drafts, 313

    sending, 312–313

Microsoft 365. *See also specific topics*

    app window, 6

    Backstage view, 7

    adjusting

        color schemes, 8–9

        default font and size, 65

    cloud and, 36–37

    searching for Ribbon commands, 10–11

    sharing documents from, 40–41

    signing in to, 38–39

    signing out of, 39

    starting apps, 4–5

    using apps with touch screen, 16–17

Microsoft 365 Indicator, 6

Microsoft 365 Web apps, 36

Microsoft Access

    adding

        fields to tables, 266

        records, 276–279

    adjusting

        form views, 272

        table views, 264–265

    creating

        blank databases, 260–261

        databases based on templates, 258–259

        forms, 270–271

        reports, 292–295

        tables, 262–263

    customizing reports, 295

    database basics, 256–257

    deleting

        fields, 267, 274

        records, 282, 283

    filtering records, 286–287

    formatting form fields, 275

    hiding fields in tables, 268

    moving fields, 269, 273

    navigating records using forms, 280

    performing Simple Queries, 288–291

    printing reports, 295

    searching for records using forms, 281

    selecting cells in, 27

    sorting

        records, 284–285

        tables, 284

        using forms, 285

Microsoft Excel
  adding
    cell borders, 138–139
    cell shading, 138–139
    chart elements, 187
    fill color, 139
    worksheets, 152
  adjusting
    cell alignment, 132–133
    chart data, 189
    chart layout, 186
    chart style, 185
    chart type, 184
    font and size, 134–135
    number formats, 136
    orientation of data, 133
    page setup options, 154–155
  analyzing data, 164–165
  applying
    absolute cell references, 172–173
    conditional formatting, 142–143
    data bars, 143
    relative cell references, 172–173
  centering data across columns, 131
  clearing cells, 150–151
  copying
    cell formatting, 135
    worksheets, 156
  creating
    charts, 180–181
    custom lists, 129
    tables, 160–161
  decreasing decimals, 137
  deleting
    rows/columns, 151
    worksheets, 157
  entering cell data, 124–125
  file types for, 21
  filtering tables, 162–163
  finding and replacing data, 158–159
  formatting
    chart elements, 188
    data with styles, 140–141
  formulas, 168–171
  freezing column/row titles on-screen, 147
  functions, 174–179
  increasing decimals, 137
  indenting cell data, 133
  inserting
    columns, 145
    notes, 166–167
    page breaks, 155
    rows, 144–145
  moving
    charts, 183
    worksheets, 156
  naming ranges, 148–149
  PivotCharts, 196–197
  PivotTables, 192–195, 198–199
  printing worksheets, 155
  renaming worksheets, 153
  resizing
    charts, 182
    columns, 146
    rows, 146
  selecting cells in, 27, 126–127
  sorting tables, 163
  totaling cells with AutoSum, 178–179
  turning on text wrapping, 130
  using AutoFill, 128–129
  viewing data trends using Sparklines, 190–191
  worksheet gridlines, 139
Microsoft Outlook
  adding
    notes, 306–307
    senders to contacts, 318
  composing messages, 312–313
  creating
    contacts, 302–303
    message rules, 322–323
    tasks, 304–305
  customizing Navigation bar, 308–309

Microsoft Outlook *(continued)*

deleting

message rules, 323

messages, 319

notes, 307

forwarding messages, 317

navigating in, 298–299

reading incoming messages, 315

replying to messages, 316–317

saving messages as drafts, 313

scheduling appointments, 300–301

screening junk e-mail, 320–321

sending

file attachments, 314

messages, 312–313

viewing appointments/tasks, 310–311

Microsoft PowerPoint

adding

animation effects, 240–241

captions, 205

charts to slides, 226–227

columns to tables, 225

rows to tables, 225

slide text, 214–215

tables to slides, 224–225

text boxes to slides, 223

video clips to slides, 228–229

adjusting

font, 216–217

font size, 217

slide layout, 210–211

slide size, 212–213

views, 206–207

aligning text, 222

applying

text formatting, 217

themes, 220

creating

custom animations, 242–243

handouts, 249

photo album presentations, 204–205

presentations, 202–203

speaker notes, 246–247

defining slide transitions, 238–239

deleting slides, 233

editing slide text, 215

formatting charts, 227

hiding slides, 233, 251

inserting

background songs, 245

slides, 208–209

moving slide objects, 230

organizing slides into sections, 236–237

printing notes, 247

recording narration, 244

rehearsing slideshows, 248–249

reorganizing slides, 232–233

resizing slide objects, 231

reusing slides, 234–325

running slideshows, 250–253

selecting

data in, 26

text color, 218–219

setting line spacing, 221

zooming objects, 252

Microsoft Publisher, 26

Microsoft Word

adding

borders, 86–87

footers, 94–95

headers, 94–95

page number fields, 95

shading to text, 87

vertical lines between columns, 89

adjusting

color of text, 64

font, 62

views in, 54–55

aligning text, 66

applying

formatting to text, 63

table styles, 92

assigning themes, 84–85

checking spelling and grammar, 106–107

clearing formatting, 77

combining reviewers' changes, 118–119

copying formatting, 76

creating

column breaks, 89

columns, 88–89

lists, 74–75

customizing AutoCorrect, 108–109

Dictionary, 111

editing text, 57

file types for, 21

finding and replacing text, 102–103

formatting with styles, 78–79

highlighting text, 100

indenting text, 68–69

inserting

comments, 101

endnotes, 96–97

footnotes, 96–97

online videos, 82–83

Quick Parts, 58–59

symbols, 60–61

table rows/columns, 93

tables, 90–91

leader tabs, 70

locking tracked changes, 116–117

Mini toolbar, 63

navigating documents, 104–105

Quick Styles, 78

Read mode, 17

Read Mode view, 98–101

removing tab stops, 70

resizing text, 63

ruler, 69

saving documents, 119

selecting data in, 26

setting

default margins, 73

line spacing, 67

margins, 72–73

Quick Indents, 68

Quick Tabs, 70

tabs, 70–71

Thesaurus, 110–111

tracking document changes, 114–115

translating text, 112–113

troubleshooting print margins in, 73

typing text, 56–57

unlocking tracked changes, 116–117

using Font dialog box, 65

using templates, 80–81

working with comments, 120–121

Mini toolbar (Word), 63

modes, switching, 45

modification techniques, for graphic objects, 34–35

moving

charts in Excel, 182

fields in Access, 269, 273

graphic objects, 33

slide objects in PowerPoint, 230

worksheets in Excel, 156

N

naming ranges in Excel, 148–149

narration, recording in PowerPoint, 244

navigating

documents in Word, 104–105

in Outlook, 298–299

records using forms in Access, 280

Navigation bar, customizing in Outlook, 308–309

Navigation pane (Access), 261

noncontiguous data, selecting in Excel, 181

Normal view (PowerPoint), 206, 232

notes

adding in Outlook, 306–307

deleting in Outlook, 307

inserting in Excel, 166–167

Notes Page view (PowerPoint), 247

Notes pane (PowerPoint), 246

number formats, changing in Excel, 136

number series, AutoFill and, 129

numbered lists, creating in Word, 75

O

OneDrive

about, 36

creating folders in, 49

opening documents in desktop apps from, 46–47

sharing documents using, 50–51

signing in to/out of, 42–43

uploading documents to, 48–49

using online apps in, 44–45

online apps, 44–46

online document tools, 37

online pictures, inserting, 30–31

online videos, inserting in Word, 82–83

opening

databases in Access, 261

dialog boxes, 13

documents

about, 37, 44

in desktop apps from OneDrive, 46–47

to share, 50

files, 22–23

operator precedence, in Excel, 169

OR criteria, 287

orientation, adjusting in Excel, 133, 154

Outline view (PowerPoint), 206

outlines, drawing, 35

Outlook. *See* Microsoft Outlook

Overtype mode (Word), 57

P

page borders, adding in Word, 87

page breaks, inserting in Excel, 155

page numbers, adding in Word, 95

pages

changing setup options in Excel, 154–155

navigating documents using, 105

paragraph borders, adding in Word, 86

passwords, 51, 117

PCs, inserting pictures from, 28–29

personal settings, 36

photo album presentations, creating in PowerPoint, 204–205

PivotCharts, creating, 196–197

PivotTables (Excel), 192–199

Playback tab (PowerPoint), 229

playing inserted videos, in Word, 83

PowerPoint. *See* Microsoft PowerPoint

presentations, creating in PowerPoint, 202–203

Presenter view (PowerPoint), 253

preset Quick Parts, 59

primary key, 277

printing

files, 24–25

notes in PowerPoint, 247

reports in Access, 295

troubleshooting in Word, 73

worksheets in Excel, 155

Program Window controls, 6

public domain, 31

Q

queries (Access), 257, 290–291

Quick Access Toolbar (QAT), 14–16, 25

Quick Analysis button (Excel), 165, 181

Quick Borders, adding in Excel, 138

Quick Parts, inserting in Word, 58–59

R

ranges, naming in Excel, 148–149

Read mode (Word), 17, 98–101

reading incoming messages, in Outlook, 315

Reading view (PowerPoint), 207

recording narration, in PowerPoint, 244
records (Access)
    adding, 276–279
    deleting, 282, 283
    filtering, 286–287
    navigating using forms, 280
    searching for using forms, 281
    sorting, 284–285
records (Access), 256
reference operators, in Excel, 169
referencing cells, in Excel, 168, 171
relative cell references, applying in Excel, 172–173
renaming
    table fields in Access, 263
    worksheets in Excel, 153
replying
    to comments in Word, 121
    to messages in Outlook, 316–317
report filter, in PivotTables, 193
reports (Access), 257, 292–295
resizing
    charts in Excel, 182
    columns in Excel, 146
    graphic objects, 32–33
    PowerPoint pane, 207
    Ribbon, 13
    rows in Excel, 146
    slide objects in PowerPoint, 231
restoring junk e-mail to safe list, in Outlook, 321
reusing slides, in PowerPoint, 234–325
Reviewing mode, 45
Ribbon, 6, 10–13, 180
rotating graphics, 34
row labels, in PivotTables, 193
row titles, freezing on-screen in Excel, 147
rows
    adding
        to tables in PowerPoint, 225
        to tables in Word, 91

    deleting in Excel, 151
    inserting in Excel, 144–145
    resizing in Excel, 146
    selecting in Excel, 127
ruler (Word), 69

S

saving
    documents in Word, 119
    files, 20–21
    messages as drafts in Outlook, 313
    work in online apps, 45
scheduling appointments, in Outlook, 300–301
screening junk e-mail, in Outlook, 320–321
search bar, 6
Search Document box (Word), 105
searching
    clearing searches, 11
    for records using forms in Access, 281
    for Ribbon commands, 10–11
selecting
    cells in Excel, 126–127
    data, 26–27
    items from galleries, 13
    named ranges in Excel, 149
    noncontiguous data in Excel, 181
    text color in PowerPoint, 218–219
senders, adding to contacts in Outlook, 318
setting
    horizontal alignment in Excel, 132
    line spacing
        in PowerPoint, 221
        in Word, 67
    margins in Word, 72–73
    tabs in Word, 70–71
    vertical alignment in Excel, 133
shading, adding to text in Word, 87

sharing documents
about, 37
from Microsoft 365, 40–41
using OneDrive, 50–51
via email, 50
via links, 51
shortcuts, creating to apps, 5
signing into/out of
the cloud, 36
Microsoft 365, 38–39
OneDrive, 42–43
Simple Queries, performing in Access, 288–291
slide objects (PowerPoint), 230, 231
Slide Sorter view (PowerPoint), 207, 233
slides
adding
charts to in PowerPoint, 226–227
tables to in PowerPoint, 224–225
text boxes to in PowerPoint, 223
text to in PowerPoint, 214–215
video clips to in PowerPoint, 228–229
adjusting
layout in PowerPoint, 210–211
size of in PowerPoint, 212–213
defining transitions in PowerPoint, 238–239
deleting in PowerPoint, 233
duplicating in PowerPoint, 209
editing text on in PowerPoint, 215
hiding in PowerPoint, 233, 251
inserting in PowerPoint, 208–209
organizing into sections in PowerPoint, 236–237
reorganizing in PowerPoint, 232–233
reusing in PowerPoint, 234–325
Slides from Outline command (PowerPoint), 209
slideshows (PowerPoint), 248–253
Sort by Color option (Excel), 163
sorting
records in Access, 284–285
tables

in Access, 284
in Excel, 163
sounds, assigning as transition effects in PowerPoint, 239
source data, in PivotTables, 193
Sparklines, 165, 190–191
speaker notes, creating in PowerPoint, 246–247
special characters, adding in Word, 61
spelling, checking in Word, 106–107
starting apps, 4–5
Status Bar, 6, 179
structure, of formulas in Excel, 168
styles
applying to graphics, 35
formatting
data with, in Excel, 140–141
with in Word, 78–79
table, 92
subtotals, in PivotTables, 193
switching
to Datasheet view in Access, 265
to Design view in Access, 264, 272
to Layout view in Access, 272
layout views in Word, 55
modes, 45
symbols, inserting in Word, 60–61
synonyms, displaying in Word, 111

T
table cells (Word), 91
table rows/columns, inserting in Word, 93
table views, changing in Access, 264–265
tables
about, 256
adding
columns to in PowerPoint, 225
fields to in Access, 266
to queries in Access, 291
records to in Access, 276–277

rows to in PowerPoint, 225
to slides in PowerPoint, 224–225
as an analysis choice in Excel, 165
creating
in Access, 262–263
in Excel, 160–161
deleting
in Access, 263
fields from in Access, 267
records from in Access, 282
filtering in Excel, 162–163
formatting as in Excel, 141
hiding fields in, in Access, 268
inserting in Word, 90–91
moving fields in, in Access, 269
relationships with, 289
renaming fields in Access, 263
sorting
in Access, 284
in Excel, 163
tabs, setting in Word, 70–71
tasks (Outlook), 304–305, 310–311
templates
creating
databases based on, in Access, 258–259
files from, 19
Microsoft Word, 80–81
text
adding shading to in Word, 87
adjusting color of in Word, 64
aligning
in PowerPoint, 222
in Word, 66
applying formatting to in Word, 63
choosing color of in PowerPoint, 218–219
editing in Word, 57
finding and replacing in Word, 102–103
highlighting in Word, 100
indenting in Word, 68–69
resizing in Word, 63

translating in Word, 112–113
typing in Word, 56–57
text boxes, adding to slides in PowerPoint, 223
text series, AutoFill and, 128
text wrapping, 33, 130
themes
applying in Excel, 141
applying in PowerPoint, 220
assigning in Word, 84–85
Thesaurus (Word), 110–111
thumbnails (PowerPoint), 251
title bar, 6
totals, as an analysis choice in Excel, 165
touch screen, using apps with, 16–17
Touch/Mouse mode, adding to Quick Access Toolbar, 16
tracking document changes, in Word, 114–115
translating, 99, 112–113
troubleshooting
AutoCorrect in Word, 109
AutoFilter in Excel, 163
backgrounds, 9
cell width in Excel, 125
endnotes, 97
footnotes, 97
inserting pictures, 29
margin settings in Word, 73
Outlook, 301
Ribbon tabs, 13
slide text, 215
track changes in Word, 117, 119
translation in Word, 113
turning on/off
automatic spelling and grammar checking in Word, 107
text wrapping in Excel, 130
tracking in Word, 114
worksheet gridlines in Excel, 139
typing
into cells in Excel, 124–125
text in Word, 56–57

U

unlocking tracked changes, in Word, 116–117
uploading documents, to OneDrive, 48–49

V

Values area, in PivotTables, 193
vertical lines, adding between columns in Word, 89
video clips, adding to slides in PowerPoint, 228–229
View Shortcuts feature, 6
viewing
    appointments/tasks in Outlook, 310–311
    data trends in Excel using Sparklines, 190–191
    notes in Excel, 167

Viewing mode, 45
views, adjusting, 54–55, 206–207

W

web apps (Microsoft 365), 36
Windows taskbar, displaying, 253
Word. *See* Microsoft Word
worksheet gridlines (Excel), 139
worksheets (Excel), 152, 153, 155, 156, 157

Z

Zoom tool, 6, 54, 207, 252